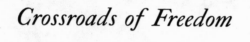

Crossroads of Freedom

CROSSROADS
OF
FREEDOM

*The American Revolution
and the Rise of a New Nation*

by

EARL SCHENCK MIERS

Drawings by Charles Waterhouse

RUTGERS UNIVERSITY PRESS *New Brunswick, New Jersey*

Copyright © 1971 by Rutgers University, the State University
of New Jersey
Library of Congress Catalog Card Number: 78-163953
ISBN: 0-8135-0699-9
Manufactured in the United States of America

Affectionately dedicated to
MASON WELCH GROSS
Enlightened scholar, kindly teacher, loyal friend
and university president without peer

Preface

How difficult it is to identify the beginnings of a romance that
has endured for more than half a century! Yet the mystery surrounding such love stories often makes them all the richer and
sweeter. In an age when, in farm communities, there were neither
Sunday movies nor radio to relieve the tedium of a drowsy summer's day, I see a boy caught up in a now almost forgotten
American pastime—the afternoon walk. The young rascal is not
quite ten. He is barefoot, and the sand at the side of the road
squirts between his toes in yellowish puffs. Wild flowers mingle
with poison ivy along the embankments; occasional meadows are
overspread with the golden glow of buttercups. Behind him,
stretched out like three caretakers from an asylum, are mother,
sister, and father, each screaming at him to avoid the melting tar
of the macadam road.

The walk, like the screechy imprecations, is all too familiar, for
having gone this way many times the boy knows that the journey
to and from the farmstead and what the New Jersey Central Railroad erroneously (but profitably) called Molly Pitcher's Well
would require three hours, twelve minutes, and forty-seven
seconds, plus whatever time a sudden summer shower might take.
Inevitably, approaching Molly's Well, his heartbeat quickens. In
his mind are the stories his paternal grandmother has told of the

events of the Revolutionary War which her grandparents experienced. He remembers, too, a tale of how his father's ancestor, John Miers, fought with the militia on this very battlefield of Monmouth where the boy now stands, on a day almost as warm as the one on which the Continental soldiers of that long ago war fainted by the roadside.

But a boy's imagination is simply whetted by the glare of the sun on sandy roads. He hears the roar of cannon, the yells of charging Britons and Hessians, the shouts of Continentals rallying to the defense of a bridge or orchard. Muskets fire, swords clash, and General Washington rides by on his white charger. For the remainder of his life, this boy will never forget how across these rolling fields from Tennent to Freehold his own flesh and blood fought and perhaps died for something still so elusive that even they could not always identify it.

Yet in the boy, as in his forebears, this love had taken root. He could never forsake it. Fully to understand its enchantment others would have to help him—say, a historian like David Ramsay:

The Americans knew but little of one another previous to the Revolution. Trade and business had brought the inhabitants of their seaports acquainted with each other, but the bulk of the people in the interior country were unacquainted with their fellow citizens. A Continental army and Congress composed of men from all the states, by freely mixing together, were assimilated into one mass. Individuals of both, mingling with the citizens, disseminated principles of union among them. Local prejudices abated. By frequent collision asperities were worn off, and a foundation was laid for the establishment of a nation, out of discordant materials. Intermarriages between men and women of different states were much more common than before the war, and became an additional cement to the Union. Unreasonable jealousies had existed between the inhabitants of the Eastern and of the Southern states; but on becoming better acquainted with each other, these in a great measure subsided. A wiser policy prevailed. Men of liberal minds led the way in discouraging local distinctions, and the great body of the people, as soon as reason got the better of prejudice, found that their best interests would be most effectually promoted by such practices and sentiments as were favorable to union.

Decades later the boy, now the father of three growing children, understood clearly what Ramsay meant. On that day of complete awakening, this so much older boy stood on the plain above the marl bluffs where the Battle of Yorktown was fought. Forty feet below, sunlight glistened on the gentle swells of Chesapeake Bay. He remembered those frightening days of early September, 1781, when the French fleet of Admiral de Grasse was in battle against a British fleet under Admiral Thomas Graves off the Virginia capes where bay and ocean join. Each ticking hour was desperate. The main Continental and French forces were on the move for what they hoped would be the climactic conflict of the long and weary struggle for union and the inalienable rights of man. Yet should Lord Cornwallis escape southward into the Carolinas, thus eluding the trap into which he had been led, triumph could turn into disaster.

No risk was too great to avoid this possible catastrophe. Washington then would be caught between the armies of Clinton and Cornwallis; and his chief French naval support would have departed. Lafayette infiltrated the British lines at Yorktown with a spy who, wearing the uniform of his enemy, must gain Cornwallis' confidence and warn him that American forces southward had been so strengthened that any foray into the Carolinas could well become suicidal. The scheme worked perfectly.

The spy's name was Charley Morgan and he lived in New Jersey. A delighted Lafayette believed that Morgan should receive an award or promotion for the hazardous mission he had performed. Charley shook his head, saying that all he wanted was the return of his old rifle.

To the older boy, who once had belonged to the same Dutch Church on the Green in Hackensack that Washington had seen in 1776 on his fatal retreat through Trenton, the Charley Morgan episode at Yorktown gave a tender ending to the ageless love story of Revolutionary New Jersey that fills the following pages.

Earl Schenck Miers

Edison, New Jersey
April, 1971

Contents

Preface   vii

Introduction   xiii

I. RESPITE AFTER TRENTON AND PRINCETON

Prelude: 1774–1776   3

1. The River Forts: November, 1776   19
2. Flight: November–December, 1776   29
3. Mount Holly: An Ace in the Hole: December, 1776   38
4. Surprise at Trenton: December, 1776   45
5. Rumors and Realities: December, 1776–January, 1777   53
6. Fox Chase in Princeton: January, 1777   60
7. Village Festival: January, 1777   66
8. A Lull Before a Storm: Winter, 1777   76
9. Impasse: Spring, 1777   85
10. Valley in Arms: May–June, 1777   92

II. THE GUNS OF MONMOUTH

Prelude: 1777–1778   101

1. Forts Along the Delaware: October–November, 1777   113
2. Conspiracy: Winter, 1777–1778   125

3. The Chase Starts: Spring, 1778   135
4. The Enigma of Charles Lee: June, 1778   145
5. Forever Molly: June, 1778   155
6. Shadows in the Night, June–July, 1778   164
7. A *Feu de Joie* and Other Matters: Summer, 1778–
   Spring, 1779   171

III. TREASON AND TRIUMPH

Prelude: 1778–1779   185
1. A War on Sleds: December, 1779–January, 1780   191
2. Huts in a Hollow: January–February, 1780   199
3. Death and Mutiny: March–May, 1780   206
4. Surprise at Springfield: June, 1780   216
5. Mutineers: July, 1780–January, 1781   225
6. A Ride to Wethersfield: January–May, 1781   236
7. March to Glory: August–September, 1781   245
   Postlude: 1781–1783   251
   Notes and Comments   257
   Index   271

MAPS

Seat of War in the North, 1775–1778   11
Seat of War in the Eastern States, 1776–1780   20
Revolutionary New Brunswick   33
Trenton, 1777   49
Operations on the Delaware   116
Fort Mercer   117
Battle of Monmouth: Parallel Lines of March   149
Battle of Monmouth: Lee's Advance and Retreat   151
Battle of Monmouth: British Advance on American
    Positions   161
Battle of Monmouth: The Last Charge   168
Robert Erskine's Map of the Morristown Area   193
Battle of Springfield, June 23, 1780   218

Introduction

The first day when the American Revolution could have been lost was July 2, 1776. On this day, in an entirely appropriate parliamentary procedure, the Continental Congress was to become a Committee of the Whole House. Thus President John Hancock could surrender the Chair to the Committee and sit with the Massachusetts delegation. Any debate or any vote taken under these arrangements would be strictly unofficial, but would indicate how the political straws were swaying. The Declaration of Independence, calling for a war to the finish, could not be effective unless unanimously adopted and no one knew better than John Adams of the vigorous opposition forming against it. Upon occasions Adams lashed his adversaries with a tongue of ridicule, making himself probably the most hated member of Congress, a circumstance in which he seemed to take considerable pride. The bull-headed resistance of New York to the Declaration produced that kind of outpouring of vituperation for which the entire Adams clan became notorious:

What is the Reason that New York is still asleep or dead, in Politics and War [John wrote an intimate friend]? Have they no sense? No Feelings? No Sentiment? No Passions? New Jersey shews a noble Ardor. Is there anything in the Air or Soil of New York, unfriendly to the Spirit of

Liberty? For Gods sake explain to me the Causes of our Miscarriages in the Province!

Pennsylvania was scarcely more encouraging, for among its seven delegates John could count only upon Benjamin Franklin and Judge John Morton of Ridley to vote affirmatively. The image John created was of slender little Jersey with her shoulders bent under the weight of two giants; but then John expected New Jersey to snap upright, popping one of the giants into a somersault and landing it on its feet while the other, for all John cared, could coast into the deeper regions of Hades.

John clomped into the July 2 session of Congress looking like one of the thunderheads lowering outdoors. Where were the Jerseymen on whom he depended and where was Caesar Rodney, who alone could break the tie in the Delaware delegation? Cousin Sam Adams, whose friends had painted their faces like Indians when staging the Boston Tea Party, found a hole in a silk stocking through which he scratched his skin irritably. Like John, Sam cast a malevolent glance at John Dickinson of Pennsylvania, whose pockets were stuffed with notes by which he expected to argue the Declaration into a verbal grave. In addition to Rodney and the Jerseymen, where, in God's name, were the great debaters *for* the Declaration like Richard Henry Lee and George Wythe of Virginia and Christopher Gadsden of South Carolina?

Delay was what John and Sam most wanted and Hancock was willing to oblige to the fullest extent of which he was capable. He spread fourteen letters before him—among them three from Washington, one from Benedict Arnold, and others from the conventions in New Jersey and New Hampshire—and read with such precision that he did not finish until noon.

Congress now became the Committee of the Whole House and Hancock handed the gavel to its chairman, Benjamin Harrison. Dickinson at once took the floor with his pocketful of notes. Sam Adams listened glumly, digging anew at the hole in his stocking as Dickinson said that he knew his action must end his political career. A message from Annapolis, announcing that Maryland had resolved to support the Declaration, cheered the entire Massachusetts delegation. Across the room John bowed solemnly to Sam. Meanwhile, despite the heat of the room or the clap of thunder outdoors, Dickinson earnestly continued his hour-long speech:

If we declare a separation without waiting to hear from France, we may be overwhelmed with debt—a debt I have computed at six millions of Pennsylvania money a year. We shall ruin ourselves, and Britain will be ruined with us. France will rise on those ruins. Britain will push the war with a severity hitherto unimagined. Indians will be set loose on our frontiers. Recollect, gentlemen, that Boston has been spared thus far. Boston will be burned!

When Dickinson finished, John arose, really having little new to say. Wind slashed the rain against the windows. John lifted his voice above the rumbling thunder. He paused once as the doors were flung open and three Jerseymen entered, dripping puddles on the floor. John reviewed for the new arrivals what he had said. Quite abusively two other spokesmen attacked the Declaration. John Witherspoon of Princeton had heard more than he could endure. Chin outthrust above the "clergyman's bib that lay wilted against his chest," Witherspoon stepped forward. John Alsop of New York had just ended an attack on the Declaration when Witherspoon's nasal voice crackled across the room:

"The distinguished gentleman from Massachusetts remarked as we came in that the colonies are ripe for independence. I would like to add that some colonies are rotten for the want of it!" Alsop's face crimsoned.

The vote to adopt the Declaration, each delegation voting as a unit, was nine for, four against. John and Sam hustled the Jerseymen across the wet cobbles to Fountain Tavern. Thomas McKean of Delaware, who had waited outside, joined the group.

"You cant make thirteen Clocks strike precisely alike, at the same Second," John had remarked upon one occasion and the ingredient necessary for that achievement, he might have added, was hard politicking. Heads bent over the table at Fountain

Tavern, the six delegates plotted how the Declaration could be saved. Suppose Dickinson of Pennsylvania would not vote for independence, asked McKean. Let Dickinson stay away, McKean said. Let Robert Morris do so also. When the test came, James Wilson would not vote against Franklin and Pennsylvania would be saved. Once Caesar Rodney arrived, the Delaware tie would be broken. That left New York, which had not supported independence "for want of Instructions from home." How could she stand one colony against twelve? Spirits lifted around the table at Fountain Tavern. Today's defeat had become tomorrow's victory.

*   *   *

The fascination of the American Revolution existed not in causes but in its enduring emotional depth. It is difficult to imagine a fourteen-year-old boy from Connecticut, who probably never had more than two or three dollars in his pocket at one time, fighting the battles of this conflict and withstanding the winters at Valley Forge and Morristown simply because of a series of taxes that touched him very lightly. The graves of many like this youth in his teens would be spread far from home until they covered an emergent nation with a staggering concept of human dignity. It is very true that committees of correspondence and writers of pamphlets had developed the struggle, but these leaders were the stuff of officers and bearers of legislative responsibilities; only the young could bear the torment of battles often separated by the agonizing tedium of wearisome waiting. There was a magic in this war, enunciated as early as 1776, when Thomas Jefferson changed the last word of the old revolutionary slogan, "life, liberty and property" to "the pursuit of happiness." In writing the Declaration of Independence Jefferson thus had given the war a purpose usually reserved for the dreams of philosophers and prophets, although the conservatives in Congress probably believed that no man could be happy unless he owned property.

Among the more puzzling perpetrators of the Revolution was the distant George III, who often was called the "mad king."

In a recent book on "the mad business," two British psychiatrists, Ida Macalpine and Richard Hunter, poke fun at members of another profession:

. . . the illness of 1765 did not attract any interest until after the King's death, when with the hindsight of later attacks a whispering campaign was started, hinting that the King may have been deranged even then. Nineteenth-century historians came to accept this speculation as if it were established fact, and George III was stigmatized as a man who had five attacks of insanity between his twenties and old age and was therefore more or less deranged throughout his life. . . . In the twentieth century this "mental breakdown" as a young man was used to support the theory that he suffered from manic-depressive psychosis. . . . Such notions could never seriously have been entertained had it been appreciated that the King was mentally deranged for the first time in 1788. . . .

Actually George III's illness in 1765, the year of the Stamp Act, was no different from the illness he had suffered three years before. A bad cough, chest pains, a fluctuating pulse, fever, insomnia, and fatigue were among its chief symptoms. Friends told the King that he was afflicted with a cold while secretly certain that he might pass on at any hour with consumption. He was "bled, cupped and blistered" until he had given enough blood to save a modern battalion. He was dosed with asses' milk, the fad then for treating all injurious illnesses. Considering all the King went through, George III must have had a sturdy constitution; he not only retained his good humor but kept the Queen "big with child." Unlike many members of his court, the King was sternly monogamous.

Only hardheadedness in all matters that involved the King personally could have led George III into a war with the American colonies. At the start of the struggle his forces consisted of 39,294 infantry, 6,869 cavalry and 2,484 artillery. These forces, moreover, were scattered as far afield as England, Scotland, Isle of Man, Ireland, Minorca, Gibraltar, West Indies, America, and Africa. The 41st Regiment consisted of twenty companies of men so aged or badly wounded that they could be used only for guard duty in Great Britain and the Scilly Islands. So George III was forced to rely heavily on the mercenaries he could hire in the

pauperized principalities of Germany and colonists who remained loyal to the throne with the result that, psychologically,
Americans not only rebelled against an oppressive king but also
resisted foreign invaders and neighborhood traitors.

*   *   *

The adversaries were required to fight the war by different
patterns. With an army that must be largely reinforced and supplied across three thousand miles of ocean, Great Britain, for all
its fabled might, could not hope to win unless it controlled the
ports from Halifax to Savannah and especially those of New
York, Philadelphia, and Charleston along with the entrances to
Delaware and Chesapeake bays. America, on the other hand,
was forced to wage a land-locked war (to a very large extent
even after the French intervened), which explained why New
Jersey became the crossroads of the Revolution and, with Morristown twice the military capital of the united colonies, the gateway to freedom.

There are historians who argue that New Jersey essayed this
role reluctantly and sluggishly and then only under duress. The
reasons for these controversies are as complex as the contradic-
tions that have swirled around George III and his madness;
whereas the methods of history may be objective the process of
presentation must be subjective and colored by the individual's
needs, prejudices and aspirations (and as an outstanding university administrator, Dixon Wecter, has observed, it takes a
brave scholar to resist the temptation of pleasing by not displeas-
ing his department head).

The basic truth is that New Jersey was aroused in 1765 at the
passage of the Stamp Act—so much so that the royal governor
ordered the stamps kept aboard a warship in New York Harbor
for "to have brought them into the colony might have precipi-
tated violence." Even though New Jersey has been pictured as a
land of farmers whose chief function was to connect New York
and Philadelphia, the State never wavered in its support of the
patriot cause during that decade when intellectual rebellion
turned into the gore of revolution. Truly Jerseymen fulfilled the

prediction of England's passionate 18th-century orator-statesman, Edmund Burke:

"We cannot, I fear, falsify the pedigree of this fierce people, and persuade them that they are not sprung from a nation in whose veins the blood of freedom circulates."

PART ONE

Respite After Trenton and Princeton

"All our hopes were blasted"

Lord George Germain
British Secretary of War

Prelude

1774–1776

The War for Independence was America's first civil war. On both sides of the Atlantic the conflict was a disruptive force, dividing families, neighbors, friends, statesmen, and those who fought its battles. Even religions were affected, and reputedly pacifistic Quakers in Philadelphia drilled to the command, "Shoulder thy firelock!" Willing to poke his nose into anybody's business, John Adams, the first of a clan that was to be dominant in American politics for a century, never minimized the dimensions of the ordeal confronting the colonies: "We shall have a long, obstinate and bloody war to go through." The enlightened guess of one of our most eminent historians, Samuel Eliot Morison, is that among the colonial population of about 2.5 million not more than 10 per cent were aggressive Loyalists, some 40 per cent deserved to be called Patriots, and the remainder were "indifferent or neutral."

The Jerseys, to which almost no one gave a second thought at the outbreak of the war, revealed conflicting passions. In New Brunswick rival bands of Tory-minded Kings and Liberty Boys engaged in the raptures of fisticuffs on numerous occasions; and students at the College of New Jersey (Princeton) enjoyed ducking under the college pump those Tories whom they characterized as "possessed swine" and in January 1774 the "steward's store of tea" was burned to the ringing of the college bell. An effigy of Massachusetts' royal governor, Thomas Hutchinson, "with a tea canister suspended from his neck" also was tossed into the fire.

Increasingly the people of the Jerseys were growing weary of their own royal governor, William Franklin, who shamed an illustrious father. To Benjamin Franklin, who could pinch words as he did pennies, Will had become hopeless—"a thorough government man." Like so many colonies, the Jerseys displayed quick indignation when Great Britain closed the port of Boston in retaliation for the fuss over tea that had hallowed these waters in patriotic hearts. A General Committee of Correspondence met at New Brunswick on June 1, 1774, not only to express its sympathy for beleaguered Boston, but also to request the governor to convene the Colonial Assembly of the Jerseys. Franklin denied the appeal in a triumph of arrogance.

Undaunted, the several counties elected delegates to an unauthorized convention that gathered at New Brunswick on July 21. The affirmation that the delegates were of "firm and unshaken loyalty to His Majesty, King George III" was inevitably the apologia that such rebellions occasioned; meanwhile, during three days of blunt oratory, the delegates condemned the money gougers in Parliament, recommended the nonimportation of taxed goods, and raised what money they could for the relief of the citizens of Boston. The governor could denigrate these proceedings as much as he wished. The downfall of William Franklin could not be blamed on the stars: with one high-handed act after another in the months that followed he finally strained to the breaking point the patience of this maverick congress.

John Witherspoon, the president of Princeton, presided over the 1775 meeting that branded the governor "an enemy to the liberties of this country" and ordered his arrest. Nathaniel Heard, of the Middlesex militia, set off for Perth Amboy to do his duty. Actually Heard offered the governor a parole if he would remain at "a fixed residence" and promise not to aid the British, a proposition Franklin arrogantly refused. There were undersurface tensions between Witherspoon and Franklin, who had planned to turn Nassau Hall over to the Anglicans. This scheme had been thwarted by Presbyterian leaders who persuaded Witherspoon to leave Scotland and become not only the head of the college but also of American Presbyterianism.

A defiant Franklin faced Witherspoon and the rough-handed farmers who composed a large part of this Provincial Congress. Bitterly Franklin accused the group of trying to usurp his authority and of depriving him of his salary. Sarcasm came easily to this reproachful man, who expected, as he wrote a friend, to be "led like a bear through the country to some place of confinement in New England." For once the Jerseymen were more than willing to oblige Franklin by exiling him to Connecticut.

*   *   *

News of the fighting at Lexington and Concord rolled across the Jerseys with the clouds of dust that followed the excited post riders. Fifty Princeton students drilled as a company on the campus grounds. "Every man handles his musket and hastens in his preparations for war," declared one devoted Rebel. Eighty-seven delegates to a second Provincial Convention, meeting at Trenton on May 23, 1775, reaffirmed its allegiance to the mother country, but after the battle of Bunker (Breed's) Hill, the delegates reassembled in August in a thoroughly different frame of mind. The time had come to levy taxes and organize military companies.

One can only guess at how many free men of military age the Jerseys then possessed. Some say the figure was as high as 27,000 before deducting 6,000 Quakers or other conscientious objectors, 1,000 "exempts or defectives," and 1,100 active Loyalists (although one source sets the figure for Jersey Loyalists as low as 284). An act of 1775 in the Provincial Congress established a State army of twenty-one regiments and nine battalions. Counties were assigned quotas: one regiment each for Bergen and Salem, two apiece for Sussex, Essex, Middlesex, Somerset, Morris and Burlington, three for Monmouth and four for Hunterdon. How the Congress reached these quotas is a difficult conjecture be-

cause the number of regiments required bore no relation to the
population of the counties. The training of recruits began that
autumn under Brigadier General Matthias Williamson of Elizabeth, whose later claim to fame was that his youngest son, Isaac,
one day became the governor of the State.

In Philadelphia the Continental Congress experienced lively
times. John Adams bedamned the bickerers and had his way.
Thus to the disappointment of at least Sam Adams and John
Hancock, who plainly coveted the position, George Washington
was named Commander-in-Chief and New Brunswick and Princeton saw him briefly in his blue and buff uniform of the Virginia
militia as he rode northward to take charge of the Continental
Army. When next these college towns beheld Washington, the
Provincial Congress had good reason for bemoaning "the cloud
of gloom and apprehension which hung over our State."

*   *   *

John Witherspoon was among the new delegation that represented New Jersey at the Second Continental Congress in
Philadelphia in 1776. Anyone who had attended a Princeton
commencement and heard orations on "all men are free by the
law of nature" and "civil liberty is necessary to give birth to the
arts and sciences," had no cause to wonder where Witherspoon's
sympathies lay. He chafed at the tedious delays before at last
the Declaration of Independence was adopted. Four days were
required to print the document while the post riders swatted at
the green stable flies and wished they could dash off with this
greatest proclamation of a century.

New Jersey (the name, combining the provinces of East and
West Jersey, was adopted in the summer of 1776) heard the
news in an exultant mood. In Bound Brook the venerable patriot,
Hendrik Fisher, then in his seventy-eighth year, read the Declaration to the hundred or so neighbors who listened as he spoke
from the porch of the Frelinghuysen House. Soft summer
breezes ruffled the white locks on Fisher's head. But his voice was
strong and resonant as he read Jefferson's poetic phrases:

When in the Course of human events it becomes necessary for one people to dissolve the political bands which have connected them with another. . . . We hold these truths to be self-evident, that all men are created equal, that they are endowed by their Creator with certain unalienable Rights, that among these are Life, Liberty and the Pursuit of Happiness. . . .

British America had never intended to separate from her mother country, but a chain of events which Jefferson enumerated and Fisher now repeated, had wrought the inevitable cleavage:

The King had refused his assent to laws, "the most wholesome and necessary for the public good."

The King had forbidden his agents "to pass Laws of immediate and pressing importance, unless suspended in their operation till his Assent should be obtained [when they could be voided by the King's whim]."

The King, in refusing "to pass other Laws for the accommodation of large districts of people, unless those people would relinquish the right of Representation in the Legislature," had asked the colonists to yield rights "formidable to tyrants only."

One can see Fisher pausing for breath, the wind blowing little clouds of dust along Bound Brook's main street. But the indictment against George III continued:

"He has called together legislative bodies at places unusual, uncomfortable and distant from the depository of their public Records, for the sole purpose of fatiguing them into compliance with his measures."

Representative bodies had been repeatedly dissolved "for opposing with manly firmness his invasions on the rights of the people."

He had refused for long periods to reassemble dissenting legislative groups, and even had "endeavoured to prevent the population of these States."

If the nods of the crowd around Frelinghuysen House grew vigorous, they became more so as Fisher sketched the objections to George III's judicial practices:

He has obstructed the Administration of Justice, by refusing his Assent to Laws for establishing Judiciary powers.

He has made Judges dependent on his Will alone, for the tenure of their offices, and the amount and payment of their salaries.

He has erected a multitude of New Offices, and sent hither swarms of Officers to harrass our people, and eat out their substance.

The Declaration enumerated specific acts by which George III had brought the colonies to open revolt:

He has kept among us, in times of peace, Standing Armies without the Consent of our legislatures.

He has affected to render the Military independent of and superior to the Civil power.

He has combined with others to subject us to a jurisdiction foreign to our constitution, and unacknowledged by our laws. . . .

The list of abuses brought against the King took many forms: the quartering of large numbers of troops among the colonists; protecting these troops from charges of murder through mock trials; cutting off colonial trade with the world; imposing taxes without the consent of the colonists; taking away charters; waging war on British America by plundering the seas, burning towns and destroying lives; by constraining citizens on the high seas and making them become "executioners of their friends"; by exciting domestic insurrection and exposing the colonists to the torment of Indian savagery. . . .

In a steady voice Fisher continued his bitter indictment of George III: as a tyrant who, in ignoring petitions for redress "in the most humble terms," had proved himself "unfit to be the ruler of a free people." Warnings that such behavior could only lead to war had been consistently ridiculed. "We must, therefore," Fisher read, "acquiesce in the necessity, which denounces our Separation, and hold them, as we hold the rest of mankind, Enemies in War, in Peace Friends." The result had become inevitable: "That these United Colonies are, and of right ought to be Free and Independent States."

The crowd before Frelinghuysen House broke into a cheer for its proud and venerable patriot. They raised Hendrik Fisher to their shoulders and carried him through Bound Brook. The bell began tolling in the Presbyterian Church. Cannon awakened echoes in the surrounding hills.

* * *

In every town the reading of the Declaration of Independence was greeted with joy and a sense of relief. In Princeton Nassau Hall was "grandly illuminated" and the ceremonies ended with a triple volley of musketry. In the Market Square in New Brunswick, where students from Queen's (later Rutgers) College mingled with farmers and townspeople, the Declaration was read by Colonel John Neilson, who was risking his considerable fortune to raise a battalion of militiamen. Sloops rode at anchor in the Raritan, a river John Adams had found "very beautiful" in his journey to the Congress in Philadelphia that had adopted this document. The spires of three houses of worship—those of the Church of England, the Dutch Reformed, the Presbyterian —rose against the brilliant summer sky; a nearby barracks, "tolerably handsome," looked "about the size of Boston jail"; and a few of the streets were paved.

An awed silence fell over the bustling marketplace as Neilson, a figure of dignity and local renown, began to read the Declaration's sentences of defiance and revolt. Mothers clung to the hands of children to keep them quiet. Farmers left their wagons to press closer to the speaker. There was no turning back now, Neilson told his audience; the choice was "victory or slavery." Cheers rang from the crowd. And soon Jerseymen were singing like other colonists:

> Vain Britons boast no longer with
> proud indignity,
> By land your conq'ring legions, your
> matchless strength at sea.
> Since we, your braver sons incens'd,
> our swords have girded on.
> Huzza, huzza, huzza, for War and
> Washington!

* * *

In September 1775 General Thomas Gage, who had led the
British to the humiliations of Concord and Bunker Hill, was
relieved in command by Sir William Howe. By nature Sir Billy
was a dawdler, always eager for an excuse to put off today's
imperative actions until a week from tomorrow, and was quite
willing to sit out the frequent cold storms and chilling winds of
a Boston winter. At the moment Howe's dilatory habits were
about the only bright spot in Washington's prospects. Everywhere the Commander-in-Chief turned in preparing Boston for
a siege he encountered discouragements: a military chest that was
"totally exhausted" so that "the paymaster has not a single dollar in hand"; new enlistments who dragged their feet in report-
ing for duty; militiamen who acted more like generals than
privates.

I have been laboring to establish and run me into one evil, whilst I am
endeavoring to avoid another, but the lesser must be chosen [Washington
wrote Joseph Reed, an old lawyer friend in Philadelphia]. Could I have
foreseen what I have and am likely to experience, no consideration upon
earth should have induced me to accept this command. A regiment or any
subordinate department would have been accompanied with ten times the
satisfaction and perhaps the honor.

Yet anybody looking down from Mount Whoredom, Boston's
highest hill, could only marvel at the genius with which Washington was shoring up the defenses of the city. The arrival of
Martha Washington with a few of her friends helped to brighten
the spirits of the Commander-in-Chief, and on Christmas Day
he was writing Joseph Reed that he could "give the enemy a
warm reception, if they think proper to come out." As Washington continued to rally an army and strengthen his defenses,
Howe began fitting out a fleet, quite willing to leave Boston in
the clutches of the cursed Rebels, and on the 30th of March
the *Pennsylvania Evening Post* exulted:

This morning the British army in Boston, under General Howe, consisting of upwards of seven thousand men, after suffering an ignominious
blockade for many months past, disgracefully quitted all their strongholds

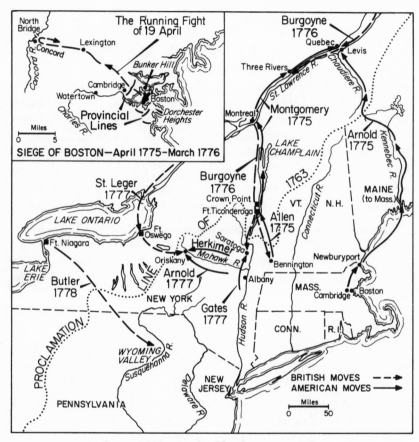

Seat of War in the North, 1775–1778

in Boston and Charlestown, fled from before the army of the United
Colonies, and took refuge on board their ships.

Among the many tokens of gratitude that Boston bestowed
upon Washington was the honorary degree of Doctor of Laws
from Harvard College. When Washington moved from Massachusetts, the patriots of the Jerseys could be proud of the number of the colony's military officers who journeyed with him:
Major General Lord Stirling, General Charles Stewart (who
had served as Washington's commissary general), General
Nathaniel Heard (who had arrested Governor William Franklin), and Colonels Philip Van Cortland, Ephraim Martin,
Stephen Hunt, Silas Newcomb, John Neilson, Frederick Frelinghuysen, Edward Thomas, Jacob Ford, Mark Thompson and
Samuel Forman. In the abortive and unsuccessful Canadian
campaigns that ended at Quebec (1775–76) three New Jerseymen also had served: Colonels William Maxwell, Elias Dayton
and William Winds. At no phase of the War for Independence
were the Jerseys unaffected and soon that conflict would be
pounding on the colony's front door.

*   *   *

Sir William Howe—"one of the greatest bus-missers in British military history"—liked guessing games and sometimes
played them well. When Howe evacuated Boston on March 17,
1776, escorted by the fleet under his brother, Admiral Lord
Howe, he headed for Halifax, awaiting reinforcements. Not
until June 7 did the British leave Nova Scotia with New York
as their objective. On July 12, the British Union Jack flapping
at their masts, the ships started through the Narrows.

This morning, [wrote Ambrose Serle, civilian secretary to Admiral
Howe,] the sun shining bright, we had a beautiful prospect of the coast of
New Jersey at about five or six miles distance. The land was cleared in
many places, and the woods were interspersed with houses, which being
covered with white shingles appeared very plainly all along the shore. We
passed Sandy Hook in the afternoon, and about six o'clock arrived safe off
the east side of Staten Island. The country on both sides was highly

picturesque and agreeable. Nothing could exceed the joy that appeared throughout the fleet and army upon our arrival. We were saluted by all the ships of war in the harbor, by the cheers of the sailors all along the ships and by those of the soldiers on the shore. . . .

Washington had marched directly on New York City from Boston. He realized not only the value of New York City (population about 22,000) as the port of entry next in importance to Philadelphia, but also that if the British controlled the valley of the Hudson, New England could be cut off from the other colonies. The American forces now in and around Manhattan numbered about 18,000, yet they offered no opposition when General Howe landed his 25,000 effectives on Staten Island. New York Harbor, the East River, and the Hudson lay under the control of his brother the admiral, "Black Dick" Howe. Washington realized both the stakes and dangers unless he could force a British evacuation. Any risk seemed warranted, so Washington ferried his army to Brooklyn and fortified its Heights.

Typical of the raw recruits on whom Washington was largely forced to rely was Joseph Plumb Martin, not yet sixteen and a private with the Connecticut forces under peppery old Israel Putnam. Although Martin had enlisted for only six months, the war seeped into his blood and he was still to be fighting after the grueling winters at Valley Forge and Morristown when Washington led his forces to the Battle of Yorktown. Martin was stationed in New York in Stone Street (which ran a single block from Broad Street to Whitehall) on the "southwest angle" of the city. Across the way was a cellar well stocked with several pipes of Madeira wine which the Connecticut boys acquired— some by payment, but more by theft—until Putnam stomped into Stone Street, "threatening to hang every mother's son of them," unless they stopped this nonsense. Martin believed him and dumped his wine. It had come in an uncleaned old oil flask and was frightfully rancid, anyhow.

Soon thereafter Martin was ordered to the Manhattan terminus of the Long Island Ferry at the foot of Maiden Lane. Here, uncovered, stood several casks of sea bread, probably made of "canel and peas-meal" and "hard enough for musket flints." Still, Martin stuffed his shirt and knapsack with them before he discovered that they could "break the teeth of a rat." He hurried down the ferry stairs, joined in three cheers with those who shared his boat, heard the cheers returned by patriots on the wharves, and sailed for Brooklyn.

The boy soldier quickly learned that a battle was not a lark: "We now began to meet the wounded men . . . some with broken arms, some with broken legs, some with broken heads." He saw a lieutenant who was acting queerly, either from drink or fear: ". . . he ran round among the men of his company, sniveling and blubbering, praying each one if he had aught against him, or if *he* had injured anyone that they would forgive him," and Martin thought: "A fine soldier you are, a fine officer, a fine exemplary man for young soldiers!" Another soldier virtually wound his way in circles, forgetful of where he had left his musket. Martin recalled a favorite couplet:

> Fear does things so like a witch,
> 'Tis hard to distinguish which is which.

Howe began the Battle of Long Island on August 27, 1776. Here Washington could have lost everything—the war, independence—save, in large measure, for the brilliant fighting of an aristocratic New Jerseyman.

*   *   *

William Alexander was born in 1726 in New York City. He traced his ancestry to a court poet and favorite of King James I who named him the first Earl of Stirling and gave him vast land grants in North America that included Long Island, Nova Scotia, and a considerable part of Canada. Perhaps a chief reason why the peerage became extinct with the death of the fifth Earl in 1739 was that William's father, James Alexander, although politically a Whig, was, as a Scot, a stanch adherent of the Stuart cause, and therefore was forced to flee England after the unsuccessful Rebellion of 1715. James prospered in the colonies, as a public official, a lawyer, and a land speculator in

New York and New Jersey, enabling his son William to gain an excellent education as a mathematician and astronomer. Among William's youthful friends and correspondents was Henry, a son of New York's Royal Governor Clinton; later, William's chum Henry Clinton was raised to knighthood and became first in command of all British forces and allies during the closing years of the American Revolution.

But much occurred between times. William joined his mother in a mercantile business in New York City, served as a commissary in the French and Indian Wars, and as an aide and secretary to Governor William Shirley of Massachusetts. Upon the death of James Alexander in 1756, William journeyed to England to reclaim his position in the peerage. More than four costly years followed in which triumph mixed with many frustrations. William gained the title of Lord Stirling under Scottish law (the name by which he was thereafter known on both sides of the Atlantic), but when in England he pressed for some part of his proprietary rights he discovered how tight-fisted and deaf to arguments kings and governments can become. His lordship was notoriously a Whig which did not enhance his reputation in palace circles, and weary of "vexatious delays," he decided to return to the colonies.

Lord Stirling's mother had been dead for more than a year when he reached New York in the autumn of 1761. A man of wealth, his social prominence increased with his marriage to the sister of William Livingston, who was to become the first governor of an independent New Jersey. Lord Stirling's report on the transit of Venus and his service as an early governor of Kings (later Columbia) College revealed that he continued his interest in higher education; and the beautiful mansion he built at Basking Ridge, New Jersey, indicated how well he prospered at farming, manufacture, and mining.

After the passage of the Stamp Act, the first of many unreasonable taxes, patriotism became one of his burning passions. As a colonel, Lord Stirling raised and equipped two regiments. In January 1776 with forty volunteers in a pilot boat he captured a British transport at Sandy Hook, and later earned a promotion to brigadier general. Congress asked him to prepare New York City against British invasion and made him its chief commander there. Under his direction Fort Lee (first called Fort Constitution) and Fort Washington (where New York's 181st Street now faces the river) were constructed. On Brooklyn Heights stood Fort Stirling.

*   *   *

In the confusion of the Battle of Brooklyn or Long Island it was not clear to Washington whether Lord Stirling had been killed or captured. To a distinguished biographer of Washington like Douglas Southall Freeman the part played by Lord Stirling in this engagement was "the most dramatic and gallant episode of the battle." To another, "Lord Stirling's brigade sustained the hottest of the enemy's fire," and in the opinion of a New York newspaper his soldiers "fought and fell like Romans."

A captive aboard Howe's flagship *Eagle,* Lord Stirling was far less melodramatic in his report to Washington. Ordered by Putnam to meet the enemy advance, he had opposed British General James Grant with two regiments established upon a ridge. At about eleven o'clock he found "that General Howe, with the main force of the army, was between me and our army." Lord Stirling saw quickly that his only chance to escape without everyone becoming a prisoner "was to pass the creek near the yellow mills." To achieve this objective he realized how "absolutely necessary" it was "to attack a body of troops commanded by Lord Cornwallis, posted at a house near the upper mills." The assault continued for quite some time and Lord Stirling appeared "on the point of driving Lord Cornwallis from his station" when British reinforcements turned the balance against the Americans. Lord Stirling attempted to edge between the house and a fort and suffered a rain of musketry on his front and both flanks, so he turned up a hill to elude this punishment and soon had outdistanced his pursuers. Realizing, however, that a complete escape was impossible, Lord Stirling "therefore went to surrender myself to General [Philip von] De Heister, the Commander-in-Chief of the Hessians."

Actually Lord Stirling had been left alone on the hills with Maryland and Delaware regiments after the Americans had collapsed on the left and center. Some of his troops, mainly Marylanders, made a courageous withdrawal across Gowanus Creek and its marshes that Joseph Plumb Martin observed: "When they came out of the water and mud to us, looking like water rats, it was a truly pitiful sight. Many of them were killed in the pond, and more were drowned. Some of us went into the water after the fall of the tide, and took out a number of corpses and a great many arms that were sunk in the pond and creek."

Why Howe delayed in capitalizing at once upon his great strategic victory in Brooklyn is one of many mysteries submerged within the almost fathomless depths of Sir Billy's personality. He not only allowed the citizens of New York to burn a large part of their city, thus diminishing the extent of his victory, but also gave Washington nearly a month to regroup his forces on Harlem Heights and arrange the exchange of Lord Stirling for Mountford Brown, Loyalist governor of Florida and the Bahamas.

Lord Stirling had returned to the Continental army less than twenty-four hours before Washington placed him in command of the flanking forces in the October maneuvering for White Plains. The result of Howe's success here left no doubt in Washington's mind as to Howe's next probable objective—to "gobble up" New Jersey. Early November found the Continentals scurrying across the Hudson to stand between New York and Philadelphia.

CHAPTER ONE

The River Forts

November, 1776

In command of Fort Lee and Fort Washington was General Nathanael Greene, who since boyhood had flashed anger at anyone ridiculing his stiff knee. Like many visibly handicapped persons young Greene exhibited a spirit of independence verging on defiance. Born in either July or August 1742 at Potowomut (Warwick), Rhode Island, the boy, growing up, saw his father as a kindly man whose "mind was overshadowed with prejudice against literary accomplishments."

Unlike his seven brothers, who were satisfied to end their education when an itinerant teacher had taught them how to read and do simple arithmetic, the youthful Nathanael also studied Latin and geometry; and at the suggestion of Ezra Stiles, the future president of Yale whom Greene met by chance in a Newport bookshop, turned to the humanistic writings of John Locke. A faithful worker at his father's forge and mill properties in Coventry, young Nathanael displayed a far more militant interest in the events leading to the Revolution than became "the son of one of the richest and most respected Quakers in America." He journeyed to Boston to buy a musket. From Henry Knox, the city's leading patriot bookseller, he bought such military works as Caesar's *Gallic Wars* and the memoirs of Marshal

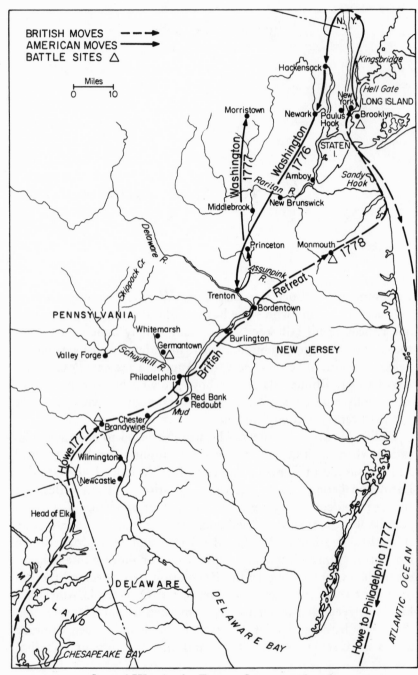

BRITISH MOVES   ----→
AMERICAN MOVES   ──→
BATTLE SITES   △

Miles
0   10

N.Y.

Kingsbridge

Hackensack

Hell Gate

Morristown

New York   LONG ISLAND

Newark   Paulus Hook   Brooklyn

Washington 1777

Washington 1776

STATEN I.

Sandy Hook

Amboy

Raritan R.

Middlebrook   New Brunswick

Delaware R.

Skippack Cr.

Princeton   Monmouth

Retreat △ 1778

Assunpink R.

Trenton

Bordentown

PENNSYLVANIA

Whitemarsh

Germantown △

Burlington

NEW JERSEY

Valley Forge   *Schuylkill R.*

Philadelphia

British

Red Bank Redoubt

Mud I.

Chester

Brandywine △

Howe 1777

Wilmington

Newcastle

Head of Elk

MARYLAND

DELAWARE

DELAWARE BAY

Howe to Philadelphia 1777

ATLANTIC OCEAN

CHESAPEAKE BAY

Seat of War in the Eastern States, 1776–1780

Turenne. For these acts Nathanael, who had now reached maturity, was well on his way to being "put from under the care of the meeting."

If Nathanael Greene regretted this religious rebuke, he did not reveal that emotion. Somewhere during his travels to and from Boston he met an unnamed British deserter who helped him organize and drill the Kentish Guards. Greene first met Washington during the long siege of Boston; here the gifts of the Rhode Island Quaker as a drillmaster earned him the rank from Congress of brigadier general and by the time the Continental Army moved to New York, he had become a warm friend of Washington because of the respect Nathanael won from such men as Henry Knox and Alexander Hamilton. A feverish illness prevented Greene's joining in the Battle of Long Island, but he took some brief part in the befuddling action at Harlem Heights before receiving his present command over the Hudson River forts.

On the last of October, a dull and rainy day, Greene wrote Washington that the British were very active around Fort Independence on the north side of King's Bridge. He had removed everything of value, he added, and cut the bridge. Should all the ground be held from King's Bridge or the garrison withdrawn into Fort Washington? This decision, Washington replied, Greene must make for himself. On the night of November 4 Washington's own sentinels around White Plains heard the rumbling wheels of British gun carriages. That night Washington's troops lay on their arms, and quickly thereafter the Commander-in-Chief learned that Howe was falling back on Dobbs Ferry.

On November 6 Washington wrote the President of Congress that Howe was returning to New York simply to close out the campaign for 1776. "I think it highly probable, and almost certain," Washington continued, "that he will make a descent with a part of his troops into Jersey; and, as soon as I am satisfied, that the present manœuver is real and not a feint, I shall use every means in my power to forward a part of our force to counteract his designs. . . ." He stormed at "the base and cowardly wretches" (Americans) who the previous night had burned the courthouse and private dwellings in White Plains and warned that "they shall . . . meet with the punishment they deserve."

Governor William Livingston heard from Washington on November 7. He was more convinced now that Howe intended to invade New Jersey, "for what has he done as yet with his great army?" The Governor, Washington warned, must place his militia "on the best footing possible," and "inhabitants, contiguous to the water, should be prepared to remove their stock, grain, effects, and carriages upon the earliest notice." The General advised Livingston: "The article of forage is of great importance to them, and not a blade should remain for their use." Washington also inquired concerning the state of the barracks "about Elizabethtown, Amboy, and Brunswic[k]" since they could be "exceedingly necessary to cover our troops."

An overoptimistic Greene wrote on November 9 of a visit the night before with Robert Magaw, the quick-tempered Irish colonel in command at Fort Washington:

The enemy seem to be disposing matters to besiege the place; but Colonel Magaw thinks it will take them till December expires before they can carry it. . . . Our giving it up will open a free communication with the country by the way of Kingsbridge. That must be a great advantage to them and injury to us.

If the enemy cross the river, I shall follow your Excellency's advice, respecting [the destruction of] the cattle and forage. These measures, however cruel in appearance, were ever my maxims of war in the defence of a country; in attacking, they would be very improper.

Greene, with his remnant of Quaker conscience, gave Washington no choice but to accept the Rhode Islander's judgment. On November 10 the Commander-in-Chief marched from White Plains, ferrying across the river below Stony Point. To guard the New York Highlands some 4,000 men under Brigadier General William Heath were stationed at Peekskill on the Hudson, about eighteen miles from White Plains. Another 7,000 troops were left at New Castle with General Charles Lee. Washington, advancing on Fort Lee, departed with about 2,000 effectives.

*   *   *

Although there was light morning frost that Sunday, the day rapidly grew sunny and warm. Captain Andreas Wiederhold, who served in General Wilhelm von Knyphausen's Hessian regiment, inspected Fort Washington on November 10 and was not altogether happy with what he observed. Both "nature itself" and "human skill" had fashioned a formidable bastion. Yet, Wiederhold knew, unless the fort were taken, "we could not keep up communication with New York, nor could we think of advancing any farther, much less get quiet winter-quarters." A violent rainstorm next day cancelled an anticipated assault; and the fort remained undisturbed when Howe arrived on the 14th and, as was his habit, revised everyone's plans.

Through cold, pelting rains Washington completed a circuitous sixty-five-mile march from White Plains to Hackensack, which was about four miles from Greene's headquarters at Fort Lee. This prosperous Dutch country was suspected of being notoriously Tory in sympathy, a fact the Commander-in-Chief might well ponder as he established his own headquarters in the home of Peter Zabriskie, who was well known for his Whig patriotism. As much as anyone, Zabriskie would know that Howe had raised a Tory regiment among these Dutchmen who were expected to serve as pilots and guides when the British invaded New Jersey.

It was difficult to believe that so much deviltry could be afoot when Washington gazed across Hackensack's peaceful village green. Here stood the old sandstone Dutch church "with its short white steeple and brass Dutch weathercock." Close by convivial voices rang in Archibald Campbell's inn. The sails of a new grist mill spun in a freshening breeze. Leydecker's farm, with its trim pole fence, was "universally allowed to be the finest place for the bigness" within miles.

Washington did not have long to enjoy the attractiveness of these surroundings. On November 15 an express rider pulled up before the Zabriskie place and within minutes Washington and four aides were galloping toward Fort Lee. The day before Magaw had told Howe's adjutant general that he intended to defend Fort Washington "to the last extremity," and Sir Billy was quite willing to oblige him in this respect. Hessian columns under Johann Rall and Knyphausen drove on Magaw from the north while British and Hessian forces under Lord Hugh Percy attacked from the south.

The sound of Lord Percy's musketry was the signal for the Hessians to assault from the north. A steep road allowed the Americans to pour down a vicious fire from two hillside batteries.

Captain Wiederhold marveled at Knyphausen's bravery, for he "at all times could be found in the thickest of the fight, where resistance and attack was the hottest, and he tore down the fences with his own hands to urge the men on. He was also exposed like a common soldier to the frightful cannon- and shrapnell-fire, as well as to the rifle shots. . . ." How Knyphausen came away alive astonished Wiederhold. A captain and a lieutenant were killed on the spot, but Wiederhold's only wound was a scratch from a broken twig, causing him to remember a homeland proverb, *"Unkraut vergeht nicht,"* which meant that "weeds are never hurt."

Night approached as Washington reached Fort Lee. Greene and General Israel Putnam already had crossed the Hudson to help Magaw prepare the defenses of Fort Washington. They were much impressed by this bastion, which covered four acres surrounded by an abatis of pointed poles. Swamps, sheer rock walls, and three earthworks, arranged in ascending tiers, protected the fort from attack. But the place also possessed weaknesses that Greene and Putnam may have ignored in their optimism that Magaw could stand off the British and Hessians for at least a month. Fort Washington claimed a wooden magazine and some offices, but lacked casements, bombproofs and barracks. Its drinking water had to be drawn from the Hudson, which lay 250 feet below.

Hours passed without any word at Fort Lee of what was transpiring across the river. With two aides Washington decided to row across the river and judge the situation for himself. In midstream he met the returning Greene and Putnam and was told that "the troops were in high spirits, and would make a good defense." The Commander-in-Chief returned to his headquarters in Hackensack.

Next morning a grumpy Washington arrived at Fort Lee. At

ten o'clock the echoing shots across the Hudson revealed that the attack on Fort Washington had resumed. The Commander-in-Chief had arrived on the New Jersey side of the Hudson believing that only 1,200 troops had been committed to the defense of Magaw; now he learned that an overoptimistic Greene had sent 1,500 reinforcements across the river.

Washington was chilled by this information. He had never intended this fort to be defended (nor had Howe expected Washington to do so), and in his heart Washington censured subordinate officers "not fit to be shoeblacks." All firing at Fort Washington ceased in less than an hour. Washington sent two courageous aides across the river with an offer to bring off Magaw's troops if they could hold out until darkness. Washington was too late—Magaw already had surrendered.

The Continental loss was tremendous: 230 officers and 2,600 troops. To this number Carl Leopold Baurmeister, a Hessian general, added:

In the fort we found thirty-two guns, two large mortars, and two howitzers, very little powder for guns and small arms, but many filled cartridges for small arms, great quantities of filled shells, hand grenades, bullets, flints, several barrels of slow-matches, quantities of provisions such as rum, flour, oil, butter, vinegar, salt meat, and fish, and fifty-three barrels full of potatoes.

While logs crackled cheerily in the tiled Dutch fireplaces of the Zabriskie house, Washington poured out his heartbreak in a letter to his brother John Augustine. Shipping "at all the lower ferries," the General wrote, had delayed his arrival in time to be of any practical assistance in the defense of Fort Washington. If Magaw had been able to get his unseasoned troops to man the lines, Washington said, "he [Magaw] would not have given up the fort." Washington admitted that he suffered "great mortification" as a result of this "most unfortunate affair"; not only had he lost Magaw's troops but also considerable artillery "and some of the best arms we had." He bewailed the slowness of the states in levying their quotas of men and he doubted if, within ten days, he would have more than 2,000 effectives with which to oppose "Howe's whole army" in Jersey and "very little" more to protect the eastern colonies by controlling the passages through the Highlands to Albany and on into the country "about the Lakes." For more than a year he had warned Congress of the necessity to engage men who would not finish their enlistments within a few months and might as well have saved his breath. The Commander-in-Chief still rankled over subordinates not fit to be shoeblacks and was "wearied almost to death with the retrograde motion of things" and if he could alter circumstances, "twenty thousand pounds a year would not induce me to undergo what I do."

Zabriskie tried to warn Washington of the danger he courted by remaining in Hackensack. As a result of the fall of Fort Washington, the Tory element had been highly activated. Zabriskie could mention a few names. The lieutenant of the King's Volunteers was Abraham Van Buskirk, son of a one-time member of the Provincial Congress and surgeon of the patriot militia. Daniel Isaac Brown, another one-time member of the Provincial Congress, was now a major in the King's Volunteers. No one could say how strong the Tories were, but once the British appeared they could come popping out like cottontails in high grass. If Washington nodded mechanically, that would not have been surprising. At this point, how important was one more problem?

*   *   *

Nathanael Greene could moan to his old Boston bookseller friend, Henry Knox, that he felt "mad, vexed, sick and sorry" over the events at Fort Washington, but the Rhode Island Quaker had a long way to go before his ordeal would be concluded. On November 20 a member of the American patrol entered Greene's tent, siezed his arm, and shook him awake. His message brought Greene out of bed on a bounce: during a cold and rainy night some 4,000 British under Lord Cornwallis had ferried across the Hudson between the western terminus of Dobbs Ferry and Fort Lee.

Cornwallis, who ranked immediately after Howe and Clinton in the military hierarchy in British America, intended to make the most of his first independent command. His Lordship, now in his thirty-ninth or thirty-eighth year (the only sure thing about his birth was the fact that it had occurred on the last dreary day in December) had paid a high price, both politically and domestically, for his presence in the colonies. Not that Cornwallis' credentials were not of the highest order, for they were: by eighteen he had studied at Eton and Cambridge and attended Turin, probably the best military academy of that age. In eight years he had risen to colonel of his own regiment, the 33rd, and his bravery in various engagements of the Seven Years' War had marked him well in royal judgment—as aide-de-camp to the king and lord of the bedchamber (1765), as chief justice of Eye (1766), and as constable of the Tower (1770). He had served in both the House of Commons and House of Lords and had won the heart of the frail but wiry Lady Jemima.

In between bearing Cornwallis a son and a daughter, Jemima had little objection if his Lordship dashed off to placate small fusses in Ireland, but she was truly flabbergasted when Cornwallis announced that he had offered to fight in the American Revolution. Even the Archbishop of Canterbury was called upon to argue against this wild idea and might have saved his time; Cornwallis felt committed to Lord North, the prime minister, and, moreover, secretly nourished ambitions of some day becoming governor and captain-general of Canada.

A contemporary portrait revealed a Lord Cornwallis with an attractive oval-shaped face, sharp eyes, an agreeable nose, and a firm but pleasant mouth. His powdered hair was pulled straight back but curled around his ears, emphasizing a high, intelligent forehead. What the portrait did not disclose, of course, was the stiffness in his gouty legs that caused him to walk with a staff or the puffiness that had crept into his cheeks and the slackness of his throat.

Nonetheless Cornwallis was a martinet in giving commands. Leaning on his staff that November 20, he waited stoically until twenty flatboats were tied to the western shore of the Hudson. Cornwallis' troops were light infantry, chasseurs or soldiers equipped and trained for rapid movement, and a brigade of guards. One hundred unarmed Tories, two engineers, twelve carpenters, and three guides completed the British invading force. Cannon had to be drawn by brute force up the steep narrow roads to Fort Lee, but Cornwallis watched this operation unmoved by the physical strain involved.

Nathanael Greene, as Cornwallis quickly discovered, had not stopped at the manner of his leaving. Breakfast kettles still boiled in the abandoned fort. Some American stragglers were found in the three hundred tents; the tents were a good haul and the stragglers were shuttled across the Hudson to rot out the war in jail. Another 1,200 drunken Americans were flushed from the woods. Cornwallis could reckon in one sense that he had fared well, for fifty loaded cannon were captured along with two large iron sea mortars, hundreds of muskets, a thousand barrels of flour, and a large assortment of shot, shell, and cartridges. A small quantity of "poor pork" was found, a few "greasy proclamations" and letters belonging to Thomas Paine, "that scoundrel Common Sense man."

Cornwallis completed his crossing of the river at about nine o'clock and Washington heard the news in Hackensack an hour later. Sadly the Continental commander prepared to leave "a very fine country" for the risks of miry and broken roads across the Aquackamong Bridge and the Passaic River before reaching Newark. A flurry of communications flowed from his pen: to Congress, pleading for a variety of provisions to replace those lost at Fort Lee; to Major General Charles Lee, asking him to move quickly into New Jersey with 3,500 troops Lee still held at White Plains; and to Governor Livingston, asking him to delay the impending end of enlistments for many members of the Jersey militia.

Washington left Hackensack on November 21. Legend insists that he stopped for a glass of wine at Archibald Campbell's tavern and afterward was delayed by a townsman who inquired whither the General was going.

"Can you keep a secret?" Washington asked.

The townsman nodded.

"So can I," Washington said and spurred his horse along the road toward Aquackamong Bridge.

CHAPTER TWO

Flight

November–December, 1776

For Washington and those who yearned for freedom, the darkest hours of the Revolution had arrived. "These are the times that try men's souls," wrote Thomas Paine, who, as an aide to Greene, participated in the humiliating flight across New Jersey. Wet, cold weather and soggy roads revealed to Paine, as he later wrote, "the summer soldier and the sunshine patriot." Within a year since the stalemate before Boston, and in less than six months since the adoption of the Declaration of Independence, the British had recaptured the initiative, for in addition to losing the Hudson River forts the Americans had been driven from Canada and their boats swept from Lake Champlain. Washington wrote to his brother that the game seemed "pretty well up."

Yet confession was often good for Washington's soul. Once he admitted the desperate depths of his adversity, he renewed his determination never to feel a British rope around his throat even if he must lead the enemy on a wild chase into the back mountains of Virginia. On November 21 Washington's letter from Aquackamong Bridge to Governor Livingston did not minimize the danger. The General preferred being caught between the Hackensack and Passaic rivers rather than between the Hackensack and the North rivers, a country which "from its levelness and openness" was "unfit for making a stand." He could not stress too strongly how inadequate was his strength compared to that of the British, and he had decided that he must fall back as far as New Brunswick, where Lord Stirling already commanded. The root of the whole trouble was that the enlistment of the "Flying Camp" belonging to Jersey, Pennsylvania, and Maryland was about to expire, which would occasion "so great a diminution of my army" that Washington begged Livingston to call for sufficient militia "to cover the country and stop the progress of the enemy, if they should attempt to penetrate." If the "defenceless" New Jersey legislature did not respond as warmly as Washington wished, the fault was not Livingston's. During the last weeks of November the Governor and his legislative colleagues wandered from Princeton to Burlington, from Burlington to Pittstown, and from Pittstown to Haddonfield before deciding on December 2 that each man should save his own neck as best he could.

The Commander-in-Chief was puzzled by the nonappearance of Charles Lee and his troops and wondered if their communications were being intercepted by spies. There were reports of enemy landings at South Amboy, an advance on Elizabethtown, and Hessians on the road to Springfield. Meanwhile, Cornwallis followed doggedly after Washington, although historians who picture Washington as leaving the south of Newark while his Lordship entered from the north somewhat distort the situation. By the testimony of Thomas Paine, "We stayed four days at Newark, collected our outposts, with some of the Jersey Militia, and marched out thrice to meet the enemy on information of their advancing, although our numbers were greatly inferior to theirs." The fact that it took the Hessians six days to move from Springfield to Bound Brook, normally a march of twenty-four hours, indicated the general sluggishness that obtained when winter weather ordinarily ended all fighting.

William Bamford, who fought with Cornwallis, was quite out of sorts with Washington's tactics:

As we go forward into the country the Rebels fly before us, & when we come back, they always follow us, 'tis almost impossible to catch them. They will neither fight, nor totally run away, but they Keep at such a distance that we are always above a days march from them. We seem to be playing at Bo peep.

Cornwallis pressed on, growing somewhat out of sorts himself. Occasionally he covered twenty miles over frigid roads in a single day, even though a British infantryman, when fully equipped, carried a load of almost one hundred pounds. At times Cornwallis outran his supply wagons and his men subsisted on flour.

News from London upset Cornwallis, who wished to be rid of this silly business and return home to an ailing Lady Jemima. But Cornwallis was ordered to halt before the Raritan and New Brunswick until Howe arrived with reinforcements. In his usual indolent manner, Sir Billy required five days for the march.

* * *

Among the first to reach New Brunswick as part of Lord Stirling's vanguard was James McMichael, a lieutenant in a Pennsylvania regiment. On November 16, somewhere near Woodbridge, the lieutenant declared he could hear the fighting at Fort Washington, which must have given him the most remarkable ears in the colonies. More credible seemed his report on settling in New Brunswick next day that the soldiers were drinking freely "of spiritous liquors" with the result that they contracted "Barrel Fever." This illness, McMichael noted, usually produced "black eyes and bloody noses." The Dutch college, Queen's, with its few remaining students and tutors, had fled to the interior of neighboring Somerset County.

Mid-November found Lord Stirling playing a frantic game of military shuttlecock across northeast New Jersey. He guarded roads from Staten Island, still a British base. On November 10 he wrote Washington from Haverstraw and a week later was back in New Brunswick. Lord Stirling's effective force had dwindled to 1,000 or fewer and like most Continentals at that time they were "broken down and fatigued—some without shoes, some had no shirts." Washington arrived at New Brunswick while Cornwallis awaited the reinforcements under Howe. The bridge over the Raritan was destroyed and Alexander Hamilton placed a battery on a hill where he commanded the river's ford, no more than knee-deep.

New Brunswick presented many problems to Washington. On the last day of November, he wrote the President of the Congress that he had left Newark three days ago when the enemy had entered "by the time our rear got out." He had departed against the wishes of his generals, who knew now that the British were sending another detachment from Staten Island. He knew also of the advance "last night" of the British as far as Elizabeth and that the Hessians were on the road from Springfield. He suspected an advance on Philadelphia. His enlisted men, whose terms did not expire until January 1, already were leaving.

As November ended Howe was contriving an elaborate campaign. He wanted a footing in Jersey for the shelter, forage, and fresh provisions it promised. Howe was thinking in terms of broad strategy: extensive operations in Rhode Island and Massachusetts, the retaking of Boston, an ascent to Albany, and, come autumn, an attack on Philadelphia. To achieve these objectives he would require 35,000 men—more reinforcements than Britain was able to send or to buy from various German principalities.

Meanwhile Washington continued his letter writing from New Brunswick on November 30. He implored Governor Livingston that day to "give orders to the officers of militia on the roads and the ferries over Delaware to take up and secure every soldier that has not a regular discharge or pass." He told the Board of War that he would not consider enlisting prisoners of war to fight on the patriot side—the suggestion was "neither consistent with the rules of war, nor politic"—and he explained why: ". . . in time of danger I have always observed such persons most backward, for fear, I suppose, of falling into the hands of their former masters, from whom they expect no mercy; and this fear they are apt to communicate to their fellow-soldiers."

Next day Washington warned poor, meandering Governor Livingston, en route from Pittstown to God knows where, that the enemy obviously held Philadelphia as their objective. Last night they were at Bonhamtown, "four miles on this side of Woodbridge"; moreover, the militia from the counties of Morris

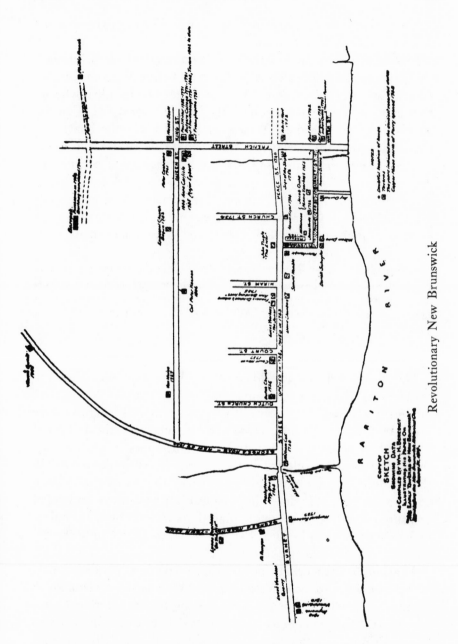

Revolutionary New Brunswick

and Sussex were enlisting reluctantly, "whether from the want of officers of spirit to encourage them, or your summons not being regularly sent to them, I cannot say"; he suspected that "designing men" had deliberately discouraged the men from Morris and Sussex. But Washington also was heartened; enlistments in Pennsylvania were very encouraging, and "General Lee is on the march down to join me." Wisely he urged that "the boats and craft, all along the Delaware side, should be secured; particularly the Durham boats used for the transportation of produce down the river."

Washington's last letter from New Brunswick was another plea to General Charles Lee, entreating him "to hasten" his march "as much as possible." Nathanael Greene mourned:

Two brigades left us at Brunswick, notwithstanding the enemy were within two hour's march and coming on. The loss of these troops at this critical time reduced his Excellency [Washington] to the necessity to order a retreat again [toward Princeton]. . . . When we left Brunswick, we had not 3000 men.

*   *   *

On November 29 President John Witherspoon called the students of Princeton to a meeting in the Prayer Room. The imminent approach of Cornwallis' forces must be recognized, he said. Dr. Witherspoon's face was as sober as those turned toward him as he offered his students "much good advice." Then the village fairly exploded with excitement as students packed their belongings, sought vehicles to carry them away, and bade fond farewell to old friends in Nassau Hall. Witherspoon loaded treasured valuables in a wagon, placed his wife in the "old chair," and rode off toward Pequea, Pennsylvania, mounted on his sorrel mare.

Washington reached Princeton three days later, knowing that he was too weak to make a stand here. He paused long enough to write a brief note to Congress, expressing his bewilderment over why he still had no contact with General Lee. Lord Stirling was left at Princeton with two brigades to hold off the British as best he could while Washington hastened on to Trenton and a crossing of the Delaware. A Continental regiment felled trees across the roads and tore up bridges.

Cornwallis, hard on Washington's heels and beginning to believe that his visit to England to join Lady Jemima must now be postponed, was not in his most lenient mood. Richard Stockton, who had given the four hundred acres on which the College stood and was a signer of the Declaration of Independence, was high on the list of those the British had marked for retribution. The Redcoats swept down on his beautiful estate, Morven, where the library was Stockton's special pride, "but libraries seem to have been anathema to the kindly British at war, and the Morven collection of books and records went up in smoke on Cornwallis' altar." Furniture and paintings were destroyed, livestock requisitioned, and Richard Stockton placed in such abusive captivity that his death followed in 1781. Houses in the village were pillaged and plundered, horses stabled in the basement of Nassau Hall, and all suspected "of being rebels or aiding and assisting them" were hustled off to prison.

*   *   *

Various descriptions of General Charles Lee have survived. To one historian this hatchet-faced soldier of fortune might have been Ichabod Crane, stepping from the pages of Washington Irving's *Sleepy Hollow;* and because of the General's quick temper the Mohawks called him "Boiling Water." In his own opinion Lee was easily the best trained military man in the colonies and he seethed inwardly with jealousy that Congress had not made him Commander-in-Chief. Certainly no one then in America had made war a more extensive career. Lee had fought with the British in the French and Indian War and in Portugal against the Spanish. He had fought in Poland and in Turkey where the imaginative Frank R. Stockton delighted in believing Lee "wore a turban and baggy trousers, and carried a great scimiter, for a man of that sort is not likely to do things by halves when he does them at all." Other fighting in Russia and

Hungary preceded his arrival in the colonies in 1773 where, two years later, he settled on a plantation in Berkeley County, Virginia (now West Virginia).

Lee accepted the rank of major general on the condition that Congress pay him £30,000 in compensation for the property losses he would suffer in England as a result of supporting the patriot cause.

Finally prodded into action by Washington's repeated pleas, and by the ultimate threat of a court-martial, Lee crossed the Hudson at Stony Point, and finding Cornwallis blocking the main road southward, decided on a circuitous route by way of Morristown, Pittstown, and Easton, covering no more than thirty-five miles in his first week's march.

At Vealtown on December 12 he spread the wagons and the camp fires of his army for an impressive distance. Lee's contempt for his weary soldiers in their "old-fashioned, full-bottomed wigs, often awry" may have explained why he preferred to lodge that night in Mrs. White's Tavern at Basking Ridge; or it is possible that he planned to become a hero by striking a lightning blow at the rear of Cornwallis' forces, thus retrieving victory that a blundering Washington had lost. Next morning, half-dressed and in his slippers, he listened to complaints in a snappish mood, breakfasted at about ten, then composed a letter to General Horatio Gates, in which Lee wrote: *"Entre nous,* a certain general is most damnably deficient." How else could one judge Washington after the succession of disasters from Long Island to the present flight through New Jersey?

About this time a cry was heard outside the tavern. A pale-faced aide told Lee, "Here are the British cavalry!" The two guards, sunning themselves on the south side of the house, were equally surprised. A British voice gave Lee five minutes to show himself or the dwelling would be burned. A woman offered to hide the General under a feather mattress, where she was certain he never would be found, but Lee preferred capture to this indignity. The trumpet sounded assembly, a hatless Lee was mounted on a horse "just as he was," and the party dashed off to New Brunswick. Drooping eyes and mouth revealed Lee's humiliation; the cold reddened his large nose, and wintry gusts whipped his dressing gown until his body was half frozen. Well might a contemporary account say:

"Oh! What a damned sneaking way to be kidnapped!"

*   *   *

Although Washington still could have no inkling of the humiliating fate about to befall his faithless friend, the Commander-in-Chief remained cheerful. "I will not despair," he told Governor Livingston on November 30, two days before the Americans entered Trenton. As soon as Washington could secure boats from Philadelphia, he informed Congress next day, he intended to cross the Delaware. On an icy Sunday five days later Washington was drawing the last of his troops across the river when Cornwallis reached Trenton with bands playing and flags waving. Convinced that he was in no immediate danger, Cornwallis left Trenton to the defense of Hessians under Colonel Johann Rall while his Lordship took up a post at "Penny Town," as he insisted on calling Pennington. Washington's first Pennsylvania headquarters were in the home of George Clymer, a signer of the Declaration of Independence, who lived in a region now a part of Morrisville.

CHAPTER THREE

Mount Holly: An Ace in the Hole

December, 1776

From the moment Cornwallis' pursuit reached Princeton, Philadelphia was a frightened city. Washington crossed to the west side of the Delaware on December 3 and at once sent the one man who he believed could allay the alarm in the City of Brotherly Love. General Thomas Mifflin, already a fourth-generation Pennsylvanian and a former member of the Continental Congress, spread the word that contrary to "the false and malicious reports" circulated "by the enemies of Congress," Washington possessed "full power to order and direct all things relative to the department [of the army] and to the operation of the war."

Like Nathanael Greene, Mifflin had been read out of the Quaker meeting for his militaristic tendencies. At the moment, Philadelphia reverberated with rumors of the Hessian atrocities that had become commonplace since the Battle of Long Island. Where shall we go, dismayed Philadelphia women asked. How shall we get out of town? Daily thereafter fear became despair and then panic.

There were few carriages available. There were "no blessed

steamboats to waft their thousands from 'Indies to the Pole.' "
Families of scant income lacked the hack or "one-horse chair"
that carried the wealthy merchant to security in rural regions.
Wrote an unnamed witness in her diary, describing the plight of
the less fortunate:

> Happy was he, who could press a market wagon, or a milk-cart, to bear
> off his little ones! My family, together with that of a friend, who had been
> obliged to abscond with the city council, were stowed, women, children,
> and servants, counting in number more than a score, into a small river craft
> called a wood-flat, whose smoky cabin did not permit the ladies with infants
> in their arms, to quite sit upright. The smoke, however, was intolerable,
> and we girls, whose hearts shrunk from no inconvenience or danger, made
> our beds with blankets upon the deck; from this enviable station we were
> driven, by a heavy fall of snow, into the hold of the boat, where we slept
> soundly on the few tables and chairs which our hurry had enabled us to
> carry with us. Innumerable were the hardships, and much would you
> wonder, could I tell you what the scattered Philadelphians endured at that
> trying season; thankful, if they could find a hut or a barn, in any region of
> security! Sometimes, those who had never spoken together in the city would
> meet in their wanderings, and then all distinctions of rank were forgotten,
> and they were a band of brothers.

Both in Pennsylvania and New Jersey the towns and villages
were flooded by Howe's proclamations offering pardon to all who
surrendered now. A rumor placed Benjamin Franklin in England,
either as a fugitive or a peacemaker. Onetime "zealous" patriots
began "growing lukewarm"—as an example, John Dickinson,
who in the belief that the Declaration of Independence had been
"premature," declined a seat in Congress from Delaware.

In the same panic that afflicted many of the townspeople, the
members of Congress collected their papers and fled from Philadelphia to Baltimore. In this refuge, before December ended,
Congress not only reaffirmed its belief in "the wisdom, and up-
rightness of General Washington" but also practically invested
him with dictatorial powers:

> Resolve, That General Washington shall be, and he is hereby, vested
> with full, ample, and complete powers to raise and collect together, in the
> most speedy and effectual manner, from any or all of these United States,

sixteen battalions of infantry, in addition to those already voted by Congress; to appoint officers for the said battalions of infantry; to raise, officer, and equip three thousand light-horse, three regiments of artillery, and a corps of engineers, and to establish their pay; to apply to any of the States for such aid of the militia as he shall judge necessary; to form such magazines of provisions, and in such places, as he shall think proper; to displace and appoint all officers under the rank of brigadier-general, and to fill up all vacancies in every other department in the American army; to take, wherever he may be, whatever he may want for the use of the army, if the inhabitants will not sell it, allowing a reasonable price for the same; to arrest and confine persons who refuse to take the Continental currency, or are otherwise disaffected to the American cause; and return to the States, of which they are citizens, their names, and the nature of their offences, together with the witnesses to prove them.

That the foregoing powers be vested in General Washington, for and during the term of six months from the date hereof, unless sooner determined by Congress.

In character, Washington wrote Congress:

I have no lust for power. I wish, with as much fervency as any man upon this wide extended Continent, for an opportunity of turning the sword into the plowshare. A character to lose, an estate to forfeit, the inestimable blessings of Liberty at stake, and a life devoted must be my excuse.

*   *   *

In those first early weeks of December, while a Philadelphia woman lamented that "massacre and starvation chilled the blood in every vein" and Thomas Paine was declaring in his pamphlet, *American Crisis,* that "Tyranny, like Hell, is not easily conquered," events were transpiring that would bring the month to a surprising finale.

One can almost hear the laughter of Howe over the manner of General Lee's capture in his dressing gown—and of the ultimate indignity in New Brunswick when Redcoats induced Lee's horse to imbibe liquor to the point of inebriation—but this bit of luck could have been one of the circumstances convincing Sir Billy that the campaign of 1776 had ended. Henry Clinton was sent with 6,000 troops to seize Rhode Island and for the next three years the British settled around Newport. Howe also

strung 14,000 troops to hold posts from Staten Island to Princeton, and thence to Pennington, Trenton, Bordentown and, briefly,
Burlington. Howe himself called rather overextended the southern end of his chain of defenses, comprising another 3,500 Hessians and Highlanders, half of whom were stationed at Trenton
under Rall and half six miles south at Bordentown under Colonel
Carl Emil Kurt von Donop. Perhaps more than Howe, Donop
was troubled by this dispersement and suggested that Trenton
should be protected on the flanks by garrisoned redoubts. Rall
responded irately:

"What need we of entrenchments? We'll at them with the
bayonet."

Washington had counted heavily on Charles Lee's support
when he crossed the Delaware with his 2,000 lean and ragged
Continentals, whom Rall called "country clowns." The truth was
revealed on December 20 when General John Sullivan, a son of
New Hampshire with an inborn streak of Irish toughness, arrived
with the troops of the captured Lee—not the 5,000 Washington
had expected but a mere 2,000! For what small consolation it
was worth, General Horatio Gates also finished his march from
Ticonderoga with another 600 soldiers.

Yet even these adversities could not leave Washington long
downcast. It was during these so often infuriating December
days that the legend of nobility now surrounding Washington
began to emerge: his amiability, his human understanding, his
ability at improvisation, his tenacity of purpose, his boldness, his
courage, his compassion. The tears in the eyes of a three-year-old
child who had been ignored when glasses of cider had been
passed around were quickly noticed by Washington. Graciously
the Commander-in-Chief bowed to permit the child to share his
portion. When offered another glass, Washington replied: "I
can drink after a child like that."

From sympathy for what the Continental troops suffered, the
Commander-in-Chief bombarded Congress for every variety of
provision. He moved his headquarters "up the river" to be closer
to the main body of his men, settling at the home of William
Keith, a substantial pointed-stone house that remained untouched

in ensuing decades "except from the tooth of time." Meanwhile, Washington scattered the countryside with agents seeking "old clothes" for his near-naked troops. Twenty-six townships were scoured for blankets against the freezing weather; they were not free by any means, and when the charge was added for cleaning them at Jenks's fulling mill, the cost became high: £678 12s. 6d. The inhabitants of Quaker Buckingham seemed readiest for this kind of business. Yet there were compensations. The Reverend John Rosebrough, who served two Presbyterian churches in Pennsylvania's Northampton County, raised a battalion largely from his congregations and marched it to Washington's assistance.

Sound military judgment led to many Continental decisions. Newtown, then the county seat of Northampton, was selected as the main base of supplies since it was screened from the view of the river and joined good roads from all important places thereabouts. With the leaves off the trees, Jericho Mountain provided an excellent lookout point for observing enemy activities up and down the Delaware. Brigades under Lord Stirling and Generals Hugh Mercer, Adam Stephen, and the Frenchman, Roche de Fermoy, guarded posts from Coryell's Ferry to Yardley's Ferry, the flanks to McKonkey's Ferry whence, ultimately, Washington would cross the Delaware on his return to Trenton. General James Ewing with about 500 men was farther south along the river, watching the ferry to Bordentown. That stout-hearted Pennsylvanian, General John Cadwalader, was headquartered at Bristol with 1,000 men (mostly newly trained militia), where he guarded the river to Dunk's Ferry below Burlington.

From these flanking posts, in part, Washington would receive an unexpected Christmas present and thereby benefit enormously.

*   *   *

The grumpiness with which Donop and Rall parted at Trenton suddenly became very important. The larger part of the troops —2,000 against 1,500—left with Donop. In short, if the Hessian troops commanded by Donop at his headquarters in Bordentown could be immobilized, the situation at Trenton would be greatly altered.

The "Battle of Iron Works Hill," fought at Mount Holly, an extremely well-to-do village some twenty miles from Trenton, was far too significant to be ignored. About 90 Hessians under the command of Captain Johann Ewald, "a scholar if not always a gentleman," came by way of Black Horse (Columbus) and Slabtown (Jacksonville) to appear in Mount Holly on December 20. Repeatedly, but without success, Mr. Cox, who owned the old mine works, had appealed to the State legislature for a guard of "50 men exempted from military service." The iron works, after all, was engaged in a necessary business, casting cannon balls, soup kettles, and fixtures for the salt works at Tuckerton.

Ewald's Hessians behaved as badly as everyone anticipated. The old benches in the Friends Meeting House showed the marks of the cleavers with which the Jaegers cut up their meat. Around one pillar were the rope marks where they hauled up the bullocks. American provisions, found in the Town Hall, were burned amid Hessian laughter. Aaron Smith was forced from his residence in the meeting house and his Bible kicked down the street for about two hundred yards—another source of hilarity for the soldiers who quenched their thirst at the Cross Keys Tavern. Mrs. James Clothier, alone at the time, appeased the vengeful Hessians by "baking an oven of bread" and serving them from a barrel of fine whiskey "in a tin coffee pot." A boy saved the brass andirons from his parlor by snatching them from the hands of a Hessian. David Housler, who had fought with Washington on Long Island, escaped incarceration in a tavern room by slipping past his guard and running "as if the Old Fellow were after me."

The "flying camp" of Americans who came down to give the Hessians battle was led by Deputy General Samuel Griffin, wounded at Harlem Heights and still a very sick man. His force could not have been much more than 450 militiamen, including many boys, who had been cajoled into the army in Philadelphia and Salem and Gloucester counties. They matched the Hessians on Iron Works Hill in a smart artillery duel, delaying for some hours a local funeral then in process. Two dead Hessians were found spread crosswise in a rifle pit on the hillside. Very likely overstating the case, the *Pennsylvania Evening Post* of December 24 declared that "the enemy were forced to retreat with precipitation, having some killed, and leaving behind them many knapsacks and other necessaries, amongst which was a hat shot through the crown." Actually the Americans had been instructed "not to fight but to fly after they had misled Donop," which they did by scurrying toward Moorestown. A confused and obviously bitter Donop, leaving a rear guard of 80 at Bordentown, marched most of his 2,000 troops next day twelve miles to Mount Holly on a fool's errand. Thus they were about twenty miles from Trenton when Rall needed them most.

Donop's confusion might have been greater that Christmas Day if Cadwalader had been able to cross at Dunk's Ferry. Almost across the Delaware, Cadwalader's men had to turn back "on account of the Ice on the Jersey shore" which would not support their artillery. If Cadwalader and Ewing could have navigated the river that day, Washington wrote afterward, he was certain that he "should have been able, with their assistance, to drive the enemy from all their posts below Trenton."

Washington did not know how well he had been served at Mount Holly as he wrote on slips of paper "Victory or Defeat," the password for his intended attack that night on Trenton. Colonel John Glover's fishermen from Marblehead, Massachusetts, were expected to handle the boats in crossing the river.

*   *   *

In keeping with Hessian custom, Christmas in Trenton had been celebrated in high spirits. Rall spent the evening playing cards. A Tory from Pennsylvania appeared with a message revealing Washington's full plan.

"The gentlemen can't be disturbed," said the Negro servant who guarded the door.

The Tory insisted that his note be taken to Rall. The servant agreed reluctantly. The Hessian commander, "excited by wine" and in the act of dealing, snatched the communication and stuffed it into his pocket, where it remained unread throughout the night.

CHAPTER FOUR

Surprise at Trenton

December, 1776

Christmas approached. Six days before this holiday which the Hessians traditionally celebrated in singing and dancing, wine-drinking and games, Thomas Paine, who had been an aide to Nathanael Greene at Fort Lee, published his new pamphlet, *American Crisis*. This publication so aroused patriotic fervor that 120,000 copies were sold in the next three months and Washington, enchanted by Paine's inspiring arguments, ordered the pamphlet read to every regiment.

Many spies visited Washington's headquarters. They brought him maps showing the water obstacles and the locations of roads on both banks of the Delaware. They laughed at the ineptness of the Hessians at any kind of carpentry. Boat building baffled them completely and they were even inexperienced at replanking a bridge. Sometimes farmers loyal to the patriot cause came looking for the Commander-in-Chief. Their purpose was to reaffirm their faith in him, even though recent events well might have dashed their revolutionary hopes. There could be no question that the loyalty of these rustic visitors greatly strengthened Washington's morale.

The Commander-in-Chief's mood grew cheerier when, three days before Christmas, General Joseph Reed, writing from

Bristol, urged Washington to act "to revive our expiring credit, give our cause some degree of reputation, and prevent a total depreciation of the Continental money, which is coming on very fast." Politely the Commander-in-Chief replied that "Christmas-day at night, one hour before day" had been fixed for "our attempt" on Trenton. "For Heaven's sake," Washington pleaded, "keep this to yourself, as the discovery of it may prove fatal to us." Washington reiterated his belief that Philadelphia would be attacked as soon as the Delaware was sufficiently frozen to permit the British to cross on the ice. There was even a rumor widely circulated by British agents that Washington would burn the city before permitting it to be captured.

On December 23 the Americans prepared rations for three days. Boats already were collected at Knowles' Cove, a well-screened inlet not far from McKonkey's Ferry (sometimes called Eight-Mile Ferry and now Taylorsville). Scouting reports on the day before the crossing placed a Hessian picket on the Pennington Road about a half mile above Trenton and another at General Philemon Dickinson's house on the river road.

Washington used part of next day in letter-writing to the President of Congress. Many of the troops who had come with Gates and the captured Lee were leaving, Washington said, and he had "not the most distant prospect of retaining them a moment longer than the last of this month." With their departure, he added, his army would consist of five regiments from Virginia, William Smallwood's regiment from Maryland, small remnants of two regiments from Pennsylvania, part of Andrew Ward's regiment from Connecticut, and the German Battalion, largely recruited in Philadelphia. In round numbers, these troops amounted to no more than 1,500 and would be joined by about 1,000 militiamen. Moreover, through "an intercepted letter from a gentleman from Philadelphia, who has joined the enemy," there remained no question of Howe's intention to occupy that city by the turn of the year. The Commander-in-Chief urged that the public papers be removed from Philadelphia if someone had not already thought to do so.

By Christmas morning—clear but very cold—the rations had

been cooked and new flints and ammunition distributed. After the regiments had paraded in the late afternoon they marched straight for the ferry. There was a rawness now to the cold and snow began falling. Soldiers without shoes either wrapped rags around their feet or went barefoot. Gradually the wind stole into the northeast and beat directly into the faces of the troops. Sleet, added to the snow, "cut like a knife."

Twenty-four hundred soldiers followed Washington to McKonkey's Ferry. In a brief note to Cadwalader the Commander-in-Chief said: ". . . I am determined, as the night is favorable to cross the River, and make the attack upon Trenton in the morning. If you can do nothing real, at least create as great a diversion as possible."

Colonel Glover's Marblehead fishermen began the crossings at about sunset. Washington went in one of the first boats. To the men piloting the craft the labor was exhausting. With all their strength they used boat hooks to push aside the cakes of floating ice. Snow pelted their faces. Around them the roar of the water and the crash of the ice made it almost impossible to hear even shouted commands. Once Washington reached the shore one source described him as sitting on "a bee-hive," wrapped in his cloak as his eyes followed every ensuing detail.

Washington had hoped to complete the crossing by midnight so that he could strike Trenton at five o'clock, but the storm and the ice scuttled these plans. The last cannon was ferried across sometime around three o'clock so that it would be daybreak now before the Americans entered Trenton. Still, there was one good side to the storm since it muffled the sounds of marching feet and the rolling wheels of the artillery.

At Bear Tavern, about a mile or so from the ferry landing, the army divided into two columns. Sullivan, who was to lead a force down the river road, was told to halt a few minutes at the crossroads leading to Howland's Ferry so that Washington, who would lose time taking a circuitous route by way of the Scotch and Pennington roads, would be able to launch a simultaneous attack. Each division was supplied with its own guide. Lord Stirling and Generals Greene, Mercer, and Stephens marched

with Washington, and so stealthily did they advance that scarcely
a word was spoken between generals or troops. One exception
occurred when an aide from Sullivan brought a message saying
that he feared the storm had fouled his muskets and what should
he do?

"Tell your general to use the bayonet and penetrate the town,"
Washington replied. "The town must be taken, and I have
resolved to take it."

*　　　*　　　*

A barking dog brought a farmer down a lane to the Pennington Road. The man was in a violent temper and quite profane
in inquiring what fools were chasing about the countryside on
such a stormy night. When apprised by Lieutenant James
Monroe that the column was part of Washington's army marching on Trenton, the farmer's attitude changed entirely.

"I am going with you," he said. "I am a doctor, and I may help
some poor fellow."

Afterward, as the nation's fifth President, Monroe completed
his tale: "In the attack I received a ball in my shoulder, and
would have bled to death if this doctor had not been near and
promptly taken up an artery."

*　　　*　　　*

With daylight came bitter cold. The troops shivered. But
Washington was elated by how perfectly his two-pronged attack
worked. "The upper division," he later wrote Congress, "arrived
at the enemy's advanced posts exactly at eight o'clock; and in
three minutes after, I found, from the fire on the lower road,
that the [other] division had also got up."

The Hessian outguards, though they continued a scattering
fire from behind houses, were clearly confused and their opposition was nominal. Hessian drums called the troops to arms.
Washington's soldiers split into two sections, entering Trenton
by way of King (Warren) and Queen (Greene) streets; Sullivan's forces likewise divided, coming up Second (State) and
Front streets. Thus the enemy was "hemmed in" by Assunpink

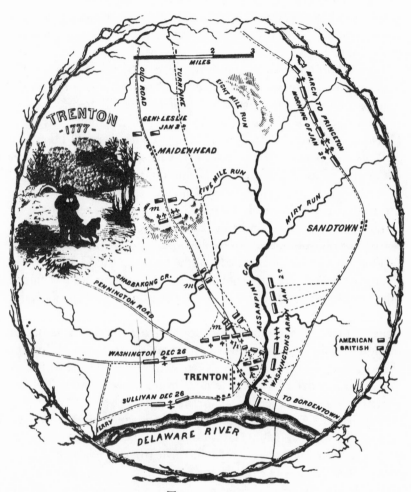

Trenton, 1777

Creek, a good-sized body of water at Trenton. Captain Forest commanded the head of King Street with a six-gun battery, and in a scramble for position Captain William Washington and Lieutenant Monroe beat off Hessian artillerymen and set up a second battery.

Like schoolboys, the Americans who remembered what the corporals of their regiments had read to them from Thomas Paine awakened the streets of the pretty little village of Trenton with the shouts of "This is the time to try men's souls." Aroused Hessians responded: "Der Feind! Der Feind! Heraus! Heraus!"

Rall, still groggy from too much Christmas wine, had to be shaken twice by an aide before Rall could comprehend the fact that the Americans were overrunning Trenton. The colonel literally leaped into his uniform. Riding up the street, where his stunned troops verged on panic, Rall cried out in Dutch:

"My brave soldiers, advance!"

The Americans approached grimly, thinning the Hessian ranks with their deadly aim. A mortal wound, tumbling Rall from his horse, compounded the confusion of the Hessian troops as Rall's body was borne to his headquarters in the Quaker home of Stacey Potts. An attempt to escape toward Princeton was beaten off by Pennsylvania riflemen. Knyphausen's men plunged through the town with John Stark's New Hampshiremen after them. About six hundred light horse and infantrymen, taking flight at the first alarm, succeeded in breaking free before Americans under General Arthur St. Clair could block the bridge to Bordentown. The British Light Dragoons, who held no love for the Hessians, managed to escape "hell-for-leather" toward Princeton before that route was entirely closed.

The main juncture of fighting was at King and Queen streets where, if Rall had listened to Donop, a redoubt would have been constructed. Through tanyards and houses the Americans made their advance under Lord Stirling and General Mercer. Americans kicked in doors to overcome Hessian snipers in the upper stories of private homes, then used the two floors of these houses to fire on the enemy.

The screams of the wounded filled the air made hazy by gun

and cannon smoke mixed with snow and sleet—to General Henry Knox, the Boston bookseller, "a most horrid scene to the inhabitants." American riflemen fired from cellars, almost completely shielded from their adversaries. Hessian deserters tried to escape through the leafless shrubbery of the gardens between houses. Some dived into the icy waters of Assunpink Creek, but more drowned than found freedom on the opposite shore. A few turned back and were rescued.

The Battle of Trenton lasted about an hour and a half. Alexander Hamilton, not yet twenty, served one of the artillery batteries. The colonel of the 3rd Virginia was Thomas Marshall, father of the future Chief Justice of the United States. Another was Captain Richard Clough Anderson, an ancestor of the future General Anderson of Fort Sumter fame.

Shaking hands with Major James Wilkinson, a happy Washington said: "This is a glorious day for our country." The Commander-in-Chief echoed the opinion of a later British historian, Sir George Otto Trevelyan, who declared it was doubtful if "so small a number of men ever employed so short a space of time with greater and more lasting results upon the history of the world."

Washington wrote to Cadwalader of the booty he had collected at Trenton:

Prisoners.	Prisoners.
1 Col.	92 Sergeants
2 Lieut Cols.	20 Drummers
3 Majors	9 Musicians
4 Captains	25 Servants
8 Lieuts.	740 Rank & file
12 Ensigns	
2 Surgeon Mates	

Total 919 [918], about 25 or 30 killed, 6 pieces of Brass Artilly, from 900 to 1000 stand arms, &c.

This age was one in which generals, once the fighting ended, reverted to being gentlemen. In this spirit Washington visited the dying Rall in Stacey Potts' home. The Hessian was greatly em-

barrassed that he had just read the letter which he had stuffed
unopened into his pocket the night before or today's results might
have been much different. Through an interpreter he asked
Washington to use his Hessian prisoners kindly and to this
request the American commander agreed. Lord Stirling remembered how well he had been treated after his capture at the
Battle of Long Island and now invited a number of Hessian
officers to take dinner with him, but the provender he could pro-
vide was scanty at best and one guest grumbled that they dined
on "Grogge and salt Beef."

*   *   *

Now that Washington had captured Trenton a very real
problem arose—what to do next? Some officers argued that
"Successes & brilliant strokes ought to be pursued," but the Commander-in-Chief, not yet aware of how a disconcerted Donop
had been rattled at Mount Holly, could not tell the strength of
the enemy at Bordentown and Princeton. Nor did Washington
order forty casks of rum staved in and their contents poured onto
the ground without reason, and among the causes listed by General Reed in leading Washington to recross the Delaware was
the fact that "There were great Quantities of Spiritous Liquors
at Trenton of which the Soldiers drank too freely to admit of
Discipline or Defence in Case of Attack." Moreover, considering
the "stroke" at Trenton as "brilliant & Successful," Washington
did not believe it was "prudent or politick even to risque the
Chance of losing the Advantages to be derived from it."

So the Americans and their captives moved back to Newtown.
Here many Hessians were quartered in the Presbyterian church
where someone wrote upon the wall in red chalk:

> In times of war and not before,
> God and the soldier men adore;
> When the war is over and all things righted,
> The Lord's forgot and the soldier slighted.

CHAPTER FIVE

Rumors and Realities

December, 1776–January, 1777

The consequences of the Battle of Trenton were exciting, surprising, and sometimes exhilarating. One wild rumor in New
York City placed Washington's force invading New Jersey at
60,000, while Sir James Grant, in command of the British base
at New Brunswick, cut this figure to a more realistic, though still
badly overexaggerated 8,000.

There could be no question that Howe was quite incensed by
the entire affair. He had returned to a New York City still soot-
coated from its fire before the conquest of the Hudson forts and
had hardened himself not to notice the ugly burned-out frame-
work of Trinity Church, which resembled a mountain of crosses
awaiting figures to be crucified. Washington's stubborn insistence
on still fighting could recklessly interrupt Howe's pleasure in
lolling in the arms of Mrs. Joshua Loring, whose husband, Sir
Billy's commissary of prisoners, was good-humoredly willing to
be cuckold for a profit. Mrs. Loring was described as a "flashing
blonde" who enjoyed Howe's raucous pleasure in gambling for
hundred-guinea stakes at City Tavern. Newspapers informing
Howe that his wife had been graciously received at the Court of
St. James allowed him (at least as one historian has observed)
to enjoy "the best of both worlds."

In New Brunswick the indignation of General Grant boiled
over because of the ineffectual—and to Grant, entirely inexcus-
able—military activities of Donop. That Hessian now was stationed at Allentown, where Sir James told him to remain unless
he found the place "impracticable," whereupon, Grant added,
Donop "must crowd into Princeton, Maidenhead [Lawrence-
ville], Cranbury, and Kingston."

General Joseph Reed, hastening to confer with Cadwalader at
Bristol, chuckled at the rapidity with which inhabitants tore down
the red rags nailed to doorways as an indication that the dwellers
therein sought protection as Loyalists in accordance with Howe's
widely circulated proclamation. The people anticipated the prospect of seeing the Hessians, in the black, scarlet, or blue coats
of their individual regiments, marching in gloom to captivity.
Plunder and pillage had been a predictable Hessian habit, and
even red rags nailed to doors had not stopped the depredations
(but then the British had not acted like angels).

Some wicked tales were related (and probably enlarged by
retelling) : of a girl at Penn's Neck strangled and ravished by a
pair of British light horsemen; of how the villages of Lawrenceville and Hopewell had been "broken up" when their houses were
robbed and burned and their children and women left naked and
without shelter; and of how many women and girls, believing
they were protecting their reputations, would not admit that they
had been raped. The Hessians had been especially contemptuous
and heavy-handed in Trenton and Bordentown, where the spirit
of revenge now burned with an almost uncontrollable intensity.

*   *   *

For both military and humanitarian considerations, Washington could not be swayed by such emotionalism. The future and
proper disposition of the Hessian prisoners, [he wrote to a
special Congressional commission]

struck me in the same light in which you view it; for which reason I
advised the Council of Safety to separate them from their officers, and
canton them in the German counties. If proper pains are taken to convince

them how preferable the situation of their countrymen, the inhabitants of those counties, is to theirs, I think they may be sent back in the spring so fraught with a love of liberty and property too, that they create a disgust to the service among the remainder of the foreign troops, and widen that breach, which is already opened between them and the British.

No one better than African-born Phillis Wheatley sensed the innate character of Washington. As a child she had been brought to Boston and sold as a personal maid to Susannah Wheatley, a kindly and intelligent woman. Phillis learned to read the Bible, studied history, astronomy, and geography and became an especially efficient student of Latin and Greek mythology and history.

A contemporary called Phillis "the great Astonishment of all who heard her," and long before her publication of a volume of poems she stood as the first towering Negro literary figure in North America. Fires burned in Phillis Wheatley that could only be quenched in writing poetry and so on the last day of December, 1776, Bostonians read her tribute to Washington:

> Yet those brave troops innum'rous as the sands,
> One soul inspires, one General Chief commands.
> Find in your train of boasted heroes, one
> To match the praise of Godlike Washington.
> Thrice happy chief! In whom the virtuous join,
> And heaven-taught prudence speaks the man divine.

*   *   *

Washington recrossed the Delaware after the Battle of Trenton to rest troops who had become fatigued to the point of illness. Colonel Daniel Hitchcock, consumptively hacking away the last fortnight of his life, succeeded between spasms in proudly mounting his horse as he led his veteran New Englanders to another encampment at Newtown. Lord Stirling complained of a lame hand and painful recurrences of rheumatism. Usually there were no bandages to protect the open wounds of the injured. A lack of woolen clothing at this season of the year produced outbreaks of pneumonia. Dysentery was commonplace; and there were occasional cases of typhus. The unwashed linen shirts of the riflemen became thickly infested with vermin.

The Commander-in-Chief understood why the medical practices of the age were distrusted and avoided whenever possible. Bleeding and drilling holes in the skull to release obnoxious gasses in the brain were still standard procedures. The best an ailing patient could expect to find in a country apothecary was a primitive drug like ipecacuanha, the root of a South American plant that possessed emetic, diaphoretic, and purgative qualities. The average doctor was so little consulted and poorly paid that if he were to eke out a living he must engage in a number of crafts. Thus was one medical practitioner of the period addressed:

> To the Rev. Jacob Green, Preacher
> To the Rev. Jacob Green, Teacher
> To the Rev. Jacob Green, Doctor
> To the Rev. Jacob Green, Proctor
> To the Rev. Jacob Green, Miller
> To the Rev. Jacob Green, Distiller.

On December 27—the day after the Battle of Trenton—Washington wrote General John Cadwalader that he had been forced to move back into Pennsylvania by "the distressed situation of my troops." Luckily fresh American forces were on the move. On this day, though Cadwalader did not know Washington's whereabouts, he crossed the Delaware at Burlington. "The landing in open daylight," Cadwalader reported, "must have alarmed the enemy, or we might have been cut off by all of their force collected at this place."

An ice-clogged river and not the risk of battle had delayed John Cadwalader. This plucky Pennsylvanian, educated at the College and Academy of Philadelphia (now the University of Pennsylvania) neglected the profitable business he conducted with his brother Lambert to embrace the patriot cause. John Cadwalader's loyalty went back eleven years, if his signature on the nonimportation agreement were counted; and he had served on Philadelphia's Committee of Safety before becoming captain of a city troop called the Silk-Stocking Company (his brother Lambert was captain of another aristocratic company, the Greens).

John Cadwalader's aggressive personality could not accept defeat; he would rather die. Apprised next morning of Donop's retreat, Cadwalader advanced on Bordentown, where he was told to await further orders from Washington. Meanwhile General Thomas Mifflin, in a fur cap and a coat made from a rose-colored blanket, followed with his high-spirited Philadelphia militia who had been promised a ten-dollar bounty and a new pair of shoes and stockings if they consented to fight.

Mifflin stayed at Bordentown while Cadwalader moved to Crosswicks. Each commanded about 1,800 troops. Nonetheless, Washington was still wary of how well he could stand up against an enemy of five or six thousand. "It is confidently said," he reported to Congress in a worry-wart mood, "they have sent the chief part of their baggage to Brunswick." Howe was reported "at Amboy" with 1,000 light troops.

*   *   *

On the last day of December, the day Phillis Wheatley published her laudatory poem in Boston, Washington returned to Trenton and by tradition established his headquarters at the "True American Inn" on Mill Hill, not far from the stone bridge across Assunpink Creek. A Connecticut sergeant was amused at how "the horses attached to the artillery were without shoes, and when passing over the ice they would slide in every direction, and could advance only by the assistance of the soldiers." But men with sore and bleeding feet wanted to keep marching until they reached home. Washington rallied them, begging the soldiers to stay a month longer since they could attain more now for the American cause than at any previous period. He addressed the troops, the sergeant said, "in the most affectionate manner." The drums beat for volunteers. Not a soldier stepped forward.

Washington wheeled his horse about. Passion underscored his words:

My brave fellows, you have done all I asked you to do, and more than could be reasonably expected; but your country is at stake, your wives, your houses, and all that you hold dear. You have worn yourselves out with fatigues and hardships, but we know not how to spare you. . . . The Present is emphatically the crisis, which is to decide our destiny.

Again the drums rolled. "We cannot go home under such circumstances," a voice muttered. By ones and twos, and then in larger groups, about two hundred volunteered. An officer asked if the troops should be enlisted.

"No!" Washington replied. "Men who will volunteer in such a case as this, need no enrolment to keep them to their duty."

*   *   *

In some instances Washington had promised bounties to recruits but could not pay them. He appealed to that Philadelphia wizard of finance, Robert Morris, who before the Revolution had been an importer and exporter with ships sailing the seas of the world.

Morris' attachment to the patriot cause began with the passage of the Stamp Act; he had been a signer of the Declaration of Independence and John Adams had characterized him as a man of "masterly Understanding, an open Temper and an honest Heart." Another contemporary account described Morris as "Bold and enterprizing—of great mercantile knowledge, fertile in experiments & an able financier. Very popular in & out of the Congress."

Morris needed all his wits and charm to solve Washington's problem. Government credit was low, his own income hard pressed. The financier appealed to a Quaker friend for a loan.

"Robert, what security canst thou give?"

"My note, and my honor."

"Thou shalt have it," decided the Quaker.

Morris forwarded the sum to Washington.

*   *   *

As December ended, Cornwallis returned to assume command of the some 8,000 British and Hessian troops remaining in New Jersey. His Lordship's mood was far from cheery, considering that his packed portmanteaus would be traveling to England without him. Likely he took scant encouragement in the discovery that Sir James Grant, in moving to Princeton to join with the troops of Donop and General Alexander Leslie, had left a mere 600 soldiers at New Brunswick to guard British stores and a military chest of £70,000.

Cornwallis spent the night in Princeton at Morven. Except for the soldiers, many of whom crowded into Nassau Hall and used its basement for a stable, the village was deserted. Far more distressing to Cornwallis was the pattering of a warm rain all through the night.

The result was as bad as Cornwallis had feared. At daybreak, marching his troops three abreast down the post road to Trenton, the men slithered and sank in the mud. It was almost ten before they reached Lawrenceville, about half the way. The presence of American snipers in a thick wood led Cornwallis to post a garrison here; then, with the Hessians in the lead, he pressed doggedly on.

In Trenton Washington awaited Cornwallis upon the high ground on the south side of Assunpink Creek. Counting undisciplined militia, Washington commanded no more than 5,000. Strong detachments under Greene, stinging the approaching enemy like a swarm of bees, delayed Cornwallis' arrival into Trenton until near sunset.

Drawing up his army into a solid column, his Lordship sent his troops down Queen Street, with stern orders to storm the bridge over the Assunpink.

American cannon roared and belched black smoke. Small-arms fire clattered while the cannoneers reloaded. At every volley the Americans set up a loud shout, creating in Cornwallis' mind the impression that they were far more numerous than he had previously believed.

By dark, with the American cannonade still shaking the ground, the British stumbled back in confusion. Vaguely they realized their casualties were higher than they had expected.

Sir William Erskine urged one more charge. Cornwallis, who never underestimated Washington, shook his head. When daylight returned, he told Sir William, it would be soon enough to "bag the fox."

CHAPTER SIX

Fox Chase in Princeton

January, 1777

That night, in order to sustain Cornwallis' delusion concerning the numerical superiority of the Americans at Trenton, extra campfires were kept burning on the hillside across Mill Pond. In his willingness to wait until daybreak to bag his fox Cornwallis had forgotten that this wary animal, when cornered, was renowned for its ability to manage stealthy escapes.

Washington hardly had to be told that he was momentarily trapped and could even be facing a desperate situation. Scouts reported that next morning three regiments from Princeton—the 17th, 40th and 55th under Lieutenant Colonel Charles Mawhood —and three squadrons of dragoons were expected to join Cornwallis at Trenton. Washington ordered the army's baggage stealthily removed to Burlington and called a council of war. The Americans were caught once again between two choices— should they withdraw into Pennsylvania or boldly throw their weight against Princeton and, possibly, New Brunswick? At any event, Washington reasoned in his message to Congress, he must "avoid the appearance of a retreat." About midnight the guards stirred up the campfires, for Washington had decided to bypass Cornwallis by moving on Princeton.

The thought of drawing forty pieces of cannon over muddy

roads took the heart out of the maneuver Washington proposed. But then luck favored the Commander-in-Chief: the wind, shifting into the northwest, froze the roads as solidly as though they had been paved with brick. Doubtless aided by Joseph Reed, Washington's adjutant general who lived in Trenton and had attended Princeton, the Americans marched around the sleeping British by a circuitous route. Cadwalader at Crosswicks also forwarded a map brought him by a spy, which outlined in detail the British position at Princeton. Washington's troops moved easterly by the Sand Town road (Hamilton Avenue) until they reached Miry Run. A track here, ominously known as the Barrens, led the Americans down a road to the east of Bear Swamp where they turned northwestward along the new Quaker Bridge road to the Meeting House at Stony Brook.

Dense woodland with tree stumps and stubs of saplings and scrubs jolted the wagons and artillery. The cursing of the drivers, though low-pitched, did not promise to unlock many heavenly gates. But the army pushed on through the intense cold with St. Clair in the lead, then Mercer, then the Pennsylvania militia. The consumptive Hitchcock, hacking out almost the last shreds of his life in the freezing night, guarded the lower fords of the Assunpink with his veteran New Englanders.

Washington had hoped to strike Princeton before dawn and was thwarted by the inevitable delays of nighttime marching. He had lost very little advantage, however. So sure were the British that Cornwallis had boxed Washington in Trenton, they had left Princeton thinly protected, expecting at worst no more than a militia raid.

*　　　*　　　*

At sunrise hoar frost covered the ground and ice buds sparkled on the twigs of trees. "Sergeant R" marched that January 3, 1777 with General Hugh Mercer, one of the most popular officers among the Continentals. Mercer, born about 1725 in Scotland and educated at the University of Aberdeen, became a surgeon's mate in the army of Prince Charles Edward. He migrated to the colonies in 1746 or 1747, settled briefly in Philadelphia and moved near to the future sight of Mercersburg, Pennsylvania. He fought brilliantly in the French and Indian War, winning fame for his hairbreadth escapes. This conflict brought Mercer his friendship with Washington, and after moving to Fredericksburg, Virginia, Mercer was an occasional visitor to Mount Vernon. Skeptics who deny that Mercer originated the plan for the battles at Trenton and Princeton still must admit that he was thoroughly active in both.

Now, this morning of January 3, Hugh Mercer reached the summit of a hill. Sighting a British light horseman gazing at him, Mercer ordered a rifleman "to pick him off" but at that instant the fellow wheeled and pounded out of range to spread the alarm of the American approach. Mercer waved to his troops, and with the others, "Sergeant R" descended a hill through an orchard. Suddenly a line of Britishers rose from behind a bank and a fence. Their muskets clattered. The enemy were light dragoons, rushed into battle and unused to fighting on foot at short range.

"Their first shots," reported the sergeant, "passed over our heads cutting the limbs of trees under which we were marching." The next volley killed a corporal at the sergeant's side.

"He seemed to bend forward to receive the ball," the sergeant said, "which might otherwise have ended my life."

Mercer formed his men in line, advanced, and after "eight rods" the dragoons retreated to their packs, "which were laid in a line." The British muskets were far more effective than the American rifles, which required greased paper to make their bullets discharge in a straight line. "Sergeant R" felt a sense of exhilaration as the American guns, reloaded "with ball and buckshot," thinned the enemy's line. A victory seemed "almost complete."

But enemy reinforcements appeared, and "in a tone of distress," Mercer called, "Retreat!"

A bullet had broken the foreleg of Mercer's horse. He rallied his men, sword in hand, but few of the men behind him possessed bayonets. Believing that Mercer was Washington, the British cried:

"Call for quarters, you damn rebel!"

Mercer's Scottish pride could not stand this indignity. He struck out with his sword until the butt of a gun brought him to his knees. Seven bayonet thrusts ended his life. A lieutenant with a broken leg was dragged from a nearby wagon and killed with bayonets. Lieutenant Bartholomew Yeates, though begging for mercy after being shot and clubbed, was killed by thirteen bayonet stabs.

*   *   *

The Battle of Princeton, which did not last more than an hour, was described by Andrew Mellick:

Able historians have made us all familiar with the miraculous escapes of Washington when exposed to a cross fire of friend and foe; have told over and over again of General Mercer's having been pinned to the earth by the fatal thrusts of British bayonets; of how the smoke rose above the combatants and hung in air, a clear, white, cumulous cloud, as if weighted with the souls of those who had just closed their eyes on the radiance of that winter morn; of the appearance presented by the British commander, Lieutenant Colonel Mawhood, who in the heat of the action rode at the head of his men on a little brown pony, with two spaniels playing before him; of Knox's training his artillery on Nassau Hall to dislodge a portion of the Fortieth Regiment which had taken refuge in the college building; and of the many other incidents crowded within the short space of time occupied in completely routing the British forces. Taking into consideration the number of troops engaged, no action during the war was so fatal to American officers. One general, one colonel, three captains, one lieutenant, and an ensign were killed; but then, officers were so numerous in this little army that, even in so short an exposure to the enemy's fire, that number of casualties was fairly to be expected. All told, the American loss was but thirty, while the British left one hundred dead on the field and nearly three hundred men in our hands as prisoners, including fourteen officers.

Washington was in high spirits. " 'Tis a fine fox chase, boys!" he cried. Once he was seen astride his white charger, in the midst of this whirlwind struggle, rallying his troops at a point about thirty yards from the enemy. A distressed aide, Irish-born John Fitzgerald, pulled him back, thanking God for the battle smoke that obscured the British vision. Unharmed, Washington remained in the saddle, waving his lines forward.

"Bring up the troops, Colonel Fitzgerald," he called to his
aide. "The day is our own."

And so it was. Hitchcock was up now, striking Mawhood's left
in a deadly drive. The Pennsylvania militia flushed the light
infantry from behind a fence. Hand's riflemen, supporting the
Pennsylvanians, mowed down the enemy. As though to add salt
to the wound of British humiliation, one of Knox's cannonballs
decapitated the portrait of George II, hanging in the Prayer
Room of Nassau Hall.

The British, Washington told Congress, "were chased three
or four miles." Two brass field pieces had to be left behind for
want of horses to carry them away. The Commander-in-Chief
added: "We also took some blankets, shoes, and a few other
trifling articles, burned the hay, and destroyed such other things,
as the shortness of the time would admit of."

*   *   *

Originally, on leaving Trenton, Washington had intended to
press on to New Brunswick, but now, believing his troops too
weary for further fighting, he turned toward the hill country of
New Jersey at Van Tilburgh's Inn in Kingston. Afterward, communicating with Congress, Washington questioned the soundness
of his judgment: ". . . six or eight hundred fresh troops upon a
forced march would have destroyed all their stores and magazines, taken (as we have since learned) their military chest, con-
taining seventy thousand pounds, and put an end to the war."

From Kingston the Americans followed a narrow road to
Rocky Hill, then marched down the valley of the Millstone. The
Indian name of this river was "Mattawang," meaning "hard to
travel," and under the circumstances the description seemed
entirely appropriate.

From every farmhouse people came out to see Washington and
cheer his victories at Trenton and Princeton. But the little army
following the Commander-in-Chief were too worn out, cold, and
hungry to enjoy this exuberance. Many fell out of line and endeavored to sleep on the frozen ground.

The wounded moaned in the lumbering wagons, trying to ease

arms in slings, or hold their bandaged heads and shattered jaws away from the sideboards, or bit on bullets to stand the pain of their fractured legs. Some pale casualties, their eyes growing glazed, lay in the straw, not much caring if they lived or died. Washington saw the marks left in the road by the bare and bloody feet of William Lyon, a Continental soldier from a neighboring county.

"My boy," Washington said, "you deserve a better fate."

"There is no danger of my feet freezing as long as the blood runs," Lyon replied.

The army passed over the Millstone River on a bridge near Griggstown and beat off a sizable British cavalry attack. The bridge was wrecked at Washington's order. Commissaries went forward to ask inhabitants to prepare food for the half-starved columns.

At dusk the army reached Somerset Courthouse (later Millstone). Just beyond the church stood the Van Harlingen House, where Queen's College students pursued their lessons after the British occupied New Brunswick. Washington stayed in the home of John Van Doren, south of the village. (Months later when British raiders crossed this way and Mrs. Van Doren refused to reveal where the family treasure was sequestered, she was hung by her heels in the cellar. Luckily, although her face had turned black, neighbors rescued her in time.)

Laggards struggled into the camp during the night. With daylight Washington plunged deeper into the hill country, marching by way of Pluckemin.

CHAPTER SEVEN

Village Festival

January, 1777

Washington approached the "blue range" of the New Jersey hills that natives insisted on calling mountains. It was rolling country over which the marching soldiers huffed and puffed, and yet, in pauses on a hilltop, the scene was wonderfully rewarding. Above the treetops rose the church spires of country villages— Lesser Cross Roads (Bedminster) and Peapack, Lamington and Pluckemin, New Germantown (Oldwick) and Liberty Corner. One easily could imagine the beauty of this land in summer with barn swallows a-twitter, cows quenching their thirst in shallow brooks, the fields burgeoning with rich harvests, and farmers scything their grain crops from sunup to dusk. Against the bleakness of winter the houses along the roadside, gray with time, seemed desolate, but not the smiling faces of the inhabitants who watched the army going by. Not since the days of the Irish prostitute who had shamed many a prominent family hereabouts had the old county of Somerset known such excitement!

Pluckemin, where Washington camped for two days, was reached that afternoon. Loungers bolted from their upturned dry-goods boxes before Eoff's Tavern, doubtless convinced that they had made one too many visits to the bar for "a leetle apple." But the cheers of the completely sober citizens of Pluckemin left no question that the hero of Trenton and Princeton was actually in their village. Houses were opened to the wounded. Captured soldiers were jammed into the Lutheran Church and British officers were incarcerated in the home of Matthew Lane.

Through the remaining daylight soldiers who had been too weak to keep up with the others drifted into the village so that by the time the drums beat tattoo approximately 2,000 troops were quartered on a hillside south of Pluckemin. Arms were stacked and the flames of campfires flickered in the darkness. Baggage wagons, caissons, and cannon lined the roadside. Here and there sounded the neigh of a tethered horse which was quieted by the sentinels. Sleep came quickly to the exhausted army.

The festival day for Pluckemin was January 5, a Sunday. From miles around people came to the village at the news of Washington's presence. Peapack and Lamington sent wagons loaded with provisions. Every face wore a look of heartiness. The more curious moved to the windows of the Lutheran Church and gazed at the imprisoned Scotsmen in their tartans and the dragoons in their colorful uniforms. The hammering sounds of the blacksmith and his assistants shoeing horses continued into the night, when their brawny figures were illuminated by the glow of the forge.

Eoff's Tavern held open table and all grades of soldiers, Continental and militia, mingled in the festival spirit of the day, no better personified than by a farmer from Bedminster who swung down the road "in his Sunday breeches of blue cloth, his red waistcoat with flapping pockets showing under an amply skirted coat adorned with metal buttons." Citizens and visitors to Pluckemin delighted in rubbing shoulders with famous figures of the war—the "tall and vigorous" Nathanael Greene, the "alert and soldierly" John Sullivan, the "broad-faced" Knox, and, above all, "the conspicuous figure of Washington, who seemed a king among men as he moved amid the throng, with high-born eye, lofty but courteous port, and a calm, strong face reflecting a mind full of the tranquillity of conscious power."

*   *   *

Washington was busy at a writing desk that Sabbath. He completed his report to Congress on his activities since recrossing to Trenton the last day of December. To Major General Israel Putnam the Commander-in-Chief wrote a cheerful letter, saying that the enemy appeared "panic-struck" and he had some hope now "of driving them out of the Jerseys." Putnam was ordered to Crosswicks to keep a sharp watch on the enemy in that quarter, and if the British remained in New Brunswick to act "with great circumspection, lest you meet with a surprise."

"As we have made two successful attacks upon the enemy by way of surprise," Washington continued, "they will be pointed with resentment and if there is any possibility of retaliating, they will attempt it. You will give out your strength to be twice as great as it is." Spies, Washington warned, should be freely used: "A number of horsemen, in the dress of the country, must be constantly kept going backwards and forwards for this purpose, and if you discover any motion of the enemy, which you can depend upon, and which you think of consequence, let me be informed thereof as soon as possible by express."

Another letter from Pluckemin went to Major General William Heath, a Massachusetts farmer who had taken his rifle to fight at Bunker Hill and since then had steadily advanced in rank. Heath was told to move toward New York "with a considerable force, as if you had a design upon the city." Four thousand New England militiamen would be needed, Washington thought. "Act with great precaution," he advised. After leaving a sufficient guard at the Highlands, General Benjamin Lincoln was to cross the North River and bring the remainder of the militia to Morristown. A final warning told Heath to gather every available boat should it become expedient for him to make a crossing at Dobbs Ferry.

*   *   *

Pluckemin's day of festival included a solemn occasion. A British officer of rank, Charles Leslie, had died and was to be buried in the Lutheran graveyard (or "Devil's Acre," as the natives called it) with the honors of war. Toward noon about forty

Americans stood at stiff attention opposite the building where lay the corpse. The light infantry acted as an escort, while Washington ordered the captive British officers in Matthew Lane's house released so that they could attend the ceremony.

To the sound of muffled drums and fifes the soldiers presented arms as Leslie's body was borne from the house. In columns of four and reversing their arms, the escort led the procession in slow step to the churchyard. Citizens and the military clustered around the bier. A hush fell over the village as the chaplain spoke: "I am the Resurrection and the Life, saith the Lord." Slowly the coffin was lowered. Soldiers turned their gun muzzles down and rested their bowed heads on their musket butts. The escort fired three volleys over the open grave.

Shouldering arms, the troops marched off. By the time they reached the main village road, the drums and fifes were playing a lively tune. Business picked up at Eoff's. The British officers were taken back to their confinement in Matthew Lane's house.

Next morning Pluckemin's brief history as the Continental military capital ended when Washington moved to Morristown, going by way of Basking Ridge, New Vernon, and the outskirts of Green Village.

* * *

The Commander-in-Chief, who had begun this eventful campaign among the Tory Dutch of Bergen County, now entered the Whig country of Morris County, where a large percentage of the population were ardent rebels. Lively tales supported this claim. When wealthy Thomas Millege was elected sheriff of Hanover, and expressed doubts of his ability to oppose George III, he was forced to leave his farm and warned that if he ever returned, "he would be drummed out of the county on a wooden horse." When in Morristown during an argument over the Declaration of Independence Parson Green discovered a critical parishioner, "who had drunk deeply of Toryism," the parson ordered the culprit banned from his church. In Mendham when David Thompson, an elder in the Presbyterian Church, became a captain of the militia, he told his men: "We can look to Jehovah

when all other refuges fail." In Whippany, Anna Kitchel watched
her father, husband, and five brothers shoulder muskets to fight
for the American cause. Washington's new winter quarters,
selected over the objection of Nathanael Greene, promised the
Virginian ample security.

Morristown had seen its first "Continentals" on December 20
when the "three regiments from Ticonderoga," intended to
reinforce the army on the west bank of the Delaware, had paused
here because Washington had believed their presence would
"inspirit the inhabitants." At the moment the Morris County
militia were some seven miles southwest, guarding the crude
wooden bridge over the Passaic River at Chatham, for an extremely sound reason: here they could fight off any Hessians or
British who might have eyes on Ford's Mill on the Whippany
River, one of the main producers of gunpowder for Washington's army.

Morristown was a village of about fifty houses that nestled
beneath Thimble Mountain. Washington's headquarters were at
Jacob Arnold's Tavern across the green from the old courthouse
with its wooden cupola and shingled sides. Close by stood the
Continental House where the powder from Ford's Mill on the
Whippany and other war matériel were stored. The Baptist and
Presbyterian churches were used as hospitals; and after decades
of wrangling with the Church of England apparently the Pres-
byterians were the hardier stock for no matter how cold the
weather, every Sabbath they held outdoor services in an orchard.

In so many ways Morristown assumed the appearance of a
military capital: in Washington's aides, who wore their cocked-
hats sidelong; in the sentries who guarded Arnold's Tavern day
and night; in the parade ground, eighty feet wide and cut from
the village's main thoroughfare, with a large liberty tree planted
in its center. The tents of officers, almost all of them taken at
Princeton, bordered this drill ground.

The main body of the army was quartered in the Lowantica
Valley in an area about two and a half miles southeast of Morris-
town and about a mile and a half northwest of Bottle Neck (later
Madison). The valley was named by the Indians for a stream

that ran southeasterly into the Passaic. Woodland, mainly of
chestnut, was plentiful, and farms were not fenced so that the
troops could spread out as they pleased. Huts were built of
notched logs, rising to a height of eight feet, and roofed with
split logs. Wood chips daubed with mud filled the cracks. Chim-
neys, reaching just above the roof ridge, were constructed of
sticks and mud, and bunks were filled with straw. Each soldier
possessed a blanket and on very cold nights the occupants "dou-
bled up" so that they were protected by two thicknesses of woolen
covering.

Outwardly life in Morristown appeared jolly. Farmers from
the neighboring countryside were delighted to sell beef for fifteen
cents a pound, butter for forty-five cents, geese and turkeys for
eight shillings. Everyone was cheered by General Nathanael
Greene's observation: "We cannot conquer the British force at
once, but they cannot conquer us at all. The limits of the British
government are their out-sentinels."

But surface appearances were deceiving. Britons and Hessians,
riding out of New Brunswick, where Cornwallis commanded,
and Amboy, where General John Vaughn commanded, raided
farmhouses and villages. And Heath, marching on Fort Independence near King's Bridge, scarcely crowned his slanting brow
with a laurel wreath. Reaching the fort, he cried out in a lofty
voice: "Twenty minutes only can be allowed for the garrison to
give their answer; and should it be in the negative, they must
abide the consequences." Ten days passed and the garrison still
had not answered. At last the enemy appeared and Heath's
troops panicked. The general tried not to hear the shouts of
ridicule.

An alarming smallpox epidemic spread through the Morristown encampment, in later years giving that part of the Lowantica Valley the name of Fevertown. Although Dr. Daniel
Sutton of England had invented a type of inoculation against
smallpox by a pin prick instead of the deep gash formerly required, the soldiers still feared this more than the illness. Washington was adamant: "Desperate diseases require desperate
remedies." Inoculated soldiers were lodged in the village despite

"the squalls of the inhabitants." For three centuries smallpox with its high death rate had a dramatic impact upon world history, and the Revolution would end before Edward Jenner found an effective preventive by inoculating patients with the milder disease of cowpox.

*   *   *

Money was a problem that forever nibbled at the edges of Washington's mind—money for food, for clothing, for equipment. Robert Morris reported on how soldiers—"and those who get their living by feeding and entertaining them"—were enlisted in Philadelphia:

These are the harpies that injure us much at this time. They keep the fellows drunk while the money holds out; when it is gone, they encourage them to enlist for the sake of bounty, then to drinking again. That bounty gone, and more money still wanted, they must enlist again with some other officer, receive a fresh bounty, and get more drink, etc. The scene is actually carrying on here daily, and does immense injury to the recruiting service. . . .

Inflation as a form of war was not a Philadelphia invention. According to Kenneth Scott, the authority on counterfeiting in colonial times, England was unique in history as the first country to attack an enemy by employing counterfeiting in an effort "to undermine confidence in the currency, and thereby the credit, of an enemy." The scheme worked so well that in a time when paper money was the universal currency Benjamin Franklin deplored how the fraud "operated considerably in depreciating the whole mass [of money], first, by the vast additional quantity, and next by the uncertainty in distinguishing the true from the false; and the depreciation was a loss to all and the ruin of many." Ultimately Washington would grumble to John Jay, "A wagon-load of money will scarcely purchase a wagon-load of provisions"; a Philadelphia mob vented its rage by parading a dog tarred and plastered with the paper currency of Congress; but such punishments as flogging, standing in pillory, branding, ear cropping, imprisonment and heavy fines did not discourage the counterfeiters. The day came when an officer complained that buying a horse would cost him twenty years' salary.

H.M.S. *Phoenix,* lying at anchor in New York Harbor in 1776, looked like just another forty-four-gun warship. Aboard her, however, was a printing press capable of producing thirty-dollar bills. So brazen were the British about using inflation as a weapon that in 1777 the following advertisement appeared in New York newspapers:

> Persons going into other Colonies may be supplied with any Number of counterfeit Congress-Notes, for the Price of the Paper per Ream. They are so neatly and exactly executed that there is no Risque in getting them off, it being almost impossible to discover, that they are not genuine. This has been proved by Bills to a very large Amount, which have already been successfully circulated.
>
> Enquire for Q.E.D. at the Coffee-House, from 11 p.m. to 4 a.m. during the present month.

Sir Henry Clinton wrote Lord George Germain, "no assistance that could be drawn from the power, or the arts of counterfeiting" would be neglected. The bad bills usually were passed by Tory gangs, and even Continental soldiers were not immune from these get-rich-quick tactics. Still the rebels fought this practice tenaciously and one raid on a farmhouse about a mile and a half from Sandy Hook netted eight prisoners and $45,000. A brother of General John Stark and a future United States senator were members of a New Hampshire ring. Newspapers telling how to distinguish between true and false bills actually benefitted counterfeiters by informing them of what errors should be corrected in their plates.

*   *   *

Washington never lacked for problems. Early in his stay at Morristown the Commander-in-Chief advised Colonel George Baylor in Baltimore that nothing so handicapped an army as a poor selection of officers. Baylor should "take none but gentlemen" and avoid "local attachments," remembering that the war was "a public, not a private cause." Washington counseled: "Do not take old men, nor yet fill your corps with boys, especially for captains." A sharp letter warned Lord Howe that

Major-General [Charles] Lee is looked upon as an officer belonging to, and under the protection of, the United Independent States of America, and any violence which you may commit upon his life or liberty, will be severely retaliated upon the lives and liberties of the British officers, or those of their foreign allies, at present in our hands.

Washington could understand why militiamen were unhappy separated from their families in winter encampment and unhappier still when it was time for spring plowing. He could understand the displeasure of a New Jersey regiment, under the command of Colonel Elias Dayton, who had spent a year on New York's westerly frontier at Fort Stanwix (Schuyler). Dayton stated his complaint in no meaching terms: "We have now the dull prospect of lingering out perhaps two months longer in the disagreeable state of a separation of soul and body; for you must certainly suppose our hearts are in New Jersey, though our bodies are on Mount Independence."

Still believing Philadelphia would be Howe's next major objective, Washington informed the state's Council on Safety: "You may be assured, that nothing but the united efforts of every State in America can save us from disgrace and too probably from ruin." He repeated this theme in a letter to Governor Nicholas Cooke of Rhode Island: "If each State was to prepare for its own defense, independent of each other, they would all be soon conquered, one by one." But, Washington added, "If I am properly supported, I hope to close the campaign gloriously for America."

In character in a home letter to John Parke Custis, his stepson, the Commander-in-Chief revealed the true depth of his pessimism:

. . . all our movements have been made with inferior numbers, and with a mixed, motley crew, who were here to-day, gone to-morrow, without assigning a reason, or even apprizing you of it. . . . I do not think that any officer since the creation ever had such a variety of difficulties and perplexities to encounter as I have. . . .

Replying to his stepson's criticism of the troops from Virginia, Washington said: "I do not believe that any of the states produce better men, or persons capable of making better soldiers, but it is to be acknowledged that they are (generally speaking) most wretchedly officered. . . ."

Unwittingly, before the month ended, Washington created a political uproar. His offense was really quite innocent: a proclamation that unless those who had been forced by Howe to take an oath of allegiance renounced those pledges within thirty days they "will be deemed adherents to the King of Great Britain, and treated as common enemies to these American States."

Foremost among Washington's critics in Congress was New Jersey's Abraham Clark, surveyor, lawyer, farmer, and signer of the Declaration of Independence, who has been described as "a leader of the dour, sensible American middle-class." Clark also was known as "The Poor Man's Counsellor" because he preferred to handle cases of common law—for the very good reason, his opponents suspected, that he never had been formally admitted to the bar.

Clark called Washington's proclamation "a violation of our civil rights" and he intended to press Congress for a resolution "strictly forbidding any officer to impose or require any oath of the inhabitants." Of Washington, Clark remarked: "I believe the General is honest, but I think him fallible."

CHAPTER EIGHT

A Lull Before a Storm

Winter, 1777

The loungers at Eoff's Tavern, driven indoors by the cold weather, peered through the windows as the stagecoach drew to its daily ten-minute stopover in Pluckemin. The plain woman who alighted, in their opinion, could have been somebody's house servant. Then to their astonishment General Washington strode forward and embraced his wife. There could be no doubt of the deep affection between Martha Washington and the husband she called her "Old Man." Such snatches of conversation that could be overheard dealt with the Commander-in-Chief's interest in his favorite horses at Mount Vernon.

Martha Washington quickly upset Morristown. The local ladies in silks and ruffles and elaborately contrived pompadours were taken aback when she met them at the door in an apron. The wives of other officers arrived and in the gaiety of their society General Washington, at least temporarily, almost forgot his apprehensions concerning the war.

Martha Dangerfield Bland, wife of the handsome Colonel Theodorick Bland of Virginia, found Morristown "a very clever little village" largely inhabited by "errantist [unmitigated] rustics." Many of the local girls, she wrote her sister-in-law, Fanny Randolph, were exceedingly attractive, "but they appear to have

souls formed for the distaff, rather than the tender passions."
Their favorite words were "desperate" and "dreadful" as in
"dreadful good water."

Washington, Mrs. Bland believed, "commands both sexes, one
by his excellent skill in military matters, the other by his ability,
politeness, and attention." Often Mrs. Bland joined the General
and his staff at "parties on horseback." Colonel John Fitzgerald
she thought "an agreeable broad-shouldered Irishman"; Colonel
George John Johnston was "witty at everybody's expense" but
could not take a joke on himself; Colonel Alexander Hamilton
was "a sensible, genteel, polite young fellow, a West Indian";
Colonel Tench Tilghman "voluntarily lives in his family and
acts in any capacity that is uppermost without fee or reward";
and, among others, Captain Caleb Gibbs, "a good-natured Yankee who makes a thousand blunders in the Yankee style and keeps
the dinner table in constant laughter."

On a riding party Washington forgot he was a hero and became a chatty, agreeable companion. "He can be downright
impudent sometimes," Mrs. Bland confessed, "such impudence,
Fanny, as you and I like, and really, I have wished for you often."

Despite riding parties, dinners, and occasional dances, Morristown's life was guided principally by the needs of the military.
No matter how dreary the winter day the flag was raised on the
parade ground. Fife and drum music enlivened the mornings
and afternoons as the soldiers went through the evolutions of
their marches. Sutlers crowded into the village and "their principal business," apparently, was "to accommodate the drinking
propensities of the Army."

The Lowantica encampment was situated in the hills rolling
northwestward to the Delaware River. Even before Washington's arrival several hill signal stations had been established
throughout the region; but the pride of the local defense was an
eighteen-pound cannon, "the old sow," stationed at Short Hills.
At night fires upon the hilltops, indicating the possibility of
enemy raiders in the vicinity, brought minutemen and militia on
the run. Morris County patriots kept a constant watch over the

bridge at Chatham so that it was difficult to imagine a location where the army could have been more secure.

Desertions increased as the winter wore on. A few deserters were shot and at least one was required "to run the gauntlet." A British officer was so certain his captors intended to poison him that he would not eat until he had wiped the plate on the flap of his red coat. Unhappily one evening this officer overindulged in applejack and attempted to escape but was apprehended and flogged next morning.

"To be put through the operation by these damn rebels," he declared, "is more than flesh and blood can bear."

*   *   *

Riding parties and official dinners, however, could not stop Washington from slipping back into repeated moods of depression, if not despair. His spirit seemed trapped by the very intensity of his uncertainties, loyalties, and devotion to the cause for which he fought. The letters he wrote from Morristown during February and March reveal the frustrations of a frequently tormented man.

No one could deny the complications of anguish that afflicted the Commander-in-Chief. His repeated efforts to gain the release of General Charles Lee amounted to a prolonged failure. Generals complained of being passed by when Congress announced new appointments and others believed that they had been demeaned by the posts to which they had been ordered.

Many persons are extremely dissatisfied with numbers of the General officers of the highest rank [John Adams wrote his wife in late February]. I don't mean the Commander in Chief, his character is justly very high, but Schuyler, Putnam, Spencer, Heath, are thought by very few to be capable of the great command they hold. We hear of none of their heroic deeds of arms. I wish they would all resign. For my part, I will vote upon the genuine principles of a republic for a new election of General officers annually, and every man shall have my consent to be left out who does not give sufficient proof of his qualification.

Washington, who did not understand the power of Mrs. Joshua Loring to keep Lord Howe quite willing to forego an

early 1777 campaign, feared a full-scale attack almost from day
to day. Thus in early February Washington asked Congress if a
company or two of Cherokee Indians could be secured, adding:
"If they can be procured they will answer two valuable purposes,
one as excellent Scouts, the other, that they will be in fact Hostages, and will secure the good behavior of their Nation." Parties
"from every quarter" were sent to collect all the wagons, horses,
cattle, and sheep that possibly could help the enemy.

Smallpox was spreading so rapidly through the army that
Washington now required the inoculation of all recruits who
never had suffered this ailment. He opposed state bounties that,
financially, placed some soldiers on a superior footing. His
Orderly Book on February 11 told his Commissary General to
recognize "the exceeding difficulty in procuring Spiritous Liquors" in Massachusetts and prohibited further issue "till supplies
can be laid in upon more easy and better terms."

Washington's problems were changeable and constant. He
argued for Springfield, Massachusetts, as the best place for a
laboratory and cannon foundry in New England since Springfield
contained "a quantity of copper, tin, and other useful materials"
and that "necessary works and preparations" could be accomplished here three or four months sooner than at any other place.
Too many foreign officers were asking for recognition of high
rank, which Washington found an embarrassment: "They sel-
dom bring more than a commission and passport, which, we
know, may belong to a bad as well as a good officer."

On February 23 he wrote Congress: ". . . I think we are now
in one of the most critical periods which America ever saw, and
because the enemy are not in actual motion (by the by I believe
they are not far from it) every body seems to be lulled into ease
and Security."

In circular letters to the governors of the independent states
he stressed his need for everything: clothing, troops, money,
ammunition. He could not, he said time and again, supply the
firearms that were needed. He would not—to his credit—punish
the Hessians harshly, asking Congress: would not the cruel
treatment of one induce the cruel treatment of his own captors?

Washington's carping tendencies at least drew a response from his old financial friend in Philadelphia, Richard Morris.

Remember, good Sir [Morris wrote], that few men can keep their feelings to themselves, and that it is necessary for example's sake, that all leaders should feel and think boldly in order to inspirit others, who look up to them. Heaven, no doubt for the noblest purposes, has blessed you with a firmness of mind, steadiness of countenance, and patience in sufferings, that give you infinite advantages over other men. . . .

I hate deception, and cannot wish any thing like it should ever escape you; but I really think if the bright side of our affairs were sometimes to be painted by your pen, or sanctified by your name, it would draw forth the exertions of some good men sooner than distress does from others. . . .

Washington replied that his best intelligence placed Howe's troops "in the Jerseys and on board of transports at Amboy" at 10,000; his force commanded from Morristown did not exceed 4,000 and must be "augmented . . . very considerably." Every circumstance favored Howe in striking against Philadelphia, a city that offered so many advantages to the patriots. Howe also would encounter little trouble in moving his heavy baggage or such necessary stores as salt and flour, all of which could be carried by water. These handicaps, Washington wrote, "I have endeavored to conceal . . . from every one else; and, that no hasty removal of the public stores should take place, thereby communicating an alarm. . . ." To withhold such judgments from Morris or Congress, in Washington's opinion, would be "criminal."

Other communications in March explained to the governor of Connecticut the falsity of the belief that "the necessaries of life" were cheaper in the south than in the north: "It is true that less clothing is sufficient for them; but as they manufacture little among themselves they are obliged to pay most extravagantly for what they wear."

For want of proper laws Washington doubted if the southern militia ever would be well regulated; nor could he place much reliance on New Jersey and Pennsylvania militia since "they come and go as they please." (In New Jersey Governor Livingston had admitted to Washington that he could not "make our assembly sensible of the importance of an effectual militia law.")

Unexpectedly a "private" letter to Mifflin revealed a personal wish to buy as many as a hundred mares. "I have many large Farms," Washington wrote, "and am improving a great deal of Land into Meadow and Pasture, which cannot fail of being profited by a number of Brood Mares. . . ." He did not wish, however, to do anything that would harm the fighting services or have his name appear in the transaction for even "the most innocent and upright actions are often misconstrued."

The month ended with a visit from an Oneida missionary, a chief and five braves, who had been given a series of reports "so falsely and variously represented" by British agents concerning the disorganized condition of American forces that the Indians had come to judge the circumstances for themselves. Consequently, stating that the Oneidas were "well satisfied with what they had seen," Washington was able to end his month's reports to Congress on an affirmative note:

Being told that France was assisting us, and about to join in the war, they seemed highly pleased; and Mr. Kirkland [their missionary] said he was persuaded it would have a considerable effect on the minds of several of the [Indian] nations, and secure to us their neutrality, if not a declaration and commencement of hostilities in our favor. . . .

*   *   *

The winter of 1777 was also a perverse time for Lord Stirling. Not only had his sister, Catherine Alexander, married a British major now serving in New York, but his eldest daughter further revealed the division of sentiments within the family by marrying a New Yorker of Loyalist sympathies. The one bright moment of the winter for Stirling came when Congress raised him in rank to major general and placed him ninth in command behind Washington, Lee, Schuyler, Putnam, Gates, Heath, Sullivan, and Greene.

*   *   *

As spring approached with flashes of green among the sassafras trees and the willows began to yellow, the numerous Ger-

mans in the area welcomed the Reverend John Peter Gabriel
Muhlenberg in his new uniform of a brigadier general. Tall and
handsome and still in his thirtieth year, Muhlenberg once had
been the lively "dancing parson" of the Lutheran churches at
Bedminster and New Germantown. For hill country Germans
who felt a sense of shame for the Hessian mercenaries who
fought against the colonies, Muhlenberg with his gay and booming voice was a symbol of their own respectability. They had lost
him temporarily to a church in Woodstock, Virginia, where he
was still serving when the war came. Before Muhlenberg put
aside his clerical gown, he preached a famous sermon, saying
that whereas there was a time to preach and a time to pray, there
was also a time to fight.

Muhlenberg raised and commanded the 8th Virginia, composed largely of Germans from the Shenandoah Valley, which he
was now marching to join Washington at Morristown. Aside
from the Commander-in-Chief it is doubtful if among the Germans of Somerset County there was a military figure more loved
than Muhlenberg. The people remembered how he had shared
their lives, always willing to fish the streams and roam the hills
for game. Youngsters he had baptized—the progeny of couples
he had married—pranced beside him. He laughed, swinging the
children in his arms. Farewells came hard with old friends, but
duty called Muhlenberg to other responsibilities and with a bitter-
sweet reluctance he led his Virginians along the road to Morristown.

With the crocuses pushing through the near-frozen ground,
a new voice of lusty robustness was heard in Morristown as
Anthony Wayne arrived with the Pennsylvania Line. "Dandy"
Wayne had been his nickname when as a boy he had attended his
Uncle Gilbert's school in Philadelphia. So happy was Gilbert
with the youth's intelligence that he laid out a program of classical studies intended to produce "a statesman, a bright particle of
genius." But Wayne showed very little interest in a classical
background except when it dealt with Caesar on the road to
Rome or Hannibal crossing the Alps. Anything that emphasized
la glorie militaire fascinated him; he liked to march around with

a rusty flintlock and make charges over a hill upon an imaginary enemy; and so Uncle Gilbert declared his cause lost and sent the boy home to Waynesboro, Pennsylvania, where the family owned five hundred acres and a thriving tannery.

"Dandy" Wayne must have learned something about mathematics in Uncle Gilbert's school for he was sent by a Philadelphia land company to survey 100,000 acres in Nova Scotia. In 1766—now in his twenty-first year—he returned to Pennsylvania to be married and to supervise the family's properties (which in time he succeeded in running into bankruptcy). But the Revolution fulfilled Wayne's wildest dreams of military life. He raised his own regiment and hammered Pennsylvania rustics into disciplined soldiers. At almost any hour of the night he would drive his wife Polly to distraction "by getting out his pistol . . . lighting a row of candles on the lawn and standing there in the dark trying to snuff them out at a distance of twenty yards."

Like Muhlenberg, Wayne was one of a new breed of generals gathering around Washington at Morristown. And so was Dan Morgan, who brought 500 sharpshooters from Virginia. Some say Dan was born in New Jersey's Hunterdon County and some believe his birthplace was in Pennsylvania's Bucks County where his father was ironmaster at the Durham Iron Works. Dan grew into a sturdy six-footer, with a streak of the hell-raiser, and after a quarrel with his sire he wandered into Virginia's Shenandoah Valley. He served as a wagoner for the British in the fighting against the French and Indians where he had first earned his characterization as "exactly fitted for the toils and pomp of war." Once, for striking a British subaltern, the impulsive Dan had been condemned to receive 500 lashes on his bare back; he told the story with relish, for he had received only 499 stripes, proving that the damned British could not even count!

The outbreak of the Revolution brought out the full warlike capacities of Dan Morgan. Within twenty-one days he raised and trained two regiments of Virginia riflemen and marched them to Boston. Here he saw the Redcoats at their worst, for the Americans, who could have been cut off from the mainland at Charlestown Neck, decimated Howe's frontal attack because he failed to place a support on this isthmus. Dan also participated in the most regrettable of American operations when he followed Benedict Arnold through the northern wilderness to the ill-fated assault on Quebec (1775). When Arnold had been wounded, Dan had taken command and had endured the humiliation of a surrender. He was released the following autumn and raised from captain to colonel, the capacity in which he greeted Washington in the hill country of New Jersey.

The romantic Muhlenberg, the excitable Wayne, the exuberant Morgan—they were like the flashes of green among the sassafras trees, the yellow of the willows, the shoots of the crocus bursting through the ground—each part of the spring and resurrection clustering around Morristown.

CHAPTER NINE

Impasse

Spring, 1777

If Washington found Lord William Howe's personality per-
plexing and confusing, the American Commander-in-Chief simply
shared an experience that was to plague historians for two centuries. Sir Billy had fought with Wolfe at Quebec in the French
and Indian War; and after his brother George Howe was killed
at Ticonderoga during the same campaign, the Massachusetts
Assembly had erected his monument in Westminster Abbey, a
fact that the family could not easily forget.

As a member of the House of Commons, Lord William Howe
represented Nottingham, a town very much in sympathy with
the complaints of Great Britain's overseas colonies. Howe had
promised his Nottingham constituents in the winter of 1774–75
that if offered command in America he would not accept it; then
in February 1775, he reneged on this pledge with the somewhat
limping excuse that "a man's private feelings ought to give way
to the service of the public at all times."

A British historian has raised questions about Lord Howe that
may persist for another two centuries:

He was, perhaps, the only British commander-in-chief with a real chance
to crush the American rebellion. Why did he fail to do so? Why did he let

slip a succession of seemingly easy opportunities to destroy Washington's army? Was he more concerned with reconciliation than with reconquest? Did his political responsibilities as peacemaker interfere with his military obligations as general?

Howe, who had married the daughter of a mistress of George I, could not blame his dalliance solely on Eros and Mrs. Loring, or explain his difficulty in devising a plan of military action on his preoccupation with gambling for high stakes. He showed flashes of British belligerency in March and April with raids on Peekskill, New York and Danbury, Connecticut. In both communities the night was filled with the leaping flames of burning dwellings, warehouses and barns; and a large amount of food, clothing and tents was either seized or destroyed. After these forays the troops returned to New York City so that any serious military intention had hardly been expected.

A unique figure in Howe's encampment was General Charles Lee, whose exchange Washington was still trying to negotiate in mid-April. To the American Commander-in-Chief, Lee, probably, would become ultimately as complex a personality as Howe. Not long before his capture Lee had told a friend: "There are times when we must commit treason against the laws of the State, and the present crisis demands this brave, virtuous, kind of treason." Liquor turned Lee's head with giddiness and loosened his tongue. Gaily he told a British officer that if after White Plains the Hessians had pushed up briskly and crushed the American left, the war would have been finished.

Lee enjoyed his place as a favorite in New York City's best social circles, and worked hard to maintain his status. No doubt to please Howe he prepared a plan for dividing the colonies, north and south, by taking Philadelphia by sea and then occupying Annapolis and Alexandria. Lee's plan might well have influenced Howe's final decision to strike Philadelphia. Meanwhile, Rhode Island militia caught Major General Richard Prescott in a bordello near Newport, an event that pleased the risibilities of at least one London poet:

> On General Prescot being carried off naked,
> "unanointed," "unanealed"

> What various lures there are to ruin man;
> Woman, the first and foremost all bewitches!
> A nymph thus spoil'd a General's mighty plan,
> And gave him to the foe—without his breeches.

Later Washington learned that through the capture of Prescott he had acquired "trading bait" for Lee.

*   *   *

April passed without an aggressive threat from Howe. To the president of Congress, Washington on the twelfth of the month delineated the problems confronting him, state by state:

New Hampshire. No returns, but a letter from Genl. Heath says they are tolerably forward [and] all their Regiments go to the Northward.

Massachusetts. About 400 Men raised to a Regt. many of those yet to undergo [smallpox] innoculation [*sic*]. Seven of their Regiments to the Northward, and Eight are to come to Peekskill for the present.

Rhode Island. Only 360 men inlisted in both Regiments the 1st April—200 of those are yet to be innoculated. Genl. Varnum writes me that he despairs of filling up the Regiments.

Connecticut. . . . about 1800 men were recruited thro the whole State, they much dispersed, many to have the small pox and recruiting at a stand.

New York. About 200 Men to a Regiment and from the peculiar Situation of that province, it will be almost impossible for them to fill up their Regiments, tho' they exert themselves very much.

New Jersey. Between 200 and 300 to a Regt.—they also lay under many difficulties on account of the disaffection of their State, but their Officers are active and diligent.

Pennsylvania. Most of the Regiments are very backward, those most so, who have been longest recruiting.

Delaware State. No Return of their Regiment.

Maryland. I have only the Return of one Regiment which consists of 200 Men, but I do not believe the others are in more forwardness. . . .

Virginia. The nine old Regiments will not exceed 1800 effective Men, and Govr. [Patrick] Henry, in a letter which I received yesterday, informs me that he did not think, that more than four of the six new ones would be filled. He proposes the expediency of raising Volunteer Companies, to serve seven, or eight Months, to make up the deficiency. But this I shall object to on many accounts, particularly, that it would be introducing a Body of Men, who would look upon themselves, at liberty to do what they pleased, and the moment their time expired, would leave us, tho' at the most critical Juncture.

*   *   *

Washington's edginess was founded on a growing restlessness in New Brunswick, which presaged the imminence of some kind of concentrated military action against him. Since that December day of rain and cold when the British had entered New Brunswick (and Simeon DeWitt, a student at the College and destined to become Washington's chief geographer, had "lost his clothes and books" in escaping to Hackensack), the townspeople had adjusted with carefully guarded grumbling to the hardships of an occupation.

The British force in New Brunswick numbered about 5,000, tented on both sides of the Raritan with a log bridge connecting their encampments. The pews were removed from the Dutch Reformed Church so that it could be converted into a hospital and then a stable. Fortifications scarred the hillsides.

A Philadelphia report stated: "By accounts from New Jersey we learn that deserters daily come over from the enemy, who are penned up in Brunswick so that they never peep out but our people have a knock at them, which as often turned out in our favor." Every community in the vicinity had woeful tales to tell of British, Hessian, and Loyalist raiders. Long lists of stolen articles were kept in the hope of gaining restitution from the government and included such items as "2 Common Bibles, 1 Testament, and 1 Psalm book," "1 clock without case, of the best kind," and "2111 lbs of pork purchased that fall."

*   *   *

To protect the people of the Raritan Valley from these marauders, on the first of March Washington sent General Benjamin Lincoln with a force of 500 to Bound Brook. Lincoln, a Massachusetts farmer with only a common school education, approached any assignment eagerly. He built a block house for his three brass cannon to guard any approach from New Brunswick, probably giving to his headquarters the designation of Battery House. The broad-shouldered, intelligent, and pleasant Lincoln, who never used profanity and would allow no soldier or officer to do so in his presence, well understood that he had been placed directly across the route the British must take in any attack upon Morristown. His patrols were strung along the Raritan for a distance of five or six miles. Guards watched the three bridges that spanned the river.

On the night of April 12, a Saturday, Cornwallis set out with 4,000 troops to oust Lincoln from Bound Brook. A battalion of grenadiers, another of light infantry, a detachment of guards, the light horse and two battalions of Hessians and Jaegers marched the two banks of the river. Cornwallis directed his troops to avoid all roads and to advance as quietly as possible. His Lordship quite obviously wished to surround Lincoln with two detachments and thus seal his escape route into the mountains while a third detachment cut down any Americans attempting to cross the Raritan.

At about five o'clock that Sabbath morning a crowing rooster announced the pinkening sunrise. At the Battery House the American sentries cried, "All's well," and the morning gun was fired. Then Cornwallis' soldiers came with a rush and the startled sentries shouted:

"To arms! To arms!"

Battery House erupted into a bedlam. General Lincoln, still in his nightshirt, mounted a horse and dashed for the mountains. Half-dressed American troops plunged through the gap in the converging British columns. Their musket firing was wild and aimless. Once reaching higher ground, however, the Americans performed creditably. Their brisk musketry began taking effect and their retreat became orderly.

Accounts of the affair at Bound Brook varied. Washington called the American loss "trifling." Lincoln gave his casualties at sixty killed and wounded, including one of his aides, in addition to all his baggage, papers, and artillery. Howe put the American loss at thirty killed and between eighty and ninety captured, whereas the British sacrificed only three Jaegers and four soldiers of the light infantry "slightly wounded." Another British officer added to the booty at "Bawnbrook" a quantity of spirits, flour, and other stores. The *Boston Gazette* fumed at the treatment of American captives:

The enemy at New York continues to treat the American prisoners with great barbarity. Their allowance to each man for three days, is one pound of beef, three worm-eaten musty biscuits and a quart of salt water.

The meat they are obliged to eat raw, as they have not the smallest allowance of fuel. Owing to this more than savage cruelty the prisoners die fast, and in the small space of three weeks no less than 1,700 brave men have perished.

With equal fervor the *Royal American Gazette* of New York City reported on the skirmish at "Bawnbrook," praising the British for their "usual intrepidity" and adding to the windfall of Cornwallis' troops "a man in irons sentenced to be shot on Sunday" and "several hogsheads of New England rum." The American prisoners, lodged in New York jails, were described by the *Mercury* as "the most miserable looking creatures that ever bore the name of soldiers, being covered with nothing but rags and vermin."

For the invaders a large part of the remaining day was spent in pillaging and in searching for notorious Rebels known to live in this neighborhood. The prize they all sought was Jacob De Groot, a captain in the New Jersey militia. The nearest the British ever came to this objective was an occasion when De Groot hid in a large oven while his wife pretended to light a fire. Apparently a thorough job of looting was done on the captain's home that April 13th for afterward De Groot inventoried his losses:

1 bay horse, 3 years old; 1 brown horse, 5 years old; 1 roan horse, 7 years old; 8 Milch cows, 1 working ox, 3 four year old cattle, 4 three year old cattle, 2 one year old cattle, 4 Calves, 1 negro man 24 years old, and many articles of clothing, dishes, etc., to a value of 234 pounds and 15 shillings.

*   *   *

And so, with the unfolding of the leaves, war advanced up the Raritan Valley.

In June an American spy, Abraham Patten, was hanged in New Brunswick. The charge against Patten was that he had given a grenadier 50 guineas to carry four letters to Washington and Putnam. The soldier apparently took the cash and carried the letters to Cornwallis. These letters outlined a disingenuous plot: Patten "proposed on a certain day to set Fire to [New] Brunswick in four places at once, blow up the Magazine, and set off a Rocket as a signal for the Rebels to attack the Town."

CHAPTER TEN

Valley in Arms

May–June, 1777

Like a snapping turtle, the British seemed to draw into a shell after the brief foray at Bound Brook. Washington's increasing vexations even found a target in Lord Stirling. From the Governor's wife, Mrs. Livingston, Washington wrote, he had received charges "of roughness and indelicacy, which I am convinced your cooler reflexion much condemns." And the Commander-in-Chief added: "Conscious that you have too much regard for your Character as a Gentleman, and too nice a sensibility of the impulses of humanity, deliberately to commit an indiscretion of the kind, I can only impute, what has happened, to a sudden transport of passion. . . ."

Actually Washington was stirring up an unnecessary tempest. Mrs. Livingston had been six months at Basking Ridge and Lord Stirling's "transport of passion" was a simple spat in which he expressed the wish that the Governor's wife would seek refuge somewhere else.

In the midst of Washington's efforts to calculate what would be Howe's next move, a "welther" of problems was dumped on Washington's writing desk. Some were so old—the impossibility of relying on state militia, the lack of clothing, ammunition and funds—that he had been answering them for two years without effect.

But new problems arose. Silas Deane, one-time successful lawyer, merchant, and socialite of Wethersfield, Connecticut, was in France on a secret mission to acquire uniforms and ammunition—for free, if his Yankee ingenuity worked; on loan to Congress, if he had need to fall back on an alternative. Europeans seeking appointments in the Continental army clustered around Deane. A few, like Lafayette, De Kalb, Steuben, and Pulaski, were excellent, but most were adventurers and Washington was left with the unhappy duty of separating the chaff from the wheat.

Washington complained, admitting his perplexity, over "a strange, unaccountable languor" which prevailed at a time when patriots should be making "the most vigorous and active exertions." He still found smallpox more destructive "than the Enemy's Sword." Messrs. "Hartshorne and Bowne of Monmouth County" he accused of loading vessels in Philadelphia and trading with Howe. And nothing disturbed the Commander-in-Chief more than the designation by Congress of Congress's Own Regiment and General Washington's Life Guards. Such names he believed highly improper since all battalions should be on the "same footing." He endorsed exempting militiamen who toiled in ironworks and could count over eighty of these works in Morris County alone.

Of special scorn to Washington were officers who had "drawn large Sums under pretence of paying their Men; but have been obliged, from extravagance and for other purposes, to appropriate this money to their own use." He did not minimize his worry over these circumstances:

The desertions from our army of late [May 3] have been very considerable. Genl. Howe's Proclamation and the bounty allowed to those who carry their Arms, have had an unhappy influence on too many of the soldiery, in a particular manner, on those who are not natives. Nor have the base frauds practised by Several of our officers, contributed a little to this, in my opinion. Many of the privates complain loudly, declaring they have not received either pay or bounty—Others not a farthing of the latter, and they have become so mutinous and uneasy in many cases, that I have been obliged to draw Warrants for money on account, to distribute among the men, not having it in my power to obtain Regular Abstracts notwithstanding the most pointed and repeated Orders.

On the other hand, some of the officers aver, they have not been able to collect and adjust yet all their Recruiting accounts. I could wish some measures could be devised, to cause more frequent desertions of their Troops.—Congress may think of some expedient.—A larger bounty might have some effect and money to the Foreigners in lieu of Land. The Bounty given by Genl. Howe to those who carry in Arms, is Sixteen Dollars, as we are told, tho' his proclamation only expresses, they shall have the full value. To the Inhabitants who will take up Arms and join him, he promises Land.

Despite Washington's mounting headaches and frustrations, by mid-May the thin winter ranks of his army had expanded to 9,000. He still was no match for Howe in a full-fledged frontal assault, although his prospects were brightening. A succession of enemy raids throughout the spring accomplished virtually nothing, but neither did they reveal Howe's intentions. Meanwhile, the "dangerously handsome" Aaron Burr set girlish hearts fluttering as he galloped over the roads of Somerset County.

*   *   *

Along the moss-covered sides of roads honeysuckle and grapevines intertwined around the tree trunks and chattering squirrels pranced through the branches, when, in late May, Washington moved his winter encampment from Morristown. His destination was Middlebrook, twenty miles to the south. Here, near the banks of the Raritan, he was in the first range of the Watchung Mountains about seven miles northwest of the British in New Brunswick.

Washington divided his immediate command into five divisions of two brigades each under Major Generals Greene, Sutphin, Sullivan, Lincoln, and Lord Stirling. Knox commanded the artillery and a force of about 8,000. Earthworks in three hollow squares fortified the valley in Washington's rear. There was an abundance of water and forage for the horses.

From the ledges of the Watchungs the Commander-in-Chief

enjoyed a sweeping vista of the land from Blue Hills (later Plainfield) to New Brunswick and on very clear days his view encompassed Amboy. But even though this advantage forewarned him of possible British movements, Washington still played a three-way guessing game with Howe. Did the Briton expect to reach Philadelphia by another march across New Jersey? Or would Howe move north to join the forces under "Gentleman Johnny" Burgoyne that were coming down from Canada? Or would the enemy assault Philadelphia from the sea?

Washington was determined to take no risks. Benedict Arnold was placed in Philadelphia with explicit instructions to keep watch on Trenton and other crossings of the Delaware. Smallwood's Maryland and Delaware brigade and Hazen's regiment under Sullivan were dispatched to Princeton. Lord Stirling "continued to act as Washington's eyes and ears" on the plain below the mountains. The Commander-in-Chief moved to the front of the Watchungs, fortified his position with redoubts, and ordered his men to sleep on their arms.

The needling probes of Maxwell and Stirling at Amboy finally taxed Howe's patience, though for all his braggadocio he did not "cut to pieces with Highland Broad Swords" Stirling's brigade. In a move toward Washington's army on June 13 Howe left Amboy with 18,000 troops. At New Brunswick he split his army into two columns, and advanced toward Millstone and Middlebush, in the hope of cutting Washington off from Princeton and thus enticing him to come down from Middlebrook.

Washington pulled back his Princeton troops in time. It was no secret that Howe was traveling light and looking for a quick victory. American guards were posted at Millstone, Pluckemin, and Quibbletown (later New Market). Morgan was at Finderne and Wayne at Mount Pleasant. Then Washington dealt Howe the meanest blow of all—by simply sitting tight he frustrated the British strategy.

*   *   *

Outwitted, Howe reacted quickly. While for the first time Washington raised before his headquarters the new flag of Stars and Stripes adopted by Congress, Howe began withdrawing toward New Brunswick. Wayne at Mount Pleasant was aware of this movement and wrote Lincoln, his division commander:

Prisoners have just been brought in. They say there is an encampment of the enemy on this side of the Raritan below the New Bridge. Can't we beat up their quarters before sunrise? I am confident we can. My people are all ready to move at a moment's notice. The light horsemen will await your orders.

From his lookout posts on the ledges of the Watchungs, Washington watched the British maneuvers. Greene was sent with three brigades to nip at British heels and then retire to Piscataway; and meanwhile Morgan and Wayne, with splendid assistance from Muhlenberg, beat back the Hessians under DeHeister who had thrown up earthworks at the Horse Shoe of the Raritan south of the bridge. On the advice of his generals, which may not have been the wisest, Washington on June 24 came down to Quibbletown to be nearer his enemy. Lord Stirling protected the American left flank from a position near Metuchen.

Now, exultantly, Howe played his trump card. On June 26 he turned suddenly toward Woodbridge and Bonhamtown (now part of Edison). Howe's intention was clear and sensible: by moving in two columns he hoped to encircle Stirling and by cutting off Washington from his mountain sanctuary to bring on a battle in the open.

Under Cornwallis about 4,000 troops rushed through Woodbridge toward Scotch Plains in an effort to outflank Stirling. Meanwhile Howe led his main body to Westfield to disorganize Washington's forces. This strategy had worked at Brooklyn. Why should it not do so in New Jersey?

The answer was Lord Stirling, who, aided by Maxwell, threw his forces across Cornwallis' route. Alexander Hamilton described Stirling as "near being surrounded" and applauded his "spirited exchanges." Even though the ground was low and the water supply unsatisfactory around Metuchen meetinghouse, Stirling gave Cornwallis what Washington liked to call "a good peppering." The Americans, forced to retreat through the passes of the Watchungs beyond Westfield and Scotch Plains, did so slowly and in sound order. Warned by the action, Washington scrambled back to safety before Howe could catch him.

Surprisingly, Stirling's casualties were slight: twelve killed, fifty wounded, fifty missing, and two or three cannon captured. How badly Cornwallis had been hurt was not known for a reason that Washington explained to his brother: "They [the enemy] are equal to Indians in concealing their loss, by a removal of their dead, and were they to take up the business of scalping they would much resemble savages, in every respect!"

*   *   *

Washington's umbrage was understandable as a disgusted Howe and Cornwallis retreated from New Brunswick, which they had held for eight months. Houses in flames and ashes as well as the shameless plundering of the soldiery marked the line of march to Amboy. Pontoon bridges, intended for the invasion of Philadelphia, provided the means of crossing to Staten Island as June advanced to a close. Yet, as Washington wrote Major General John Armstrong, there was a bright side to the situation:

> The evacuation of Jersey at this time seems to be a peculiar mark of Providence, as the Inhabitants have an opportunity of securing their Harvests of Hay and Grain, the latter of which would in all probability have undergone the same fate with many farm-Houses, had it been ripe enough to take Fire. The distress of many of the Inhabitants, who were plundered not only of their Effects, but of their provision of every kind, was such that I sent down several wagon loads of meat and flour to supply their present wants.

Washington, with a land-locked army, was confronted with guessing the objective of Howe's sea-borne army—a military situation unique for its time—but the American Commander-in-Chief was not overwhelmed by this predicament. If Howe intended to join Burgoyne, Washington wrote Schuyler, "General Howe must speedily throw off the Mask, and make his preparations for going up the North River." Washington doubted such a maneuver since "a Man of General Burgoyne's spirit and

Enterprise would never have returned from England, merely to execute a plan from which no great Credit or Honor was to be derived. . . . If we can keep General Howe below the Highlands, I think their schemes will be entirely baffled." So Washington played his original hunch—Howe's objective was Philadelphia.

Meanwhile the Commander-in-Chief moved back to Morristown. On a bright July day he stepped from Jacob Arnold's Tavern. On its staff in the middle of the parade ground the Commander-in-Chief's flag ruffled in the breeze of an early summer morning. Washington smiled: Today was the first anniversary of the adoption of the Declaration of Independence.

PART TWO

The Guns of Monmouth

"At the first news of this quarrel,
my heart was enrolled in it."

Marquis de Lafayette

Prelude

1777–1778

In an age when strong men shed tears and often embraced, no more romantic figure reached the colonies than Marie Joseph Paul Yves Roch Gilbert du Motier, the Marquis de Lafayette. His story reads like an historical novel. Born September 6, 1757, at the Chateau of Chavaniac in Auvergne (Haute-Loire), France, Lafayette was at the age of thirteen among his nation's wealthiest orphans. Awkward and shy and earnestly eager to do what was expected of him, he attended the Collège du Plessis in Paris, joined a company of the King's Musketeers and by pre-arrangement married at the age of sixteen. Marie Antoinette found him a most amusing addition to the court life at Versailles: drink befuddled his head and tangled his dancing legs.

In the American Revolution, Lafayette saw an opportunity of repaying "perfidious Albion" for the humiliation France had suffered in the Seven Years' War. Louis XVI, however, was obstinately opposed to having the wealthy young nobleman travel overseas. Anyone with an annual income of 120,000 livres and a yearning for a military career could shrug his shoulders at the King's obduracy. The Declaration of Independence warmed Lafayette's blood more than the finest wine in France; he was soon in an intrigue with Silas Deane, an American agent who promised him a commission in the colonies; and he built his own ship, *La Victoire,* to carry him and others to North America. When the King ordered Lafayette arrested, the youth sent his ship from Bordeaux to a neighboring port in Spain, whither he fled in disguise.

Throughout Europe courts tittered over Lafayette's rebellion and the publicity certainly did not harm the American cause. In mid-June, 1777, the nineteen-year-old nobleman, after landing in South Carolina, hastened to Philadelphia. Washington had made well his point that a hard look should be taken at every foreign adventurer promised a commission by Silas Deane.

Congress received Lafayette coolly. The respectful, charming youth asked no favors. He was willing to begin in the ranks as a private serving without pay. It was not Lafayette's physical appearance that finally won the heart of Congress in granting him a commission: he was tall, thin and rather big-shouldered; his face was agreeable rather than attractive, with a large and slender nose, and a receding brow already emphasized the future sparseness of his reddish-brown hair.

Lafayette wore the scarf of an American major general when Washington first met him at a dinner in Philadelphia late in July, beginning an affectionate friendship that would last a lifetime for both. Events since Howe had left New Jersey gave the American Commander-in-Chief need for a diverting companion. As early as July 3 "a great stir" had occurred among the British shipping in New York harbor. A fortnight passed for Howe "in dalliance with Mrs. Loring, while the troops were lying on board the transports crowded together in the sultry heat of summer."

Although Washington scarcely believed a report that Fort Ticonderoga had fallen, he still had to move northward in anticipation of Howe following the same course. Washington marched almost to West Point before he learned the truth. Ticonderoga *had* fallen and Howe's probable movements had been misjudged. Not until July 24 was Washington informed that Howe, embarking with between 15,000 and 18,000 men, had passed Sandy Hook. So Philadelphia was Howe's objective, after all! Heavy detachments were rushed to the Quaker City.

Six days later, reaching the Delaware, Washington began doubting his own judgment for there had been no sight of Howe in Delaware Bay. On July 31—the day Lafayette and Washington first met—Howe was reported off the capes of Delaware Bay and Washington ordered the army to Philadelphia; but Howe disappeared again and eleven days passed with Washington camping in meadows near the Neshaminy River without clarifying Howe's intentions. Then the mystery was solved: Howe was passing through the capes of Chesapeake Bay and landing fifty-five miles south of Philadelphia! Washington reacted sensibly, advancing to place his forces between Howe and the city.

New enlistments had raised Washington's army to about 16,000. The Commander-in-Chief was saddened by the shabbiness of his soldiers and to spruce them up ordered a green sprig—an emblem of hope—worn in their hats. Drums and fifes were told to play a quick step. Sixteen abreast, "without *dancing* along, or totally disregarding the music," the Americans entered a cheering Philadelphia. Under any circumstances John Adams would have found some basis for criticism:

Our soldiers have not yet quite the air of soldiers. They don't step exactly in time. They don't hold up their heads quite erect, nor turn out their toes so exactly as they ought. They don't all of them cock their hats; and such as do, don't all wear them the same way.

*   *   *

Like a play on a revolving stage the war now entered new scenes and encountered new episodes that changed its denouement. Old characters disappeared and, in some instances, were replaced by other *dramatis personae*.

Two trips across the Atlantic, and perhaps some rather unscrupulous political infighting, were required before John Burgoyne gained command of the British army in Canada. It has been easier for historians to stereotype Gentleman Johnny as a "playboy general" than to deal with the motives or objectives of this highly complicated personality. That Burgoyne's northern campaign, intended to seize Albany, was to receive Howe's immediate support was the mistaken afterthought and not the plan of 1777.

Howe was expected to take Philadelphia before lending any substantial cooperation to Burgoyne. At the time the fervent belief of Lord Germain and George III was that by conquering Albany to the north and Philadelphia to the south, the war could be ended.

Burgoyne yearned to succeed in three careers—as a general, a politician, and a playwright—and came within a single toss of the dice of winning this ambitious gamble. His plays, though obviously contrived as was the fashion of the time, sparkled with a wit and satire that revealed an ability to stand back from the British social scene and view it objectively. The highlight of his more than thirty years in Parliament had been his censure for conducting one hostile campaign for reelection by holding a pistol in each hand to intimidate his rivals, but again he believed that he was only acting like a realist. Burgoyne was equally unemotional in judging the enemy he was about to fight:

Composed as the American army is [of men so skilled at using axes and shovels that they could speedily throw up an earthworks], together with the strength of the country, full of woods, swamps, stone walls, and other enclosures and hiding places, it may be said of it that every private man will in action be his own general, who will turn every tree and bush into a temporary fortress, from whence, when he hath fired his shot with all the deliberation, coolness, and certainty which hidden safety inspires, he will skip as it were to the next, and so on for a long time. . . .

A man of Burgoyne's several interests and ambitions naturally accumulated a wide variety of adversaries. Even his birth was surrounded by scandal, some declaring that he was the bastard son of Lord Bingley. At least one published news tidbit portrayed Burgoyne as a sharpster who hung around his London clubs until he could find some tipsy fellow member whom he easily flim-flammed at cards. His military experience, coming in that part of the Seven Years' War fought in Portugal against the French and Spanish, was downgraded by such ridiculing nicknames as "General Swagger" and "Julius Caesar Burgonius." He was far brighter than his critics realized, especially on the battlefield where he was entirely competent in the employment of cavalry, light infantry, and artillery.

Boastfulness and self-indulgence combined to make Gentleman Johnny his own worst enemy. He knew perfectly well that he was exaggerating when he declared he could conquer America in "a hop, step and jump." A contemporary pictured "jolly" Burgoyne at this time as spending "half the night singing and drinking and amusing himself in the company of the wife of a commissary, who was his mistress, and, like himself, liked champagne." The fall of Ticonderoga really resulted more from St. Clair's stupidity than Burgoyne's sagacity. The American neglected to reinforce Sugar Hill, which dominated the fort, so Burgoyne ordered a cannon dragged to its summit and thus held St. Clair and 3,500 troops at his mercy. The occasion surely did not justify George III bursting into the queen's chambers with the boyish shout: "I have beat them, I have beat the Americans!"

While St. Clair's troops scampered through the Green Mountains, leaving behind 120 cannon, Burgoyne faced serious troubles. In moving toward the Hudson, he set his hatchet men to chopping a road through dense forests. Why he did not proceed along the easier route by way of Lake George is another of the perplexities that confound historians. Even the lusty profanity of the axemen could not hurry the progress when Burgoyne's personal baggage (including the champagne he and his mistress so thoroughly enjoyed) required thirty wagons. In twenty-four days the army advanced twenty-three miles. One of his Indian guides, Wyandot Panther, scalped a pretty Loyalist girl, which did not endear Burgoyne to other Tories in the neighborhood. At the end of the month the situation grew desperate. Burgoyne's army verged on starvation and even hay for the horses had to be carted from Canada.

Burgoyne cast covetous eyes on Bennington, about twenty-five miles east of the Hudson in that part of the colonies known as "the New Hampshire grants." Here were the provisions that Burgoyne needed and he sent 600 Hessians to capture them. What Gentleman Johnny did not know was that tough old John Stark had returned to Bennington.

Stark had fought with the Americans from Bunker Hill to Trenton, then had returned home when Congress failed to raise him in rank. Stark looked upon Hessians as he did upon all skunks—the faster they were killed the less scent remained. He rallied around him the kind of ill-assorted lads the Green Mountains produced—boys in small-clothes fastened just below the knees to long stockings that ended in cowhide shoes ornamented by large buckles. They carried a variety of weapons, ranging from a heavy Queen's Arm captured in Canada twenty years before to French pieces dating back to the reduction of Louisburg in the French and Indian War. Powder horns were more prevalent than cartridge boxes. Only occasionally was a bayonet seen. Such swords as appeared were hammered on the anvils of village blacksmiths.

Clearly contemptuous of these farmer-soldiers, the Hessians walked into two hours of what Stark described as "the hottest [fighting] I ever saw in my life." Guns roared like thunderclaps as Bennington turned into a slaughter pen. An aghast Burgoyne poured another 500 men into the battle. The rout continued. At Bennington Burgoyne lost about 800 men. The American casualties were no more than 70.

*   *   *

Washington was cheered by Stark's victory at Bennington before the Commander-in-Chief set off to block Howe's occupation of Philadelphia. Informed that the enemy were landing in Maryland at the Head of the Elk [Elkton], Washington, accompanied by Lafayette and Greene, reconnoitered the country to within two miles of Howe's camp and was forced by a heavy rain to spend an uncomfortable evening in a Tory household. Luckily, surrounded by friends as well as foes, the trio escaped before their presence could be divulged.

The American army gathered at Wilmington, Delaware. A false alarm indicated a battle forming along Red Clay Creek, but the maneuver proved to be a feint "to amuse" Washington while Howe turned the American right flank and wedged his forces between Washington's army and Philadelphia. The Virginian pulled back at two in the morning, choosing to make his stand along the Brandywine, some eight miles northwest of

Wilmington. Several small fords littered this creek but with Greene in command, Washington decided to center his army at Chad's Ford, the main crossing. Wayne's Pennsylvanians occupied a nearby hill and the Virginians under George Weedon and Muhlenberg were posted directly to the east of the ford. Other divisions protected the Brandywine from Wistar's Ford on the north to the steep heights of Pyle's Ford on the south.

That night the Reverend Joab Trout left no doubt as to which cause God favored when preaching on the text, "all that take the sword shall perish by the sword," for he added loudly: ". . . the doom of the British is near!"

The sun burned through the fog at eight-thirty on the morning of September 11, promising a hot and sultry day. The action before Chad's Ford heightened—again a feint that Washington did not clearly comprehend until the forenoon had passed. Then a farmer, Squire Cheney, his broad shoulders bursting through the clothes he had hastily donned, arrived with the disconcerting news that Howe, who had camped the night before at Kennett Square, was marching on Birmingham Meeting House, a stone building about three and a half miles north of Chad's Ford that the Americans were using as a hospital. Squire Cheney also declared that he had seen the enemy marching up the west side of the Brandywine but he knew a defile where they could be held off with no more than 200 men. Washington derided both tales, yet they were true.

The strategy that had worked in Brooklyn but had failed in New Jersey, Howe was willing to try once more. This time it succeeded as Cornwallis commanded the flanking movement. Cannon balls plowed the fields. The tops of trees were blown away. Grapeshot scattered leaves as though the first days of winter had arrived. A Quaker wagged his head sadly at the sight of "such a number of fellow beings lying together severely wounded and some mortally." Among them was Lafayette, shot in the leg. Washington, with between 1,200 and 1,300 men lost, knew how badly he had been crushed. Howe acknowledged only 89 killed.

Why suddenly the carpers failed to take Washington to task

for his inability properly to analyze the information he received or to use his Light Horse more effectively is one more of the baffling questions surrounding Brandywine. "Scotch Willie" Maxwell, who was drunk that day, was denounced as "a damned bitch of a general," but Congress was inclined to look upon the fighting at Brandywine as sufficiently worthy to send the army thirty hogsheads of rum. Meanwhile Congress dispatched its papers to Bristol while its members moved to Lancaster and then to York.

As part of the aftermath of the battle Washington ordered Wayne with 1,500 men and four fieldpieces to harass Howe's rear. Wayne posted his troops in a forest clearing near Paoli Tavern and was not more than "a spit and a holler" from his own home. At midnight on September 20 three British battalions found Wayne's soldiers asleep. A bayonet attack killed at least fifty before a humiliated Wayne could lead the way through the night to the safety of Chester and thereafter no one wondered why Wayne was known as "Mad Anthony."

Six days later Howe seized Philadelphia. The honor of entering the city with 3,000 troops fell to Cornwallis. Another 3,000 occupied the Jersey side of the river. Washington wondered why everyone seemed so euphoric; to him the fall of Philadelphia was among "the most fatal consequences to the cause of America"; and with Howe's forces now reduced to about 8,000, Washington was determined to free the city.

The Battle of Germantown, fought October 4, followed. The operation was confused at best. Washington's plan called for a simultaneous advance the night of October 3 along four roads. Men already overwearied now marched another sixteen miles along strange roads. Adequate communications could not be maintained for all that the Americans wore white papers in their hats as a mark of identification. Fog thwarted Washington's expectation of a charge with bayonets at sunup. Wayne's men, about 300 strong, crying "Have at the bloodhounds! Revenge Wayne's affair!" had some brief success before being hammered back. Private Joseph Plumb Martin, serving with the Connecticut regiment, could not recollect much about Germantown:

Affairs went on well for some time. The enemy were retreating before us, until the first division that was engaged had expended their ammunition. Some of the men unadvisedly calling out that their ammunition was spent, the enemy were so near that they overheard them, when they first made a stand and then returned upon our people, who, for want of ammunition and reinforcements, were obliged in their turn to retreat, which ultimately resulted in the rout of the whole army.

On this occasion Washington cheered Congress: "The day was unfortunate rather than injurious."

* * *

"This army must not retreat."

In this spirit Burgoyne left Canada on his expedition to Albany. The ease of his conquest at Ticonderoga led the general to conclude that America contained "no men of military science." After the affair at Bennington on August 16 cost him one-tenth of his army, Burgoyne should have experienced second thoughts —or at least have retraced his steps to the easier route by way of Lake George—but Burgoyne, said one American officer, was "puffed up with vanity" and did not respond in an emergency like ordinary men. What he would have called professional pride and honor excluded any turning back to Burgoyne (although what he expected to do with Albany, if he captured it, was not quite clear).

Burgoyne never had been fully supported. He had asked for 8,000 regulars and received 7,000, for 2,000 Canadians and received 650, for 1,000 Indians and received 500. The countryside was nowhere as Loyalist as he expected for all that his bombastic proclamations condemning Rebels for engaging in "the compleatest form of Tyranny that ever God in his displeasure suffered." His relation with Howe never was fully explained by Germain, no matter what the Secretary of War later said.

Gentleman Johnny's best hope was that 1,800 Tories and Indians under the command of Colonel Barry St. Leger could push their way from Fort Oswego on Lake Ontario to Fort Stanwix on the Mohawk River since the fall of Stanwix would open the way to Albany, 110 miles distant. Tigerish defenses by

Colonel Peter Gansevoort and General Nicholas Herkimer
denied Stanwix to St. Leger; and the good old Dutch curses of
Herkimer's soldiers plus the booming of the cannon at Stanwix
drove off the Indians at Oriskany. Burgoyne crossed to the west
bank of the Hudson on "a bridge of boats."

Somehow General Horatio Gates, blinking myopic eyes behind
thick-lensed glasses, found an excellent defensive position for his
Americans on Bemis Heights at Stillwater. Gates, who had been
driven beyond his capacities by an overambitious wife, defended
his sense of insecurity with a stubborn grumpiness that led
soldiers to refer to him as an "old grandmother." Burgoyne
unleashed a furious assault on Bemis Heights on September 19
and encountered Dan Morgan who rallied his Virginia riflemen
to battle with a turkey call. In a conflict that offered no quarter
from start to finish, Morgan shared the day's honors with Benedict Arnold.

Both leaders were old Indian fighters. A battle in a woodland
and field still partially covered with stumps and fallen timbers
was no particular handicap in their experience. "They are asses
in lions' skins, Canadians and Tories," Arnold told Morgan.
"Let your riflemen cure them of their borrowed plumes." Morgan's Virginia sharpshooters routed the advance within fifteen
minutes. The "Old Wagoner" was not so much excited by the
howls of the retreating enemy as by Arnold's reckless charge
upon the English and Germans. Gates' refusal to send reinforcements "infuriated" Arnold; he bore the brunt of the battle himself "inspired with the fury of a demon"; and that night Burgoyne fell back, still trapped. His day's losses must have totaled
500.

The feud between Arnold and Gates burned deeply. When on
October 7 Burgoyne launched his second assault, Gates told
Arnold: "I have nothing for you to do; you have no business
here."

Anger spread across Arnold's cheeks. Then, by God, he would
fight as a volunteer with Morgan! Arnold mounted an iron-gray
horse and left Gates blinking through his thick lenses. Arnold was
with Morgan when the center of the British lines was broken;

Arnold, virtually a one-man army, ousted the Hessians from two stockaded cabins; but a leg wound ended his usefulness.

Burgoyne, his army torn apart, surrendered at Saratoga. Gates offered Burgoyne and his soldiers free passage to Britain on the promise that they would not serve again in North America "during the present contest." What was to keep Burgoyne and his men from replacing other British troops who could then fight in the colonies Gates found impossible to explain. Never had he acted more like an "old grandmother."

*   *   *

In 1777—the year in which Britain expected to end the American Revolution—the mother country received two important military visitors from the colonies, one before and one after Burgoyne's disasters at Bemis Heights and Saratoga.

First to appear, early in the year, was the friend of Lord Stirling's youth, Henry Clinton, who intended to resign his military commission because he was bone weary from arguing military strategy with Howe. "I am a shy bitch," Clinton once said of himself and it is difficult to quarrel with this self-description. The reticence with which Clinton masked his deeper emotions may have fooled others but not himself. When his wife died as the result of five pregnancies in five years, Clinton verged on insanity.

As the only son of Admiral George Clinton, once Royal Governor of New York, Henry Clinton was born to the aristocracy and warmly accepted by the court party. A member of the House of Lincoln, his peerage went back to Henry VII. After the death of his wife (1772), Clinton's friends warned him that he could avoid a breakdown only by finding some forceful purpose in life, and apparently they advised him well, for two years later George III sent Clinton to visit Catherine the Great, who was then organizing a war between Russia and the Turks. Catherine had no mercenaries to sell George III for the prospective military suppression of his American colonies, and Clinton found the Queen in agreement with Frederick the Great of Prussia who scorned such business as "trafficking in blood." So George III turned to the pauperized leaders of the almost three hundred German principalities that were part of the old Holy Roman Empire, where he bought 20,000 troops who were all called, mistakenly, Hessians. A number of principalities other than Hesse-Cassel supplied these mercenaries.

Clinton has been accused of possessing "some curious alchemy," which meant simply that he likely had a better mind for military strategy than any of his fellow generals. Clinton was perhaps overtalkative in London, particularly about Cornwallis' blundering in New Jersey, but he at least convinced Lord Germain, who would not accept Sir Henry's resignation. The war secretary shuddered over the tragic consequences that could accrue if Clinton were not in the colonies to take supreme command should any fatal mishap befall Howe. Clinton, looking "very grum" (Germain's phrase), received the Order of Bath although George III was also somewhat in a grum mood since he was running out of ribbon. In much the same spirit Clinton sailed back to North America.

Lord Cornwallis returned to England after Burgoyne's surrender at Saratoga. Lady Jemima's health was failing rapidly, and Cornwallis told her frankly: "I am really so bilious as to think our army in America, Fleets everywhere, Possessions in the West Indies, &c., &c., &c. will be frittered away and destroyed in Twelve months." Germain and the court party had to find some scapegoat other than themselves for Burgoyne's failure. Howe became their logical victim and his "gross and mortifying blunders" were ridiculed "as if valour consisted in a military jig."

Cornwallis could not be accused of betraying Howe even though he was exposed to harsh examination by the Ministry, and at times his Lordship appeared to be dancing his own military jig as he criticized the Ministry more severely than he was prone to judge Howe. Lady Jemima still pressed her husband to remain at home but the whips were cracking in the War Office in Whitehall and Cornwallis had no choice but to return to North America. Their leave-taking was the last time Cornwallis saw his wife alive. She died, some said, of a broken heart.

CHAPTER ONE

Forts Along the Delaware

October–November, 1777

Unaware of the doom destiny was preparing, Howe entered Philadelphia after the fighting at Germantown and Washington withdrew twenty-four miles to Pennypacker's Mill. New situations called for new strategical planning by generals, often obscure to the average soldier who dragged from one day to the next with a sense of dreary aimlessness.

Private Joseph Plumb Martin now experienced one of those interludes and complaints poured from him like sweat in summer. After two days without eating he admitted that nothing so "galled" him on a retreat as "to be obliged to run till I was worried down." Once beyond the reach of the enemy's shot Martin "had no more fear of their overtaking me than I should have of an army of lobsters doing it." Satisfied that Howe had moved all his forces inside Philadelphia, Washington on October 15 encamped at White Marsh, about twelve miles to the north of the Quaker City. The days were so breathless that the smoke from campfires caused serious cases of eye-burn, and the loamy ground, "converted into mortar," made "any hogsty . . . preferable to our tents to sleep in."

Reports that a party of Howe's troops had advanced to an encampment on the west side of the Schuylkill River again placed

Martin and his Connecticut friends in motion: "We marched from camp before night as light troops, light in everything, especially in eatables." Reaching Barren Hill, some twelve or fifteen miles from Philadelphia, they were ordered to wade the river and then to wade back—officers being what they were—so they returned to Barren Hill, not only famished but also freezing. Reinforcements came up that night and a day's rations were issued—a pound of beef, including the fat and bone, and a pound of flour.

Without utensils the soldiers became experts in improvised cookery. The flour, mixed with water, was daubed on a flat stone and scorched on one side, which was "patriot's bread" if one needed a name. The fat beef was broiled on a stick in the fire. That night they again waded the Schuylkill, but then after a stumbling night march they were spotted by British outriders and waded back. Next day the march was resumed in the hope the British would consider the American party too insignificant to warrant an attack. At noon Martin found a black walnut tree and happily gorged himself on the nuts covering the ground; but at sunset the order came once more to wade across the Schuylkill. The quartermaster sergeants brought up casks of liquor in wagons and Martin explained why everyone did not receive an equal share:

The intention of the quartermaster sergeants was to give each man a gill of liquor, but as measuring it out by gills was tedious, it was dealt out to us in pint measures, with directions to divide a pint between four men. But as it was dark and the actions of the men could not be well seen by those who served out the liquor, each one drank as much as he pleased; some, perhaps, half a gill, some a gill, and as many as chose it drained the pint.

Martin and his brigade moved five miles to another encampment. Tipsy from drinking whiskey on empty stomachs, they made a bawdy, somewhat brawlish group. A five-rail fence down a lane beside water-filled fields provided a challenge, for "not being able, many or most of them, to keep a regular balance between head and heels, they would pile themselves up on each side of the fence, swearing and hallooing, some losing their arms, some their hats, some their shoes, and some themselves." Luckily the enemy did not appear.

That night the Americans were ordered to defend the forts along the Delaware, which they reached by crossing the river between Bristol, Pennsylvania, and Burlington, New Jersey. Another nightfall brought them to Haddonfield, where Martin's happiest memory was of a captured goose (called a "Hissian" in the army), which they plucked and cooked. Martin's share was one wing. They were nearer to battle than any of them realized.

* * *

With genuine concern Howe recognized how thoroughly the Americans were fortifying the shores and miry islands of the Delaware to cut off the shipping of supplies to Philadelphia. Moreover, the ship channel of the river which swirled between these islands and forts was obstructed by *chevaux-de-frise,* iron-pointed wooden beams embedded in huge crate-like structures loaded with stones. Sunk in the river within a few inches of the water surface and pointed downstream, the *chevaux-de-frise* were intended to impale or rip away the bottoms of approaching enemy ships. Sometimes spiked barrels strung together were employed as obstructions. Above the fortifications at about Gloucester, gamely ready to give battle, floated that assortment of sloops and other converted vessels known as the American navy.

Toward mid-June, 1777, John Hancock, then president of the Continental Congress, had directed Governor Livingston to employ 500 militia in hurrying the construction of the fort at Billingsport, about twelve miles below Camden.

Once in virtual control of Philadelphia, Howe reacted swiftly. Two regiments under the command of Colonel Sterling were ordered to cross the river from Chester, Pennsylvania. They moved speedily, attacking the fort from the rear. Taken by surprise, the Americans spiked their guns, set fire to their still unfinished barracks, and fled in panic along the stone road near the river's edge.

The ensuing contest at Fort Mercer in Red Bank (not to be confused with the community of the same name in Monmouth

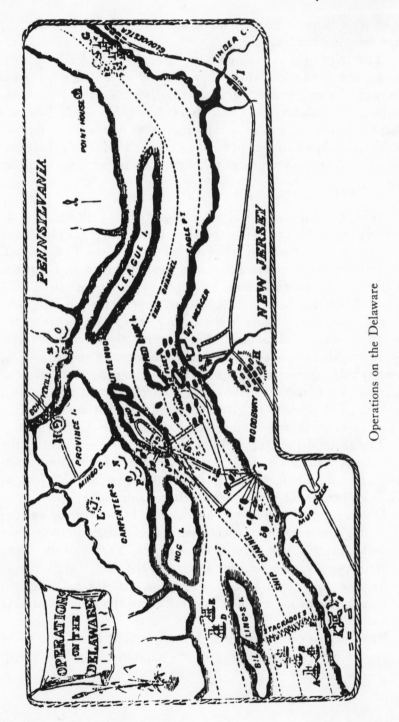

Operations on the Delaware

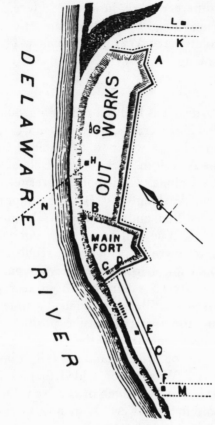

FORT MERCER.

PLAN OF FORT MERCER, AT RED BANK, NEW JERSEY.

References.

A. End of the fort at which the Hessians entered.

B. Small ditch, cross embankment and location of the masked battery.

C. Remains of the hickory-tree used during the battle as a flag staff.

D. Ruins of a brick wall in the middle of the artificial bank.—Gateway.

E. Count Donop's grave.

F. Louis Whitall's house.

G. Monument, erected in 1829.

H. Pleasure-house.

I. Marks of the trenches in which the slain were deposited.

K. Road the Hessians marched to the attack.—Reeve's old road.

L. Tenant House.

M. Road to Woodbury.

N. Direction of Fort Mifflin.

O. Farm Road.

NOTE.—The works represented extend about 350 yards in a right line.

Fort Mercer

County) was a different story, however. "Here," wrote Joseph Plumb Martin, "was fought as brilliant an action as was fought during the Revolutionary War . . . Bunker Hill to the contrary notwithstanding."

*   *   *

Fort Mercer, which was built on the high ground between Big Timber and Woodbury creeks, was not more than five miles above Billingsport. Howe was now determined to make a complete sweep of the American works on the Delaware. On October 7, in a letter to Colonel Christopher Greene, distant kin of Nathanael Greene, Washington stressed the importance to "proceed with all expedition and throw yourself into that place." Washington wrote: "You will find a very good fortification at Red Bank; but if anything should be requisite to render it stronger, or proportion it to the size of your garrison, you will have it done." A French expert had been sent to correct any flaw in the garrison's artillery. A moment's time should not be lost in improving the fort's defensive position. "Any delay," Washington warned, "might give the enemy an opportunity of getting there before you, which could not fail of being most fatal, in its consequences." Washington added that he had written to Brigadier General Silas Newcomb of the New Jersey militia "to give you all the aid in his power." If by now Christopher Greene was not alert to his dangers, Washington added: "The whole defense of the Delaware absolutely depends upon it [defending Fort Mercer]; consequently all the enemy's hope of keeping Philadelphia and finally succeeding in the object of the present campaign."

Actually the Marquis de Chastellux, a fine French engineer, had been sent in the company of Lafayette and others to review the worthiness of the works at Fort Mercer. Chastellux had reported favorably, but had added that dependence should not be placed alone on the steepness of the bastion's sides, and recommended that *chevaux-de-frise*, along with cannon-mounted river galleys, should protect the escarpment. To the Frenchmen the Americans simply were not sufficiently practiced in war to plan such a fortification. The whole post, Chastellux added, required "a good earthen rampart raised to the height of the cordon" with a *fosse,* or ditch, and abatis in front. Somewhat to Chastellux's disconcertment he noticed that "a great portion of the garrison" were "negroes and mullatoes and all were in a ragged, destitute condition."

Colonel Carl von Donop with four regiments of Hessians, or about 2,000 men, crossed the Delaware at Cooper's Ferry on October 21 where he acquired a Negro slave, Old Mitch, to lead him that evening to Haddonfield. Donop was a tall, handsome, impressive man, trained to the finer points of conduct by his experience in the courts of Europe, and he was often remembered for his kindliness. The inhabitants of Haddonfield generally were anxious to have some officer spend the night with them for in this way they were protected from the rank-and-file Hessians who, regarding Americans as "semi-barbarous," were wanton in their destruction of property. Farmers of the region often grew terrorized of these enemy soldiers, and when the Hessians swore in German and the farmers protested in English a genuine international impasse resulted.

The roll of Hessian drums next morning announced the continuance of the march on Fort Mercer. American pickets destroyed the lower bridge over Timber Creek, requiring Donop to make a four-mile detour. Thus the Hessians were delayed and it was near noon before they reached the edge of the woods confronting Fort Mercer. A ridiculous military extravaganza followed when a soldier with a drummer and flag approached the bastion.

"The King of England," he cried, "orders his rebellious subjects to lay down their arms, and they are warned that if they stand the battle no quarters whatever will be given."

The voice of Colonel Christopher Greene sounded from within the fort:

"We ask no quarters, nor will we give any."

With this proper exchange of military amenities, the fighting began.

*   *   *

Christopher Greene, supported by Brigadier General Silas Newcomb of the New Jersey Militia so that the number of his troops may have been 400, braced against Donop's inevitable assault. Although the outworks were unfinished, the interior of the redoubt was far from an inferior work. A Hessian battery opened a sharp play upon the north of Mercer, where the fort was protected by a nearby morass. Donop advanced to the outworks and made his first mistake by deciding that the Americans had been frightened away. The Hessians cheered, prematurely.

Still, the German drums beat a lively rataplan. Donop's troops rushed the fort where not a man could be seen (although a flag flew from the stripped branches of a hickory tree). The Hessians began to scramble up an embankment.

That was the moment when all hell broke loose. At an angle of the old embankment on the Hessian left a half-masked battery opened fire. Grapeshot and musket balls poured down like a sudden autumn hailstorm. It was a terrible barrage and Hessians fell like hay before the sweep of a scythe. Anguished officers trying to rally their men were clearly seen from above by the Americans, and among them the figure of Donop in his colorful uniform was most conspicuous. At the same time another Hessian column attempted to attack from the south in an assualt "more fortunate than the other [for it] passed the abatis, traversed the *fosse* and mounted the berm [a path or ledge] when they suddenly stopped." Later a Frenchman, puzzled as to why the attack had stopped, set off on an investigation. What he found was

about twenty Hessians standing on the berm and stuck up against the shelf of the parapet. These soldiers, who had been bold enough to advance thus far—sensible that there was more risk in returning and not thinking proper to expose themselves—were taken and brought into the fort.

Meanwhile amid "the deplorable spectacle of the dead and dying heaped one upon another" a voice, speaking in English, was heard:

"Whoever you are, draw me hence."

The voice of Donop! American soldiers rushed down to rescue the fallen Hessian leader. A bullet had shattered his hip.

The severe attack was stopped almost immediately. Donop said:
"I am in your hands. You may revenge yourselves."

A Frenchman, who spoke English badly, answered kindly in
his own language which the Hessian understood.

Donop smiled and responded in French: "I am content; I die
in the hands of honor itself." Close to death, Donop was carried
to the same Quaker-owned dwelling in Haddonfield where he had
stayed on his way to Fort Mercer. He was only thirty-seven. "It
is finishing a noble career early," Donop reputedly said, again
in French, "but I die the victim of my ambition and the avarice
of my sovereign."

The Americans counted their losses at eight killed and twenty-
nine wounded, many by the bursting of a cannon within the fort.
One captain, reconnoitering, was captured. The Hessian casualties may have been as high as 1,100.

An elegant sword voted to Christopher Greene by Congress
was never received, for the colonel later was murdered in an
attack by Tories near Croton River in New York's Westchester
County. Many of the Hessians wounded at Red Bank were
placed in an old brick schoolhouse in Woodbury and when they
died they were interred in a field known for generations as the
Strangers' Burying-ground.

*   *   *

For years only the swaying of the green reeds indicated the
presence of Great and Little Mud Islands where the ship channel
of the Delaware sweeps toward the Jersey shore between Billingsport and Gloucester. On the larger of these midriver quag-
mires rose Fort Mifflin, designed by a French engineer, François
Louis de Fleury, a mean fellow who carried a cane with which he
swiped at any inferior who passed nearby. Mifflin, under the command of Lieutenant Colonel Smith, was not a strong redoubt. It
was surrounded by only a wet ditch without abatis and the block-
houses at each of its angles were badly constructed.

Private Martin, passing through Woodbury on his way to
Mifflin, declared:

I endured hardships sufficient to kill half a dozen horses. . . . In the cold
month of November, without provisions, without clothing, not a scrap of
either shoes or stockings to my feet or legs, and in this condition to endure
a siege in such a place as that was appalling in the highest degree.

Martin maintained that he went a fortnight in the mud without
enjoying a wink's sleep. And every time he saw Fleury with his
cane, Martin leaped a ditch and ran for his life.

Howe grew more determined to be rid of these forts along the
Delaware. Opposite Mifflin the British erected five batteries with
six heavy guns and a bomb battery with three long mortars. Up
the river at Hospital Point they placed another battery of six
guns. A floating battery of twenty-two twenty-four pounders was
moved within forty yards of an angle of Mifflin. Meanwhile at
Hog Island, a flotilla was gathered consisting of the sixty-four-
gun *Augusta,* the *Roebuck* and two other frigates, the sloop
Merlin and a galley. Guns also were placed on Province Island
between Mifflin and the Pennsylvania shore.

Heroic fighting followed—the more so, if one accepts the
judgment of Surgeon Albigence Waldo of Connecticut: "Mifflin
was a Burlesque upon the art of Fortification." By land, by water,
the British opened a shattering bombardment on November 10
that continued for six days. Smith, the commander, fought with
about 300 men and must have made them seem a thousand. The
first day the chief of artillery was killed and a barracks partially
burned. Next day the enemy changed the position of fire, knock-
ing down palisades and demolishing a cannon. Smith came within
a tick of losing his life while writing to his old Rhode Island
friend, General Varnum; a ball, passing through the chimney
and scattering bricks in all directions, knocked Smith senseless.
The lieutenant colonel was transported to Fort Mercer and his
command transferred to Connecticut's Lieutenant Colonel Russell, already exhausted by illness, and to Rhode Island's Major
Thayer, who stood by voluntarily to take Russell's place if
necessary.

The six-day encounter was not a one-sided contest by any
means. The sixty-four-gun *Augusta* became impaled on the
chevaux-de-frise planted in the ship's channel. She drifted help-

lessly toward the Jersey shore. Exuberantly the gunners placed a hot shot on her deck. Flames leaped upward. A few moments of awesome silence followed. Then the fire reached the man-of-war's powder magazine. For miles around the ground shook as though an earthquake had struck the countryside. There was an upward shaft of red and orange flame. Parts of the ship could be seen rising skyward, intermingled with the arms, legs and heads of those who had been aboard her. "A volume of thick smoke," Thomas Paine wrote, "rising like a pillar, spreading on top like a tree, was seen ascending to heaven."

The *Merlin* blew up in a similar manner. Windows were broken for miles around.

*   *   *

Martin could say that the grapeshot came down "like a hail" and "ate us up," but Waldo believed that "our people defended themselves with unparallel'd bravery." November 15 was the climactic day. Then, wrote Waldo, Mifflin was attacked "by 4 ships, 4 Batteries, & 1 Gally [sic]" against which "our people" replied from "1 Battery, 12 Gallies & two Shearbacks or small ships." The fighting was "incessant" all day, there was "a continual storm of Balls," and at the height of the fray a "Capt. Stephen Brown [of the Fourth Connecticut Line] was kill'd by a shot from the round-top of a Ship that had hauled up in pistol shot of the Fort."

A British deserter, who had suffered "much," falsely awakened American hopes. But on that fatal November 15, an East India-man of twenty twenty-four pounders acted in concert with the guns on Province Island. Mifflin could no longer stand such abuse which continued "far into the gloom of night"; soon the only two dismounted cannon in the fort "shared the fate of the others"; and "every man who appeared on the platform was killed by the musketeers in the tops of the ships, whose yards almost hung over the American battery." All palisades were swept away; all embrasures were ruined; the whole parapet was leveled; all block houses were destroyed. Captain Thayer of the Rhode Island Line sent all but forty of his men from Mifflin to Mercer; then a cannon ball added a wounded hip to Thayer's shattered wrist; by midnight the destruction of "every defence and every shelter" at Mifflin, along with 250 men of the garrison killed or wounded, ended the defense of the forts on the Delaware. "The loss of the British was great; the number was not certainly known."

In retreat, Surgeon Waldo, who was not impressed by "the wiffing wind of fortune," cited the case of a hermit in Mount Holly who had lived for twenty-seven years in a hole in the ground. The old man, who expected to survive here until he was eighty, had gathered around him many books but would not light a fire even in the coldest weather. He spoke English poorly, but conversed fluently in German or Latin. Local legend proclaimed that the hermit was doing penance because years ago he had murdered his sister.

Washington at White Marsh was like the old hermit in his hole at Mount Holly; the Commander-in-Chief was similarly isolated in any desire to send reenforcements to his embattled forts along the Delaware. He could celebrate the victory at Saratoga with a thirteen-gun salute but at the time neither Washington nor Howe could tell how, in so many ways, Burgoyne's defeat had changed their careers.

CHAPTER TWO

Conspiracy

Winter, 1777–1778

At least the campaign of 1777 was tailing off. There were still numerous skirmishes, quick and annoying, but no more effective than a dog's fleabites. Washington's generals could not agree on a suitable site for a winter encampment; the Commander-in-Chief took upon his shoulders one more responsibility. A bridge of thirty-six wagons connected by rails provided a way of crossing the Schuylkill and led the Americans with their ragged tents to a place called "the Gulph" on Gulf Creek, about three miles beyond the river.

In the cold, with snow falling, Surgeon Waldo tried to cheer himself with the maxim, "Pain succeeds Pleasure, & Pleasure succeeds Pain," and ended by begrudging every weary step he trudged. There was, of course, some skirmishing—there was always some skirmishing in which the Americans fought at a disadvantage through a lack of certain essentials—for Waldo contended that "were Soldiers to have plenty of Food & Rum, I believe they would Storm Tophet." Insofar as this place outside Jerusalem had become synonymous with hell, the comparison fitted Waldo's present disposition toward the Gulph. The surgeon was fatigued and ill, itching when he was not vomiting; the smoke from the campfires made his eyes smart; he resented the lack of whiskey, and wondered what impulse of idiocy had led him to this wretched hole when he could have been in Connecticut enjoying the comforts of home and family.

Prisoners and deserters were constantly appearing. To the surgeon, newcomers of whatever variety, despite their fatigue, displayed an unexpected "spirit of Alacrity & Contentment from so young Troops." Waldo groused over "poor food, hard lodging, cold weather, nasty cloaths [sic], nasty cookery," and then intermingled with his complaints a sudden, subdued philosophy:

There comes a bowl of beef soup—full of burnt leaves and dirt, sickish enough to make a Hector spue—away with it Boys—I'll live like the Chameleon upon Air. Poh! Poh! crys Patience within me—you talk like a fool. Your being sick Covers your mind with a Melanchollic [sic] Gloom, which makes every thing about you appear gloomy. See the poor Soldier, when in health—with what cheerfulness he meets his foes and encounters every hardship—if barefoot, he labours thro' the Mud & Cold with a Song in his mouth extolling War & Washington—if his food be bad, he eats it notwithstanding with seeming content—blesses God for a good Stomach and Whistles it into digestion. . . .

Waldo foresaw his own sad ending: ". . . I shall soon be no more! and all the reward I shall get will be—'Poor Will is dead.'"

* * *

A week before Christmas Washington led his army a few miles northwest of the Gulph to Valley Forge, an area the British had stripped of food and supplies in September. Close by was an eminence delusively named Mount Joy. But Surgeon Waldo was delighted on his arrival at Valley Forge—a roasted pig was served—and bleak though the prospects were otherwise, Waldo commented on how much worse they could have been elsewhere:

Our brethren who are unfortunately Prisoners in Philadelphia meet with the most savage and inhumane treatments that Barbarians are Capable of inflicting. Our Enemies do not knock them in the head or burn them with torches to death, or flee them alive, or gradually dismember them till they die, which is customary among Savages & Barbarians. No, they are worse by far. They suffer them to starve, to linger out their lives in extreem [sic] hunger. One of these poor unhappy men, drove to the last extreem by the rage of hunger, eat his own fingers up to the first joint from the hand, before he died. Others eat the Clay, the Lime, the Stones of the Prison Walls. Several who died in the Yard had pieces of Bark, Wood, Clay & Stones in their mouths, which the ravings of hunger had caused them to take in for food in the last Agonies of Life! "These are thy *mercies*, O Britain!"

Not that Valley Forge resembled paradise! Morning and night the soldiers subsisted on the same menu of firecake and water. "No meat! No meat!" they shouted and the surrounding hills echoed back: "No meat! No meat!" As a result of the mixture of cold and smoke from the campfires, Waldo declared, "my eyes are started out from their Orbits like a Rabbit's eyes."

On December 22 the surgeon admitted:

I am ashamed to say it, but I am tempted to steal Fowls if I could find them, or even a whole Hog, for I feel as if I could eat one. . . . Ye who Eat Pumpkin Pie and Roast Turkies [sic], and yet Curse fortune for using you ill, Curse her no more, least she reduce your Allowance of her favours to a bit of Fire Cake, & a draught of Cold Water, & in Cold Weather too.

Waldo had a strange reason for thankfulness on Christmas: "We avoid Piddling Pills, Powders, Bolus's Linctus's Cordials and all such insignificant matters whose powers are Only render'd important by causing the Patient to vomit up his money instead of his disease."

It was not alone the cold, the ice and snow, and the slowness of building huts to replace tattered tents that brought misery to Valley Forge. By now inflation had reduced paper currency, whether issued by Congress or the states, to near worthlessness. A counterfeit thirty-dollar bill could be distinguished from the original by the fact that Congress had spelled the name "Philadelpkia" whereas on the bogus bill it was spelled correctly. Businessmen would deal with American officers and soldiers only on a basis of "hard money," which, of course, they did not possess. So the merchants, knowing that British pounds were as solid as Gibraltar, carried their trade to Howe in Philadelphia.

Soldier talk at Valley Forge followed predictable patterns. Wrote Private Joseph Plumb Martin:

We stayed at the quartermaster general's quarters [Thomas Mifflin's] till sometime in the afternoon, during which time a beef creature was butchered for us. I well remember what fine stuff it was, it was quite transparent. I thought at that time what an excellent lantern it would make. I was, notwithstanding, very glad to get some of it, bad as it looked. . . .

And Martin recalled an incident on foraging patrol:

There was a little Negro boy belonging to the house, about five or six years of age, who, the whole time I was there, sat upon a stool in the chimney corner; indeed, he looked as if he had sat there ever since he was born. One of the wagon masters said to the landlady one day, "Mother, is that your son that sits in the corner?" "My son!" said she. "Why, don't you see he is a Negro?" "A Negro! Is he?" said the man. "Why I really thought he was your son, only that he had sat there till he was smoke-dried."

On the last day of 1777 Waldo was granted a furlough while learning how to darn stockings and greeted the new year with poetic grace:

MARTIAL GLORY

The hint taken from the following line of Pope:
"Gun, Drum, Trumpet, Blunderbuss & Thunder."

Soldiers! would you acquire a lasting fame;
Would you be pleased with a Hero's name;
Have you a wish, to be a Martial Wonder;
Rush furious on your foes, & fearless blunder,
Thro' Gun, Drum, Trumpet, Blunderbuss and Thunder.

*   *   *

Lord Stirling, always conscience-ridden when loyalty and duty were involved, warned Washington that a group of officers, making capital of the misfortunes at Brandywine and Germantown, were organizing a conspiracy against him. At the base of this cabal, Lord Stirling said bluntly, was Thomas Conway, a man of many confounding peculiarities. Although born in Ireland, Conway had been taken to France at the age of six. Here, in his midteens, he had served in the army and reached the rank of colonel after the German campaigns of 1760–61.

Apparently Silas Deane was attracted by Conway's boasting of his skill in military discipline, especially with infantry. In April, 1777, Congress named Conway a brigadier general, and, on first meeting the Irishman at Morristown, Washington had liked him as "a man of candor," but after watching Conway in action at Brandywine and Germantown the General-in-Chief had found Conway more of a braggart than a military genius. Friction between the two started when Washington declined to raise him to major general. In matters of military administration, Washington would not pussyfoot. Twenty-three brigadiers stood ahead of the Irishman in line for promotion.

Huffily, Conway submitted his resignation to Congress, who refused to receive it and instead raised him to major general. John Adams rather liked having Washington cut down to size, writing his wife: "Now we can allow a certain citizen to be wise, virtuous and good, without thinking him a deity or a savior." Those who criticized Washington for remaining on the west bank of the Schuylkill instead of crossing and seizing Derby drew a sharp rejoinder from Dr. Waldo: "He knows better than to leave his post and be catched [sic] like a damned fool cooped up in a city."

That the controversy started by Conway was filtering down into the ranks signified its intensity. Like Waldo, most of the soldiers idolized Washington; he was not so high and mighty that he would not participate in their games and actually was very good at cricket.

Like a faithful husband, Washington was the last to know the full extent of his betrayal. In some respects, the pettiness of the cabal was ridiculous. A few historians have difficulty in believing that such an intrigue ever existed. But unrest among the generals was widespread. For example, Thomas Mifflin was inordinately jealous of the respect Nathanael Greene or Henry Knox enjoyed within Washington's official family. The "full tide of cynicism" that beleaguered Washington after the somewhat fabled account of Gates's success at Saratoga is difficult to believe. In the vernacular of the Pennsylvania Dutch, the Commander-in-Chief's critics went after him "dail foremost."

Thus the Attorney General of Pennsylvania could exclaim, "Thousands of lives and millions of property are yearly sacrificed to the insufficiency of our Commander-in-Chief."

Thus James Lovell, a member of Congress and one of Washington's bitterest enemies, could set Horatio Gates's near-sighted eyes to blinking: "This army will be totally lost unless you come down and collect the virtuous band who wish to fight under your banner. . . ."

Thus James Wilkinson [Lord Stirling's original source of information] could quote from a letter by Conway to Gates: "Heaven has determined to save your country; or a weak General and bad counsellors would have ruined it."

Thus an overexcited Surgeon General Benjamin Rush pleaded with John Adams: "For God's sake, do no suffer him [Thomas Mifflin] to resign!"

Thus Washington wrote Richard Henry Lee: ". . . as an officer [Conway] and his importance in this army exist more in his own imagination than in reality. . . ."

*   *   *

Up to a point Washington enjoyed a good intramural fight. He always began where such contests should, with the original culprit, and not mincing words he wrote Conway of the statement attributed to him in a letter to Gates.

Conway denied the charge, adding: ". . . you are a brave man, an honest man, a patriot, and a man of good sense. . . . I believe I can assert that the expression, *weak general,* has not slipped from my pen." Washington did not answer the letter. Congress endeavored to wriggle out of its hasty action by stipulating that Conway's promotion had been made "on the staff" and not "in the line." Twice Conway visited the Commander-in-Chief at Valley Forge. Washington received him icily. When Conway complained to Congress, Washington replied that if the Irishman meant "that I did not receive him in the language of a warm and cordial friend, I readily confess the charge."

Horatio Gates grew all a-flutter. Washington must help him catch the "wretch" who had "stealingly copied" from his letters. Gates, who did not deny the statement attributed to Conway, gave signs of hysteria. Somewhat to Washington's surprise, since he believed there had been only one letter, Gates sent copies of *all* his letters with Conway to Congress. The Commander-in-Chief said frankly that the first news of the Conway cabal had come from Lord Stirling, whom he believed to be a stranger to Gates. Washington branded Conway as "a dangerous incendiary."

Now Surgeon General Benjamin Rush, laying such facts as he chose before the governor of Virginia, declared that the army needed the leadership of a "Gates, a [Charles] Lee, or a Conway." He asked that once read, his letter be thrown into the fire. Instead, Patrick Henry sent the letter to Washington.

An effort was made to draw even Lafayette into this conspiracy when, without consulting Washington, Congress offered the Frenchman an independent command in Canada if he would accept Conway as his second in command. Lafayette refused to be part of such an intrigue. Other foreign officers found Conway's conduct "criminal and unpardonable" as it affected Washington.

While still holding together a half-starved, half-frozen army at Valley Forge, the Commander-in-Chief told his old friend Henry Laurens, "My enemies take an ungenerous advantage of me. . . . They know I cannot combat their insinuations, however injurious, without disclosing secrets it is of the utmost moment to conceal." In the belief that "next to being strong, it is best to be thought so by the enemy," Washington held his ground. "Why should I expect to be exempt from censure?" he asked Laurens. But his heart told him he was right. He would offer no other excuse. (Ultimately on the second anniversary of the Declaration of Independence Conway, finally rejected by Congress, fought a duel with loyal old General Cadwalader, and Conway, believing that he verged on death, begged pardon for his "wrong-doing.") Before then, however, Washington's fate—and that of his Continental Army—had been altered by the appearance at Valley Forge of another foreigner who could not speak a word of English.

* * *

His name was Friedrich Wilhelm Ludolf Gerhard Augustin, Baron von Steuben, although he sometimes called himself Friedrich Wilhelm August Heinrich Ferdinand, and in America gave Frederick William Augustus von (or de) Steuben as his name. He arrived in the midst of the conspiracy against Washington, highly recommended by Benjamin Franklin and Silas Deane. Steuben was then a balding man with a big nose and a seventeen-year-old secretary, Pierre Duponceau, who was his translator. A large Italian greyhound trotted at the baron's heels and a dazzling, bejeweled Star of the Order of Fidelity of Baden glittered on his blue uniform. Historians would murmur that most of what he claimed was not true, but they did so softly, for none could deny that before he had finished at Valley Forge he had given Washington one of the finest armies in the world.

Steuben was not, as he had told Franklin, a lieutenant general who had served the King of Prussia for twenty-two years; he was a captain without a job or a cent to his name. His title of baron came from a principality so sunk in poverty that its leader dismissed his court and traveled incognito to avoid financial embarrassment. Yet Steuben, well-schooled and well-read, as the son of an accomplished Prussian officer, had been trained in a system that was second to none in its military excellence. His experience in war had begun at the age of seventeen; he was now in his late forties.

Using the commercial concern of Hortalez & Company as a decoy, Beaumarchis, a French dramatist, was giving secret financial aid to America. It was from this corporation (in which Benjamin Franklin and Silas Deane also were involved) that the penniless baron received his passage money on the understanding that once he reached the colonies he was on his own. Steuben shrugged. How could he be any worse off?

The baron's chances of success were not hurt by Franklin and Deane writing that Steuben had been "recommended to us by two of the best judges of military merit" in France. Steuben's note to Washington stated that he was eager "to deserve the title of a citizen of America by fighting for the cause of your liberty" as a volunteer. Washington, enmeshed in the Conway conspiracy, told Congress it must be the judge of what should be done with this latest foreign import. Henry Laurens, president of Congress, found Steuben "a man of military knowledge and acquainted with the world." Congress named him Inspector General. Within four days at Valley Forge the Commander-in-Chief and the baron were close friends.

Steuben's strict military Prussianism left him scandalized at the behavior of Washington's ragtag soldiers. Nobody did anything right, which, interpreted in terms of the baron's upbringing, meant that everyone did as he pleased. If any state possessed a code of military conduct, it was not shared by any other state. By the most cumbersome system of composition imaginable— from vernacular German translated into literary German, from vernacular French translated into literary French and finally from vernacular English translated into literary English—Steuben organized the creation of *Regulations for the Order and Discipline of Troops of the United States* (for generations, popularly known as the "blue book," the manual of American drill and field service regulations).

Steuben wrote his lessons one at a time. He picked one hundred troops for his first students. What drove Steuben half crazy was that in Prussia when you told a soldier, " 'Do this,' . . . he doeth it." In America a drillmaster had to explain: "This is the reason why you ought to do that." If the American agreed, he responded.

From six in the morning to six at night Steuben's booming voice dominated the parade ground at Valley Forge. A few profanities in French and German were thrown in when his patience was exhausted; and when these words were unavailing he appealed to Captain Benjamin Walker of New York: "My dear Walker, come and swear for me in English." He reduced standard military drill to these commands:

1. Poise Firelock. 2. Shoulder Firelock. 3. Present Arms. 4. Fix Bayonet. 5. Unfix bayonet. 6. Load Firelock. 7. Make Ready. 8. Present. 9. Fire. 10. Order Firelock.

By the end of March Steuben had the whole army drilling in unison, and battalion by battalion they were at least equal, if not superior to any force the British could put in the field. Half-frozen, half-starved soldiers forgot other miseries in their expanding pride. In Revolutionary times a *salamander*—really a hot toddy—took its name from the iron stick with which the concoction was mixed. Many were raised in Steuben's honor.

CHAPTER THREE

The Chase Starts

Spring, 1778

Under the occupation of Howe, life in Philadelphia passed gaily. Loyalist families were invited to the festivities as the British "killed dull hours at the dance, the faro-table, and the theatre." Any thought of a serious assault on Valley Forge was laughed off. Pleasure, not George III, ruled. The minuet and the Virginia reel enlivened weekends at the City Tavern; crowds gathered at the cockpit in Moore's Alley; gambling parties disrupted the quiet of night at the Bunch of Grapes and the Indian Queen; the London Coffee House glowed with lights for the more conversationally minded; and the Old South Theatre featured such productions as *The Mock Doctor* and *The Deuce is in Him*.

Across the Atlantic, in London, a grimmer mood existed during these weeks. Burgoyne's defeat at Saratoga had given France an opportunity for recognizing the independence of the American colonies and, inevitably, financial, military, and naval support must follow. Neither George III nor Lord Germain would accept the responsibility for enlarging the war, so Howe had to become the scapegoat and the papers were prepared for Sir Henry Clinton to succeed him. The court party was so thoroughly shaken that Commissioners of Peace were secretly dispatched to America, reaching Philadelphia on June 6. The distinguished group included Frederick Howard, Earl of Carlisle; George Johnstone, former governor of West Florida; Sir William Eden, later Lord Auckland and Under-Secretary of State; Lord Howe and Sir Henry Clinton; and Doctor Adam Ferguson, Professor of Moral Philosophy at the University of Edinburgh.

Washington refused to allow Dr. Ferguson to carry a letter and the bills of petition to Congress. First Congress must read the communications and decide whether they wished to receive the Commissioners, Washington declared. So the documents, craftily sealed with "the image of a mother caressing her children," were dispatched to Congress; but the Commander-in-Chief, a crafty politician in his own right, had forced the Commissioners to recognize the legal existence of Congress.

The documents (George III later claimed they were written without his authority) were an astonishing assortment of petitions. They guaranteed Congress every freedom it sought, including representation in Parliament, and stopped only at acknowledging the independence of the colonies. But then the Commissioners stumbled; at a slightly slurring remark about the King of France the perusal of the documents stopped; and the members ultimately resolved: "That Congress will not in any degree negotiate with the present commissioners in America for restoring peace."

Congress' resolution was widely approved. Said patriot Governor George Clinton of New York: "[Prime Minister] Lord North is two years late with his political maneuvers." Said Governor Trumball of Connecticut: "There was a day when even this step might have been accepted with joy and gratitude, but that day, sir, is passed irrevocably." Said Robert Morris, the financial genius of Philadelphia, "No offers ought to have a hearing for one moment unless preceded by an acknowledgement of independence."

But Benjamin Franklin made the shrewdest comment. When told that the war might last ten years, the Philadelphia sage smiled, bowed, and replied that it would be better for the colonies to fight fifty years than to abandon independence.

When the Commissioners of Peace left America, they issued

a statement berating those disloyal to the King. Governor Livingston gave his copy of the proclamation to his son with which to make a kite.

*   *   *

The warmth of spring stole up the Schuylkill to Valley Forge. Food and new clothes arrived, recruits traveled overland, and the pride felt in learning drill formations under Steuben aroused the spirits of the men. Many wives of officers now were in camp: Martha Washington, Mrs. Nathanael Greene, Lady Stirling. And there was the hilarity of the day of a mock battle when Steuben's near-sighted secretary, Pierre Duponceau, seeing red petticoats hung on a fence to dry, mistook them for the British and alarmed the encampment to a false attack!

Washington, pressing his Commissary of Prisoners, Elias Boudinot, to arrange the exchange of General Charles Lee for General Richard Prescott, could not know that within a few days of his release (March 29) Lee had given the Crown remarkable details on how to conquer America:

"If the Province of Maryland or the greater part of it is reduc'd or submits, and the People of Virginia are prevented or intimidated from marching aid to the Pennsylvania Army the whole machine is dissolv'd and a period put to the War." He advised sending men to Alexandria and Annapolis, and joining these forces with others "to take Baltimore or post themselves on some Westward bank of the Susquehanna. . . ." Such was the Lee whom Boudinot led into Valley Forge on Sunday, April 5. Washington sent a party of horse under his aide, Lieutenant Richard K. Meade, to meet the general. For two miles officers lined the sides of the road to honor Lee, whom Washington greeted "as if he had been a brother." That night Lee spent with the Washingtons and when he overslept next morning breakfast was delayed. Boudinot was disgusted:

When he came out, he looked dirty, as if he had been in the street all night. Soon after I discovered that he had brought a miserable dirty hussy with him from Philadelphia (a British sergeant's wife) and had actually taken her into his room by a back door, and she had slept with him that night.

In swearing renewed allegiance at Valley Forge, Lee suddenly withdrew his hand from the Bible, saying "as to King George I am ready to absolve myself from all allegiance to him, but I have some scruples about the Prince of Wales." And when Washington's informants within Philadelphia verified the gossip that Clinton had replaced Howe in command, a strange compulsion led Lee to write:

General Lee presents his most sincere and humble respects to Sir Henry Clinton. He wishes him all possible happiness and health and begs, whatever may be the event of the present unfortunate contest, he will believe General Lee to be his most respectful and obliged humble servant.

Steuben would have wished Clinton a sharp bayonet between his shoulder blades.

*   *   *

On May 8 a committee from Congress came to Valley Forge for a council of war and conceded that the storming of Philadelphia would be unwise. Ten days later Washington wrote Lafayette that there no longer could be any doubt of Clinton's intention to evacuate Philadelphia. But whither then? An excursion into Pennsylvania to disperse the Continental Congress at York? A move to the south or to the north up the Hudson River? Gates feared for the desolation of New England.

Clinton had his problems, especially from officers who believed that any retrogressive movement would be an indignity. But Sir Henry's orders were explicit: he was to reoccupy New York City. A lack of transport tonnage, Admiral Howe said, prevented an evacuation by water unless Clinton was willing to march his entire army forty miles to an embarkation at New Castle, Delaware. The proposition was ridiculous, considering the baggage and the fear-stricken Loyalist sympathizers Sir Henry must carry with him, Loyalists "too obnoxious to the rebel rulers to expect the smallest chance of even personal safety should they be left behind." Also there was the cavalry to be saved. Sir Henry could wish that Washington would fight him in an open field, but Sir Henry was not a fool who expected to gain this chance.

Actually, for the first time in the war Washington held a numerical superiority over the enemy. Considering all forces, including militia and recent reinforcements of the line, Washington commanded 16,000 effectives. Among his generals only Lee objected to meeting the British on a foot-to-foot, horse-to-horse, cannon-to-cannon basis.

British baggage wagons (there would be 1,500 drawn by 5,000 horses and stretching for twelve miles) began crossing the Delaware on June 8. Rebellious battalions from Anspach and Bayreuth and Britons too sick to march were transported by vessels to New York. All wagons and light artillery had crossed the Delaware by June 12; all horses by the 15th, along with Hessians still expressing deep "discontent." The Peace Commissioners left June 18.

The *New Jersey Gazette* of May 27 carried an extremely knowledgeable comment: "The Militia of this State are desired to be particularly attentive to signals, as a movement of the enemy is soon expected." Attentive they were, knowing that Clinton had sent two brigades of Hessians to Haddonfield at a crossing of the Delaware on June 17. Provisions for six weeks· had been issued to Clinton's army, proof that Sir Henry did not know what to expect. Half his force had to be used to protect his baggage. The British moved across New Jersey in two columns —one under General Alexander Leslie along the road to Bordentown and another under Clinton and Cornwallis on a parallel road from Allentown.

The forces that followed Sir Henry and his Lordship included England's finest: the Grenadiers, the Coldstream Guards, the Black Watch, the Hessian Jaegers, the Sixteenth and Seventeenth regiments of horse, the Queen's Rangers as well as several brigades of light infantry. The last Briton to leave Philadelphia was Cosmo Gordon. He was still sleeping off the previous night's drunk.

The scars of British occupation were everywhere visible in Philadelphia when the American Light Horse under Benedict Arnold rode into the abandoned city on June 18. General Knox and his wife could not bear the stench of the place. Houses had been torn down to permit the construction of redoubts and fields laid waste. The British and Hessians, wailed residents who remained, had "introduced new fashions and made old vices more common." Homes used for stables had holes cut in the floor so that the filth could be swept away.

But Clinton put the thoughts of such scenes behind him as he started a flight across New Jersey.

*   *   *

The Jersey Blues under William Maxwell needled the retreating British whenever possible. Bridges were knocked down. Felled trees littered the roads. Wells were filled with rock and sand. With the American advance marched Joseph Plumb Martin, who remembered reaching Princeton:

Some of the patriotic inhabitants of the town had brought out to the end of the street we passed through some casks of ready-made toddy. It was dealt out to the men as they passed by, which caused the detachment to move slowly at this place. The young ladies of the town, and perhaps of the vicinity, had collected and were sitting in the stoops and at the windows to see the noble exhibition of a thousand half-starved and three-quarters naked soldiers pass in review before them. . . . They were *all* beautiful. New Jersey and Pennsylvania ladies are, in my opinion, collectively handsome, the most so of any in the United States. . . .

Originally Clinton had expected to reach Staten Island via the Raritan, but the pressure of the Americans, the delay in clearing roads, and numerous skirmishes with the cavalry, forced him to change his course to a route toward Monmouth Court House (Freehold) and the Navesink to Sandy Hook. The weather, a mixture of steamy rain and temperatures in the 90's, added to Sir Henry's abominations. Heavily clothed British and Hessians fell exhausted by the roadside. Often mosquito bites so bloated the faces of the prostrated soldiers that they became unrecognizable.

Washington's pursuit with the main army began when he crossed at Coryell's Ferry to Lambertville. Riflemen under Dan Morgan and horsemen under that jovial Irishman, Colonel

Stephen Moylan, were sent to harass the enemy. They must have raised some deviltry for Clinton was reported to have been found drunk in the home of Mrs. Bunting at Crosswicks—half-dressed Britishers rushed about in confusion and Sir Henry was sobered up by a plunge in the creek. Washington's light-clad troops, unhindered by torn-up bridges, could move faster on a route that paralleled Clinton's, but it was not Washington's intention to match the British in a dress parade across New Jersey. Another American council of war was held at Hopewell, near Princeton.

This meeting, in Alexander Hamilton's estimation, might have done credit to a "society of midwives," but he acknowledged its military significance. Lee opposed any direct assault on Clinton's troops, although he conceded that pressure on the enemy's flanks might well be increased; he believed that no military risk should be taken that might upset the diplomatic advantages that could be gained from France's recognition of American independence; and he argued that the only logical course for the main army was to march straight for the Hudson River. Lee's prestige gave great strength to his opinions, especially among the younger officers. But there was a group of generals, including Greene and Wayne, who agreed with Lafayette that it "would be disgraceful and humiliating to allow the enemy to cross the Jerseys in tranquillity."

Washington held the same opinion. "People expect something from us," Greene said. Brandywine and Germantown still rankled Washington; he would enjoy giving the British suitable retribution for those discomfitures. The Commander-in-Chief planned an advance corps that added 1,500 men under Brigadier General Charles Scott to the 1,000 under Maxwell and 600 under Morgan. Later 1,000 of Wayne's Pennsylvanians joined the force.

Lee refused the command, not yet aware that Wayne was to support the advance; Lord Stirling, likewise unaware of Wayne's assignment, declined on the ground that he belonged with the main army. Busy with the duties of a quartermaster general, Greene could not be spared. So Washington turned to Lafayette, not yet twenty-one; the responsibility was awesome for one so

.young but the Frenchman accepted eagerly. Hamilton, told to assist the Marquis, met Lafayette near Robin's Tavern, some eight miles from Allentown. Part of the British army, Hamilton reported, were on their way to Freehold.

*   *   *

Not since the Reverend William Tennent went to heaven and returned had Monmouth County known such excitement. The Reverend William lies buried under the center aisle of the church that traces its history to a royal charter granted by George II in 1750 and still stands on the battlefield. Opinions, then and now, differed concerning the Reverend William who at least had the sound sense to pass on before war swept over his beloved fields and orchards. Some said he was the child of the angels and some that he was the tool of the devil, while others maintained that no matter which way one looked at it, the Reverend William still remained the biggest liar in the county.

The facts of his story were easily stated. Apparently in the midst of a word during a conversation in Latin with his brother concerning the nature of the soul, the Reverend William "fainted and died away." Laid out on a board, as became a corpse in those times, the Reverend William awaited burial in a properly dug grave. But a doctor friend, who claimed he could feel a "warmth" under the Reverend William's armpits and around his heart would not allow the burial to continue (to the disgust of the parson, who doubtless had composed an extremely laudatory graveside eulogy). Three days later the parson returned and the Reverend William, again on his burial board, looked deader than dead. The doctor friend begged for one more hour of patience, which might have been denied except that the Reverend William —for all that his eyes were closed, his lips discolored and his body cold and stiff—chose this moment to sit bolt upright on his board and emit a mournful groan. The parson fled.

Several weeks passed before the Reverend William, a wraith-like figure, could totter about. He possessed no memory of the past or present and had to be taught anew how to read and write. Then one day, slapping a hand to his forehead, an awareness of his lifetime experiences returned. Reverend William was extremely reluctant to discuss the period of his trancelike paralysis when, he confessed, he had ascended to heaven. Vaguely he described being "wafted along" under the direction "of a superior Being"; he "felt joy unutterable and full of glory"; songs and hallelujahs surrounded him; they were, he said, "ravishing sounds." The closest the Reverend William ever came to revealing what heaven had taught him was the declaration, in a sermon, that the Bible was "not of Divine authority, but the invention of man."

To this countryside British and American armies now advanced to create their own combination of folklore and history. Afterward tales would be told about them that almost equal the legend of the Reverend William.

Old Tennent Church marked the end of the battlefield whence the Americans approached. The British gathered around and immediately above Monmouth Court House or Freehold. Only two of the original buildings, the Court House (which was then a wooden structure) and the old English church on Throckmorton Street (which the British used as a hospital) still survive. There were perhaps as many as forty houses in the township. In addition, Freehold contained a blacksmith shop, a wheelwright's shop, two taverns, two schoolhouses and three stores.

No one today can recognize the Revolutionary battlefield that lay between Old Tennent and Freehold, for many changes have come to this region, one of the finest farming lands in New Jersey. In 1778 this section was dominated by three ravines, each of which played a particular part in the ensuing battle. Dense woods, thick briars and underbrush covered much of the region. The farm land that intervened promised a rich harvest.

The British troops that clustered about four miles from Monmouth Court House covered almost twelve miles of roadway. They approached in this order: foot, horse and artillery, provision train, baggage, army wagons, numerous private carriages, a large number of bathorses (that is, horses carrying belongings of officers or a baggage train), bakeries, laundries and blacksmith shops on wheels, large hospital supplies, boats, bridges, magazines, female camp followers and "every kind of useless stuff." At that time—a fact Clinton did not recognize—the road to the Raritan was still open. Sir Henry moved his headquarters, about two miles at a jump, along the Smithburg Road from the Rising Sun Tavern (about six miles south of Freehold) to the home of Thomas Tomson and then to the home of William Covenhoven on the western edge of the village.

*   *   *

The heat remained at oppressive heights and was mixed with brutal thunderstorms, which held Clinton in check when by a march of sixteen miles he could have made a complete escape to the high grounds of Middletown.

Meanwhile, Charles Lee was having second thoughts now that he realized the imposing size of the American advance corps. Under the circumstances he believed that Lafayette should step aside and allow Lee to take a command which, by rank, was properly his.

Graciously Lafayette consented.

CHAPTER FOUR

The Enigma of Charles Lee

June, 1778

Hero or traitor?

In determining the truth of what happened at Monmouth much depends on whether one sees the engagement as General Charles Lee believed he fought it or accepts the evidence others gave at his court-martial.

On Saturday, June 27, Lee encamped at Englishtown, not far from Old Tennent and about five miles from Monmouth Court House. Washington, marching along the Cranbury road since sunrise, was about the same distance from Englishtown and had established his headquarters at Penelopen (Manalapan). Here he summoned Lee to a conference. The Commander-in-Chief ordered two days' rations prepared. The password for the coming battle would be "Lookout" and the countersign "Sharp and keen." After Brandywine and Germantown, Washington admitted, he must handle the enemy roughly or he would "sink his military reputation into obscurity and drop out of public sight." Lee was told that he would strike the enemy first, even though Maxwell, through his seniority, should have the honor of opening the engagement. But half of Maxwell's New Jersey troops were unseasoned in battle; and Washington believed "a very happy impression" would result if the attack was begun "by a picked corps."

Washington called Lee to a second meeting at five o'clock that afternoon. Lee's forces, he stressed, should be ready at all times to anticipate an assault, even at night. There must be no disputes regarding rank. Lee returned to Englishtown, briefed his brigadiers in the substance of his discussions with Washington, then relaxed in a chair with his favorite dog at his feet. Despite previous communications with the British, Lee gave no evidence that in any way he nurtured a scheme of treachery.

*   *   *

In the miserable heat of the morning Private Joseph Plumb Martin was marched around as if no one knew where he was going but he finally reached Englishtown. A report that somehow the enemy had gained a position in the American rear produced more marching until the rumor was squelched. Booths were built with poles and blankets as protection against a scorching sun. Martin was told to leave his baggage with a guard, for a battle could start at any moment.

*   *   *

Resting beside her sleeping husband, Mary Hays wondered if she had done the right thing in following him to Englishtown. She was only twenty-four, and no great thinker, for her heart always ruled her head. But night thoughts were clearer, if often more frightening, and to forget the scratchy, sandy ground— one could almost believe that the Atlantic Ocean once had come this far inland—Mary allowed her mind to wander.

The journey had given the young wife a chance to visit her German parents on the Trenton farm where as Mary Ludwig she had been born on October 13, 1754. Growing up, she had worked hard and cheerfully at chores both in the fields and in the house, not experiencing even a rudimentary schooling, and life on the farm became grim and skimpy. So, nearing the age of fifteen, Mary Ludwig struck out on her own, becoming a maid to an Irish physician, Dr. William Irvine of Carlisle, Pennsylvania.

John Caspar Hays kept the barbershop in Carlisle. A local
biographer thoroughly relished the romance that developed:

When the patter of her fairy feet was heard on the Irvine steps, or the
swish of her broom on the sidewalk, it was not long before John Caspar
Hays found himself gazing out the window of his little shop. And Mary, it
seems, found a good deal of work necessary outside the house. Both being
frank and sincere, they found their devotion mutual, and Mary seems to
have been a bride-elect at about sweet sixteen [fifteen].

Their marriage license was dated July 24, 1769.

Probably nowhere in the colonies had there been deeper feelings of patriotism than in Cumberland County where Carlisle
was located. Dr. Irvine joined the militia and rose to the rank
of brigadier general. Mary stayed in Carlisle while John fought
one term and reenlisted with Washington as a cannoneer. Then
when the army moved from Valley Forge, John had asked his
wife to join him.

Mary had far too much spunk to fear attack from either wild
animals or army deserters during the long, difficult journey over
lonely, winding mountainous roads to join John. A happy re-
union with her family in Trenton broke the tedium of the trip
before she found her husband, serving with Proctor's Pennsylvania Artillery. Mary leaned her back against a tree, disappointed that even nightfall had not greatly cooled the weather.
Gradually her eyes closed and, to her surprise, when they reopened the dawn had crept above the horizon.

*   *   *

June 28 was one of the worst days citizens of Monmouth
County could remember. Some said the temperature reached 110
and residents dropped dead within their homes. At least fifty
soldiers died of thirst and many fought with swollen tongues.
Martin had slept through the night in the furrow of a ploughed
field and commented on the weather next morning:

The first cleared land we came to [once the march began] was an Indian
cornfield, surrounded on the east, west and north sides by thick tall trees.
The sun shining full upon the field, the soil of which was sandy, the mouth

of a heated oven seemed to me to be but a trifle hotter than this ploughed field; it was almost impossible to breathe.

General Lee could not ask for a finer spirit than existed among his troops that Sabbath morning. Martin testified:

The men did not need much haranguing to raise their courage, for when the officers came to order the sick and lame to stay behind as guards, they were forced to exercise their authority to the full extent before they could make even the invalids stay behind, and when some of their arms were about to be exchanged with those who were going into the field, they would not part with them. "If their arms went," they said, "*they* would go with them at all events."

The New Jersey militia under Brigadier General David Forman led the assault and Virginia's Colonel William Grayson, with two brigades, caught up with them at Old Tennent church around six that Sabbath morning. Many of the militia had advanced about a mile to the bridge of Spotswood Brook where the road began to rise. A message from General Dickinson was sped to Washington and Lee, saying the enemy had left Freehold and were on the march to Middletown. The Continental generals acted in unison, telling the troops to drop their packs by the roadside and charge on Freehold at full speed.

The air was so still that not a leaf stirred. The birds did not leave their branches as they warbled their morning carols. Wild flowers, scenting the road, swayed neither to the right nor left. Meanwhile Grayson marched strenuously to meet Dickinson and his militia at the bridge. At this advanced post, near seven-thirty in the morning (and with the temperature already in the 80's) firing was heard ahead. Grayson believed that the militia might need help, and ordered his 600 men to go forward. Rhode Island's Lieutenant Colonel Jeremiah Olney climbed the rise and ordered his cannon pointed at the enemy. Theodore Thayer, a present-day historian, explained the confusion that resulted:

Whether they knew it or not, the Americans were being attacked by Simcoe and his Rangers, who had camped not far away. Before Grayson's men had a chance to fire, word came that they were being attacked by a

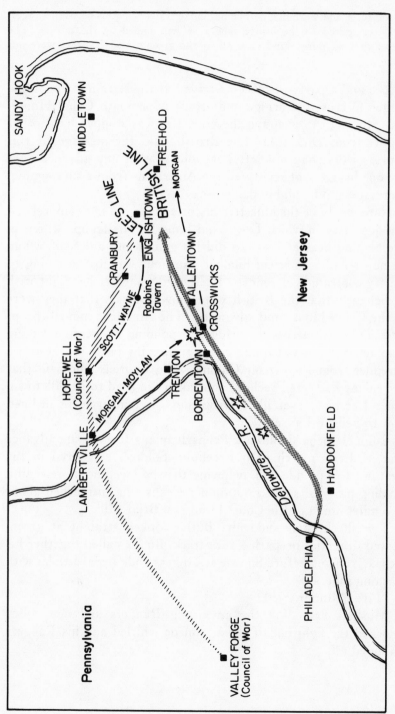

Battle of Monmouth: Parallel Lines of March

strong force and were likely to be outflanked. Believing his corps in danger, Grayson retired to the bridge where he was joined by the militia. The enemy did not pursue and soon all of the green-coated Rangers were out of sight. . . .

Lee and a party of officers arrived at the stream at this time. Eager to cross the bridge and attack Monmouth Court House, thus striking the enemy in the rear, Lee was stopped by another report from Dickinson. The British, said the message of this express rider, had not left Freehold so that any advance over the one bridge that separated the Americans from a surrounding morass would be highly dangerous.

Rare would be the objective historian who did not comprehend the quandary in which Lee found himself. His troops wilted in the blazing heat and so too did his guides and aides, of whom he never had a sufficient number. An hour was lost in trying to clarify contradictory reports. Lee heard whatever he might wish to believe—that the British were moving away, that they were at the Court House and advancing. The American moved troops back and forth across the bridge, responding to these conflicting dispatches. Somewhere he had to anchor his faith and he chose a report from Lieutenant Colonel John Laurens who said that the enemy had left Freehold and taken the road to Middletown. Since Lee had never liked Dickinson, his temperament inclined him to believe Laurens.

Colonel Richard Butler's Pennsylvanians formed the advance unit of Lee's march onto Freehold. Soldiers staggered in the heat but Lee plodded on, believing that he faced no more than a holding party of some 2,000 under Cornwallis entrenched about two miles north of the Court House on Briar Hill.

The shock came suddenly. Butler looked straight at green-coated dragoons preparing for attack. Butler pulled together his Pennsylvanians before Simcoe's Rangers rode toward them with slashing sabers.

"Fire!" Butler cried.

Muskets flamed at the advancing Rangers and one volley knocked the fight out of them. Simcoe whirled and his Rangers galloped off.

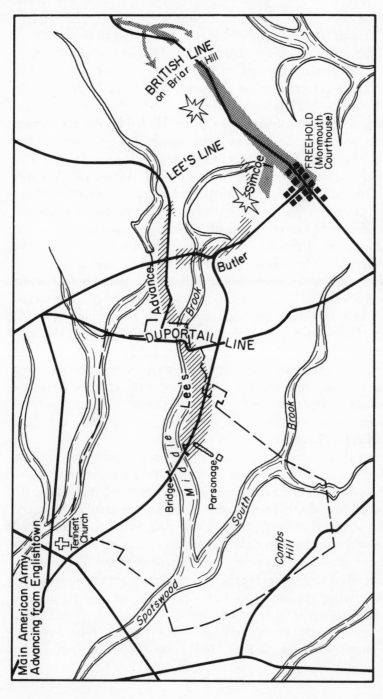

Battle of Monmouth: Gen. Charles Lee's Advance to Briar Hill and
Retreat to the Duportail Line

Now Lee heard a report that Simcoe had taken the road to Middletown, where Cornwallis was also reputed to be marching. Lafayette was sent to investigate. The Marquis crossed the third morass and came into view of the country around Briar Hill. Distantly he detected enemy columns and a large body of horse on the road to Middletown.

Lee received this information calmly. He led his division across the causeway over the morass and formed on the east rim of the ravine. Maxwell's troops, atop a hill, were left as a reserve. The morning had advanced to about ten o'clock. Lieutenant Colonel Eleazer Oswald, a Massachusetts man already a veteran at the age of twenty-three, had a battery of two cannon on a knoll whence he could lob shots into the forming enemy lines.

Lee believed that with only 2,000 British and Hessians on the hill, he could strike a bold, decisive blow. He would circle to the left with part of his division and fall on the enemy's rear while the remainder of his division attacked the front. He asked Wayne to keep Cornwallis engaged without frightening him into a general encounter. Any order of restraint brought out the bullheadedness in Mad Anthony. He chafed but he obeyed.

Clinton misread the American intention, deciding that they were after his baggage. The result was that Sir Henry started back toward Freehold with most of the cavalry and several regiments that included such famous fighting forces as the Grenadiers and the Coldstream Guards.

Short of aides and messengers, and with his horses quickly wearing out under the intense heat, Lee told Lafayette to move Wayne's men to the right in front of Freehold, but failed to inform all his subordinates of this change. Meanwhile, convinced that he opposed no more than a covering party, Lee continued his encircling movement. Scott, one of the uninformed subordinates, thought Lafayette was retreating and began withdrawing his own men across the ravine. Anger almost equaled the sun in driving the blood to Lee's face, for Scott's action had isolated Grayson farther up the ravine.

All at once everything fell apart for Lee. A rider brought word that the forces on Briar Hill were far stronger than the general had suspected. Hearing of Scott's retirement, Lafayette also began to fall back. Lee abandoned his encirclement, grateful to have a ravine and a morass at his back. Stubborn British cavalry charges threatened to turn his flanks. Lee thought of forming a battle line in Freehold where he expected to find houses of stone, so familiar in Pennsylvania. To his discouragement there were only wood houses which Clinton could easily burn. Wayne vociferated loudly but vainly in trying to change Lee's mind.

Lee took steps to correct what, in his opinion, was an untenable situation. Since Washington had not yet appeared on the field, Lee wanted a position that would bring him into more immediate contact with the Commander-in-Chief. A French engineer, Colonel Louis Duportail, told Lee to make his defense along a heights running from where the Catholic Cemetery on Highway 522 now stands, a position a mile or so from Freehold. Scott claimed that horses with fieldpieces were bouncing wildly over the road. Other officers said they did not receive orders telling them what to do. Lee also blamed the confusion on a lack of flags identifying regiments on the field, but his heaviest resentment was against the breakdown in communications:

. . . had not our system been so defective in these points, and the number of my aide-de-camps been competent, I could (such was the excellent temper of the troops) have conducted the whole of the maneuvres of this day with as much ease as ever they were performed in a common field of exercise.

And perhaps he could have. American artillery and British artillery were dueling rather ineffectually. American muskets repulsed another charge of British dragoons. A local man, Peter Wyckoff, sought out Lee. He advised a stand on the back of the west morass (advice Washington later followed). Lee likewise agreed with Wyckoff but could not bring his deteriorating command into effective cooperation.

*   *   *

To this point, by any objective view, Lee had fought bravely and with sound military sense. Such errors that he had made were the kind that any general, including Washington, might have made. But army jealousies had become deeply rooted after the Conway cabal (in which Lee had been implicated at least by inference) ; reminiscences of old officers and old soldiers tended to emphasize festering wounds of emotion; and even some historians accepted these prejudices too literally.

One historian portrayed Lafayette disputing his commander's decision of withdrawal after Clinton turned back on Freehold; Lafayette, asking permission to fall on the enemy's rear, was overruled by his superior.

"Sir," Lee allegedly said, "you do not know British soldiers; we can not stand against them; we shall certainly be driven back at first, and we must be cautious."

Reputedly Lafayette replied in the same bookish language: "It may be so, general; but British soldiers have been beaten, and they may be again; at any rate, I am disposed to make the trial."

Virginia's Charles Scott, asked if he ever had beheld Washington enraged, nodded.

Yes, once [Scott said]. It was at Monmouth on a day that would have made any man swear. Yes, sir, he swore on that day till the leaves shook on the trees, charming, delightful. Never have I enjoyed such swearing before or since. Sir, on that ever-memorable day, he swore like an angel.

But Private Martin did not believe that Washington grated "Damn him!" as he galloped down the road to meet Lee. "It was certainly very unlike him," Martin recalled, "but he seemed at the instant to be in a great passion; his looks if not his words seemed to indicate as much."

Under the circumstances Washington's excitability was perfectly understandable. Monmouth was the first time that the Army under Washington had engaged the British in open combat. Well might the battle prove to be the turning point of the war.

CHAPTER FIVE

Forever Molly

June, 1778

Near one o'clock that afternoon Washington and the main army reached Old Tennent. Lee was falling back to make a stand at the bridge crossing Spotswood Middle Brook. A frightened young fifer came down the road with a blistering face red with heat and fright. Lee's troops, he shouted at Washington, were tumbling backward in a disorganized retreat.

The boy's story was worth as much credence as anyone wished to give it. Washington responded skeptically. But now parties that had failed to stop at the Middle Brook bridge rushed down the road, their faces not much different from that of the young fifer. It was among these troops that Washington, spurring his horse across the bridge and up a rise, first met Lee. In obvious anger the Commander-in-Chief demanded an explanation for the retreat.

"Sir—sir—," Lee sputtered, obviously not comprehending the question.

Thus began the "sensational" meeting of the two generals based upon the testimony of New Jersey's General David Forman. Lee tried to explain the nature of the ground and the pursuing British. Washington ridiculed Lee as having been misled by only a strong covering party. Even in that case, Lee replied stiffly, the enemy still were too overpowering for him to engage. But Washington, in his "great passion," accused Lee of disobeying orders. The Commander-in-Chief, riding toward the parsonage of Old Tennent, mounted a hillside to view the full extent of the retreat. He saw columns of American troops rushing toward the bridge. He misjudged as part of the enemy the forces of Cadwalader and Tilghman, so widely were they extended from the highway. From the parsonage Washington could well believe reports that the enemy were not far behind. He posted Pennsylvanians under Colonel Walter Stewart and Marylanders under Colonel Nathaniel Ramsay at a nearby point, then rode back for a second meeting with Lee.

The witness who declared Washington had called Lee "a damned poltroon," at their first meeting, must have been surprised at the civility with which the Commander-in-Chief, his anger cooled, now greeted Lee. While Washington rode back to form the main army in line, would Lee again take command of the front? More than that, Lee said, he would do all within his power to stop any rout. Alexander Hamilton, riding up at this point, apparently spoke to Lee like a character out of an old romantic novel:

"I will stay here with you, my dear General, and we will all die with you on the spot. Let us die rather than retreat."

Within the same context Lee replied edgily:

"When I have taken proper measures to get the main body of [the Continental troops] in a good position, I will die with you on this spot, if you please."

Lee rode off followed by his pet spaniel. Not long thereafter Hamilton was put out of action when a bullet struck his horse.

*   *   *

Washington, mounted on the fine white horse Governor Livingston had presented to him, stemmed the tide of retreat. His orders were rapid, firm, calm, clear. "Never had I beheld so superb a man," Lafayette said, describing how the Commander-in-Chief "rode along the lines, amid the shouts of the soldiers, cheering them by his voice and example and restoring to our standard the fortunes of the fight."

As the battle developed it became a breath-taking spectacle. British grenadiers flashed red uniforms, the Scots wore green and plaid. The Hessians were white-wigged, and the fierce-bearded German Jaegers looked like descendants of the Huns of Attila. Continental regiments also could be distinguished by the colors of their uniforms: the 13th Virginia in coats of blue cuffed and faced with yellow; the 6th Virginia in coats of black and the 3rd Virginia in coats of green; the 9th Pennsylvanians in brown coats faced with red, a uniform not dissimilar from that of the 5th Maryland; the Jersey troops, mostly in blue; and Colonel Moylan's 4th Regiment in red waistcoats and buckskin breeches. Among the Continentals Washington and his aides were quickly identifiable in their uniforms of buff and blue.

The enemy [wrote Dr. James McHenry, one of Washington's most likable aides], who were advancing rapidly, elated by our retreat, were to be checked—the most advantageous ground to be siezed—the main body of the army to be formed—the enemy's intentions and dispositions to be discovered—and a new plan of attack to be concerted—and all this too in the smallest interval of time—But it is in those moments of a battle that the genius of a general is displayed, when a very inconsiderable weight determines whether it shall be a victory or a defeat.

At about this time Sir Henry Clinton, waving his sword, was described as galloping around "like a Newgate jockey." By now Washington and Wayne—whom the Commander-in-Chief signaled out for special commendation in his report to Congress—had decided to make a new stand on the left near a wood. Regiments under Colonel Walter Stewart and Lieutenant Colonel Ramsay were rushed to supporting positions at a time when no more than 400 yards separated the British from Lee. A great mixture of "hallooing" was heard on both sides. Lieutenant Colonel William Harcourt (who had captured Lee in his night-shirt at Basking Ridge in 1776) commanded a raiding party of the 16th and 17th Regiments with their light dragoons. Early in the fray Stewart of the 13th Pennsylvania was wounded and carried from the field while his command was taken by Lieutenant Colonel Lewis Farmer.

That reliable Marylander, Ramsay, now found himself besieged and gave ground slowly and grudgingly. With a horse shot from under him, Ramsay was charged by a British dragoon, pistol in hand. Luckily the bullet missed its mark. With his short-bladed sword Ramsay cut the Redcoat from his horse, mounted it, turned the horse about, and offered to give single-handed battle to the entire British party, but was easily captured (and quickly pardoned by Clinton because of the Marylander's bravery).

Private Martin was part of this action in weather "almost too hot to live in." Cannonades on both sides shook a woods, a low meadow and an orchard. Colonel Joseph Cilly of the New Hampshire Line finally found the Connecticut and Rhode Island men with whom Martin served.

"Ah," Cilly cried, "you are the boys I want to assist in driving those rascals from yon orchard."

Martin wished that Cilly had looked the other way. About 500 strong, the men emerged from their concealment and charged the British, who retreated. A tangle of fences prevented a general pursuit, so the Americans divided and Martin remembered:

We overtook the enemy just as they were entering upon the meadow, which was rather bushy. When within about five rods of the rear of the retreating foe, I could distinguish everything about them. They were retreating in line, though in some disorder. I singled out a man and took my aim directly between his shoulders. (They were divested of their packs.) He was a good mark, being a broad-shouldered fellow. What became of him I know not; the fire and smoke hid him from my sight. One thing I know, that is, I took as deliberate aim at him as ever I did at any game in my life. But after all, I hope I did not kill him, although I intended to at the time.

The British hauled up a small piece of artillery, called a "grasshopper," which could rip off a thigh bone as easily as a head. These were Scotsmen firing and Cilly cried: "Come, my boys, reload your pieces, and we will give them a set-off."

Martin did not wait for a second invitation:

"We did so, and gave them the parting salute, and the firing on both sides ceased."

Martin found a wounded captain and asked a sergeant why he did not carry the officer to the surgeons.

He would do so directly, the sergeant said.

"Directly!" Martin yelled. "Why he will die directly!"

Martin helped to carry the officer to Old Tennent church, but only "tarried a few minutes to see the wounded and two or three limbs amputated."

*   *   *

From knoll to knoll cannon roared and the casualties on both sides rose alarmingly. It was likely at this point that Mary Ludwig Hays, serving beside her husband and fetching water from a nearby spring to cool the guns and quench the thirst of the cannoneers, won immortality as "Molly Pitcher." Some historians have dealt harshly with Molly, labeling her a camp follower who chewed tobacco and swore like a trooper (as though she alone, among the uneducated, used profanity as a substitute for a vocabulary deficiency). Others have declared her name was not Hays but Maban, Hanna, or McCauley, probably confusing her with women who won attention for service in other battles of this war in which babies sometimes were born on the roadside while the guns fired. Private Martin is as responsible as anyone for libeling Molly Hays when he recalled:

A woman whose husband belonged to the artillery, and who was then attached to a piece in the engagement, attended with her husband at the piece the whole time. While in the act of reaching a cartridge and having one of her feet as far before the other as she could step, a cannon shot from the enemy passed directly between her legs without doing any other damage than carrying away all the lower part of her petticoat. Looking at it with apparent unconcern, she observed that it was lucky it did not pass a little higher, for in that case it might have carried away something else, and continued her occupation.

Poor Mary Hays! Certainly with her stoutness and redness
she was no beauty. But her loyalty scarcely deserved to be im-
pugned. When her wounded husband toppled forward, and
orders came to have his fieldpiece dragged to the rear, she
reputedly told her mate: "Lie there, my darling, while I revenge ye." Snatching up her husband's ramrod, "she worked like
an Amazon," inspiring all around her. Among her affectionate
nicknames were "Sergeant," "Molly Pitcher," and "Major
Molly." A poet of the time helped to spread her fame:

> "Wheel back the guns," the gunner said,
> When like a flash before him, stood,
> A figure dashed with smoke and blood,
> With streaming hair, with eyes aflame,
> With lips that falter the gunner's name,
> "Wheel back his gun that never yet
> "His fighting duty did forget?
> "His voice shall speak though he be dead,
> "I'll serve my husband's gun," she said.
> Oh, Molly, Molly, with eyes so blue,
> Oh, Molly, Molly, here's to you!
> Sweet Honor's roll will aye be richer,
> To hold the name of Molly Pitcher!"

Greene commended Molly to Washington. Some say that the
Commander-in-Chief gave her the rank of lieutenant with half
pay for life and that she wore an epaulette and was called
"Captain Molly"; others reduce her compensation to "a piece
of gold" and her commission to sergeant while fascinated French
soldiers "filled her chapeau with silver coin as she passed in
front of their ranks." To Albigence Waldo she was a "Spartan
heroine." After the war the Pennsylvania legislature settled
a small lifetime pension on her.

*   *   *

It was fortunate for Washington that superior generals like
Lord Stirling and Nathanael Greene had come up to support his
fighting at Monmouth. Lee's badly battered troops were sent
back to Englishtown to rest, though Lee, for once at least with

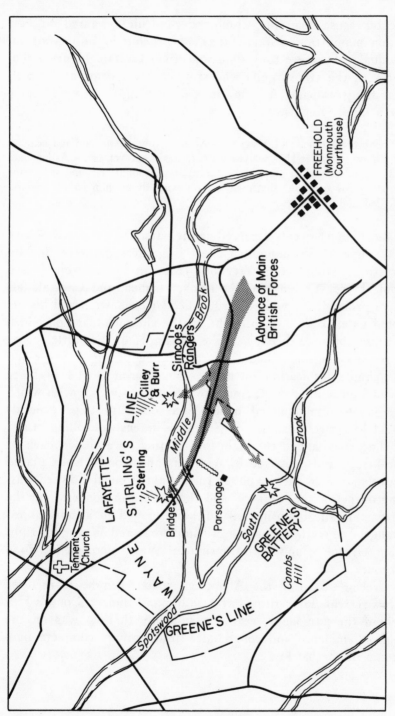

Battle of Monmouth: British Advance on American Positions

greater sense than his Commander-in-Chief, wanted to halt
within supporting distance at Tennent church. Stories of individual valor were told. One concerned Captain Henry Fauntleroy of the 5th Virginia who stopped for a drink at the well
near the parsonage. A young man of burning thirst paid dearly
for a kindly impulse:

> Seeing the parched and weary enlisted men crowding around and begging
> for a drink of water [he] waived his turn again and yet again. As he stood
> aside unselfishly while others took the cooling draught, a round shot came
> bounding toward him, shattered his hip and threw him to the ground
> mangled and dying.

But happier events occurred at the parsonage, for it was here
that some of Washington's finest brigadiers gathered for instruction: Muhlenberg, Weedon, Jedediah Huntington, Enoch
Poor. Here Washington met Knox, Steuben, and Cadwalader.
Here probably his white charger died of exhaustion and his devoted valet, Billy Lee, brought up the chestnut mare on which
Washington rode throughout the remainder of the battle.

As Washington rallied his forces to new positions, never had
the simple inspiration of the Commander-in-Chief's presence
seemed more important. And now from the aptitude with which
the Continentals moved crisply into other postings generals
could be grateful anew for Steuben's intensive drilling. Lord
Stirling commanded the main line, resting on a rise in back of
the bridge and protected by orchards and woods. Knox placed
a twelve-cannon battery under Lieutenant Colonel Edward Carrington below the infantry, and the American gunners and the
British on the opposite hill quickly engaged in a spirited exchange. Lafayette supported Stirling's rear and Wayne his right
wing. Greene's line was to the right of Wayne across Spotswood
Brook.

Greene was near the Allentown road when he learned of
Lee's retreat. He returned at a gallop and climbed Comb's Hill
behind the parsonage, realizing suddenly that he was on the
highest eminence and commanded practically a complete pan-
orama of the battle.

Greene knew how to use his advantage. A battery of from eight to ten cannon, under the command of Chevalier Duplessis Mauduit, was lugged up Comb's Hill.

The hour was now three. Clinton, eager to gain renown as Britain's new commanding general, ignored the strength of Washington's horseshoe position. Gamely Clinton threw attacks on the flanks where Greene and Stirling stood.

Cornwallis came along Wemrock road to get at Greene. Rolling drums added to the tenseness on Comb's Hill. The flying flags of the advancing troops—the Grenadiers under Sir John Wrottsley and the Scots Foot Guards under Colonel Cosmo Gordon—cast an almost hypnotic spell. Then Greene nodded to Mauduit.

The cannon roared on Comb's Hill.

CHAPTER SIX

Shadows in the Night

June–July, 1778

Cornwallis' advance stopped like an interrupted drumbeat. One round from Greene's gunners was placed so accurately that it struck the muskets from the hands of an entire platoon. One stricken drummer muttered: "Well, I wonder who they'll get to accept of our grenadier company now [as a drummer]. I'll be damned if I would!" Hamilton admitted that he had "never known or conceived the value of military discipline till that day."

Clinton shied off from Greene and pounded harder at the other flank. The balding Lord Stirling—"mild in private conversation and vociferous in the field"—made his voice roundly heard. His gunners aimed at Grenadiers and Highlanders trying to cross the bridge over the Spotswood Middle Brook in an effort to reach the orchard.

Washington acted to relieve a serious moment. Colonel Joseph Cilly with his New Hampshiremen and some Virginians, totalling about 1,000, marched off to strengthen Stirling's extreme flank. British cannon, firing heavily at the brook, might have hurt Cilly more if the smoke and the thick stillness of the heat had not obscured the maneuver. Two rail fences were torn away.

No one would have been prouder than Steuben at the manner in which Stirling's men used the screen of artillery smoke to march, muskets on shoulders, toward the British. At times one foe could not see the other.

Battle cries sounded blood-chilling. The hills echoed the American yells. In a charge that reputedly changed the course of the war "tall Grenadiers" and "bonneted Highlanders" felt the cold thrust of Continental bayonets.

Full credit at this awesome moment belonged to Lieutenant Colonel Aaron Burr, who accompanied Cilly. One day President Thomas Jefferson would bring an unsubstantiated claim of treason against Burr, but on this day the New Yorker, only twenty-one, heroically led a regiment into the thick of the fight. His alert eyes noted a party of the enemy, detached from the main force, coming through a thicket to the south. Burr, leading his soldiers across a marsh on a flooring of logs and rails, already suffered heavy fire from the British batteries. He pushed on with the stubbornness that led to his eventual downfall, many years later.

Ascending a hill, the Americans came into view of the British. The firing grew terrific, littering the ground with dead and wounded. By a stroke of luck Burr tumbled safely from an injured horse. Lieutenant Colonel Rudolph Bunner, in the lead with his Pennsylvanians, fell dead from a musket ball. Washington pulled back the force over Burr's vigorous objections. British round shot peppered the ground as the Continentals withdrew.

Meanwhile, the British, running out of ammunition in their charge on Stirling, began to fall back, but Clinton's forces were so hard pressed by the Americans that at one point a mere fifty yards separated Washington from the enemy. Wayne crossed the bridge over the Middle Brook and sought refuge behind a hedgerow near the parsonage. Greene, Stirling, Wayne, were all fighting simultaneously. Ahead of Wayne's Pennsylvanians the British were formed in rows, chiefly the second battalion of Grenadiers led by the competent Lieutenant Colonel Henry Monckton.

Waving his sword, Monckton called: "Forward charge, my brave Grenadiers!"

"Steady, steady," Wayne warned. "Wait for the word, and pick out the King birds!"

A wave of the enemy swept forward. When they were within some forty paces of the hedgerow, Wayne shouted: "Fire!" Britishers fell like autumn leaves. But their spirit was unbroken. Re-forming, they again charged the hedgerow. Some of Wayne's boys now also huddled behind a barn about twelve feet back of the parsonage.

The grapeshot from the British mixed with the leaden balls from Pennsylvania rifles. Colonel James Barnes of the 1st Pennsylvania took the shock of the assault. Maxwell's New Jerseymen and Scott's Virginians came to Wayne's support. Again the British fell back and their "high sergeant," standing seven-feet-four, was slain. The next attack ended in savage hand-to-hand combat. Then Monckton's body was seen forty yards from the parsonage and dragged within American lines (he was later buried in Tennent churchyard). Wayne held back from chasing the Grenadiers and, unknowingly, saved his force from being outflanked.

Another attempt by the Queen's Rangers and a brigade of light infantry to turn Lord Stirling's left was called back by Clinton. After hours of merciless duelling in the sweltering heat, the British knew that they were played out. For one local resident who watched the fighting atop a tombstone in Tennent churchyard the end of the battle did not come quickly enough, however. A bouncing cannon ball knocked him off the gravestone and he died soon afterward on a pew bench in the church (in later years vandal-minded souvenir hunters carried away what remained of the headstone).

*   *   *

Washington still wanted to carry on the attack, even though both enemy flanks were protected by thick woods and morasses. Washington, as he reported to Congress, ordered General Poor, with his own and the Carolina brigade to move around upon their right and General Woodford upon their left, and the artillery to gall them in front. But the impediments in their way prevented their getting within reach before it was dark. They remained upon the ground they had been directed to occupy during the night, with the intention to begin the attack early the next morning . . . [but] tho' General Poor lay extremely near them, they effected their retreat without his knowledge.

The British left behind their wounded—four officers and forty privates—as they slipped out of Freehold like shadows in the night. Discarded firelocks, knapsacks, and other tools of war marked the route they marched. A pontoon bridge enabled them to cross the Shrewsbury River to the protecting heights of Middletown. They reached Horseshoe Cove, formed by Sandy Hook, just as their fleet arrived from the Delaware.

The colorful and exciting embarkation was watched from nearby hills by scores of local citizens. The royal cross of St. George flew from the mizzens of the awesome men-of-war. Scows, longboats and yawls, pulled by the brawny arms of British tars, hauled the troops, baggage, artillery and tents of Clinton's army. Wagons that could not be transported were burned on the beach and their horses driven to swim. So for the British did the Battle of Monmouth end, rather spectacularly, with the warships towing the small boats and, guided by ropes, the horses swimming behind.

*   *   *

Stiff with ground aches, General Enoch Poor awoke next morning to discover that Clinton's army had slipped away. Here and there he saw fresh graves, probably dug with bayonets for want of spades. Last night, however, Sir Henry had moved off without any thought for his casualties. The wounded were carried to the Court House for the local residents to nurse and the British dead were buried in a pit on the southeast corner of what is now Throckmorton and Main Streets.

Washington, who had slept under an oak that night, arose and shook the dirt from the cloak in which he had been wrapped.

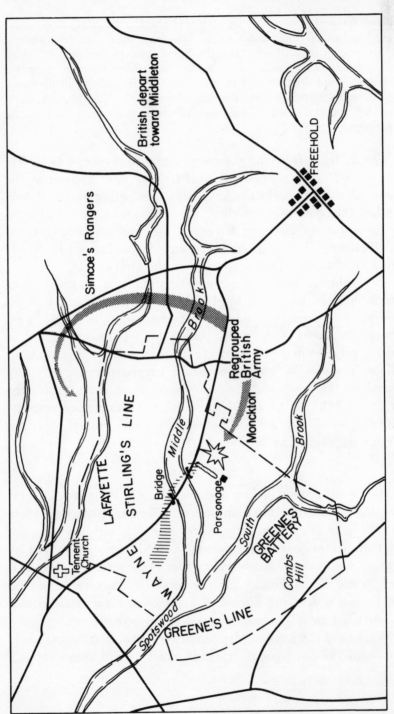

Battle of Monmouth: The Last Charge

Naturally Clinton's escape was a sore disappointment, but pursuit seemed senseless now that the British, by stealing off "as silent as the grave" had got "a night's march on him." In his letter to his brother, John Augustine Washington, the Commander-in-Chief took a bright view of Monmouth "which, from an unfortunate and bad beginning, turned out a glorious and happy day."

Wayne was letting his imagination run wild when he wrote that "by the most moderate computation their killed and wounded must be full fifteen hundred men of the flower of their army." Actually Clinton placed his losses at 174 killed (including fifty-nine who died from heat exhaustion), 170 wounded and fifty-eight missing. The Hessian, Baurmeister, believed their dead numbered 358. The generally accepted Continental casualties were sixty killed and 150 wounded, although some British were almost as flamboyant as Wayne in raising these numbers.

The chief conjecture, still argued, is whether Washington could have won more at Monmouth, if, indeed, he had won a victory. Insofar as Clinton had reached New York with his main force intact, had the battle been better than a stalemate? But this is hindsight history; at the time Washington's success at Monmouth was news joyously received in the colonies.

*   *   *

Tuesday, June 30, was a harrowing day for Washington. Lee now had nursed his fancies to the point of outraged indignity and demanded "some reparation" for what he had suffered during the battle. Washington, Lee charged, was "guilty of an act of cruel injustice towards a man who certainly has some pretensions to the regard of every servant of this country." Washington was accused of listening to "dirty earwigs"—meaning, specifically, Lafayette, Wayne and Scott.

Two of the "dirty earwigs," Wayne and Scott, poured out to the Commander-in-Chief their feelings toward Lee in an effort to prove that on June 28 the lack of early success was due to Lee's mistakes and "not occasioned by the want of numbers, positions, or the wishes of both officers and men to maintain that post."

As icily as Washington had dealt with Conway at Valley Forge, the Commander-in-Chief treated Lee:

I am not conscious of having made use of any very singular expressions at the time of my meeting with you, as you intimate [Washington wrote]. As soon as circumstances will permit, you shall have an opportunity, either of justifying yourself to the army, to Congress, to America, and to the world in general, or of convincing them that you were guilty . . . of misbehavior. . . .

Lee, balancing his chances, asked for a court-martial. The decision, he said, "would be clear-cut and final." Washington agreed, listing the charges he would bring against Lee:

    1. Disobedience of orders in failing to attack the enemy;
    2. Misbehavior before the enemy; and
    3. Disrespect in his letters to the Commander-in-Chief.

The army was excited; no event since the Conway cabal had so aroused its officers. Meanwhile on July 1 Washington began his twenty-mile march from Englishtown to New Brunswick. The heat still burned down and every footstep kicked up a puff of dust. The first sight of water was at South River, about midway on the march.

CHAPTER SEVEN

A Feu de Joie *and*
Other Matters

Summer, 1778–Spring, 1779

A dust-covered Washington rode his chestnut mare into New Brunswick on July 2. At the sight of the Raritan, soldiers who had not bathed for weeks broke into cheers. Soon their tents lined both banks of the river. The troops were led down to the water in squads and their leaders were strict in not letting them romp in the river, during the first days, for longer than half an hour. In everyone's mind was the fearful memory of the thirst-crazed soldier at Monmouth who drank so greedily at a cold spring that he fell dead.

Colonel John Laurens, son of the president of Congress, was cheered by being in New Brunswick. He found the town and its surroundings "a delightful country" and wished that his father could ride along its splendid river. Washington ordered "a *feu de joie* of the whole line" on the second anniversary of the Declaration of Independence.

The day was a gay one in New Brunswick. A salvo of thirteen cannon made the ground rumble. Soldiers on parade wore green sprigs in their hats—the symbol of hope they had employed

when marching through Philadelphia before Brandywine. What
they may have lacked in appearance they compensated for in
high spirits since Washington also had declared: "A double
allowance of rum will be served out."

The occasion was really a celebration for another reason,
since the people were still overjoyed that the British had been
driven from the field at Monmouth. When later Sir Henry
Clinton reported how he "took the advantage of the moonlight" to depart from Freehold, a wave of hilarity swept the
states and John Trumbull, one of the Hartford wits, explained
why in a canto added to his *M'Fingal*:

> Go on, great general, nor regard
> The scoffs of every scribbling bard.
> Who sings how gods, that fearful night,
> Aided by miracle your flight;
> As once they used in Homer's day,
> To help weak heroes run away;
> Tells how the hours, at this sad trial,
> Went back, as erst on Ahaz' dial.
> While British Joshua stay'd the moon
> On Monmouth's plain for Ajalon.
> Heed not their sneers or jibes so arch,
> Because she set before your march.

Actually the moon set at fifty-five minutes past ten on June 28.

*   *   *

On the second birthday of the Declaration of Independence
the court-martial of General Charles Lee began at Mynders
Vorhees' inn in New Brunswick. During the next two months
sessions were held wherever elements of the army assumed defensive positions. Thus, in New Jersey, the court met three
times at New Brunswick and six times at Paramus; and, in New
York, three times at Peekskill and fourteen times at North
Castle.

Lord Stirling acted as president of the court, assisted by Generals William Smallwood, Enoch Poor, William Woodford, and
Jedediah Huntington, and nine colonels. Lee was tried under
three articles of war:

Section II, Article 5. Any officer or soldier who . . . shall disobey any lawful command of his superior officer shall suffer death or such other punishment as shall according to the nature of his offense, be inflicted upon him by the sentence of a court-martial.

Section XIII, Article 13. Whatsoever officer or soldier shall misbehave himself before the enemy and run away or abandon any fort or guard which he or they shall be demanded to defend or speak words inducing others to do the like . . . every such offender being duly convicted thereof . . . shall suffer death or such other punishment, as by a general court-martial shall be inflicted on him.

Section II, Article 2. Any officer or soldier who shall behave himself with contempt or disrespect towards the general, or other commander-in-chief of the forces of the United States or shall speak words tending to his hurt or dishonor shall be punished according to the nature of his offense by the judgment of a court-martial.

Lee pleaded not guilty on all counts. Twenty-six persons testified against him at the trial, including Generals Lafayette, Steuben, Scott, Wayne, Forman, and Maxwell. Thirteen defended him, including Generals Duportail and Knox. The trial dragged on until August 12 when after twenty-six sessions Lee was declared "guilty of disobedience," "guilty of misbehavior before the enemy," and "guilty of disrespect to the Commander-in-Chief." Congress approved the verdict and a sentence that dismissed Lee from the army for one year.

Clinton and his British officers called Lee's treatment unfair. Again, among historians, rose another controversy that never would be fully resolved. Lee devoted his remaining years to trying by letter and petition to clear his name, but sensed the cause was hopeless insofar as "no attack . . . can be made on General Washington, but it must recoil on the assailant."

*　　*　　*

What effect should the war have on higher education? No one was more anxious to have this question answered than John Witherspoon of Princeton. Dividing the years from 1776 to 1782 between the College and the Continental Congress, where he served on more than one hundred committees, Dr. Witherspoon and the trustees of Princeton were early advocates of exempting college students from military service. Letters in the *New Jersey Gazette* signed by "Cato" and probably written by Witherspoon not only advanced the argument that parents would be unlikely to enter students into college if at any moment they were subject to draft into the militia, but also stressed the idea "that the minor service they can render the nation as soldiers is putting an embargo on the seat of the muses and preventing the development of future leaders"—reasoning that would raise a lively ruckus today!

Dr. Witherspoon won his way and an advertisement in the *Gazette,* January 27, 1779, announced that "the Representatives of this state have enacted a law by which Students of College are exempted from military duty." Among Witherspoon's first acts in Congress was to press for compensation for military damage to the college and he won a settlement of £7,250 or $19,357 in Continental currency. The payments were made in three installments in 1779 and revealed how grievously inflation had shaken the country with the paper dollar now worth only five cents in hard cash. Typical bills for the restoration of Nassau Hall were astonishing: $4,178 for window glass, $1,077 for lime, $1,076 for nails, $3,571 for carpenter's work, $2,200 for ordinary labor, $330 for glazing. Students reoccupied Nassau Hall in the fall of 1778 and shivered in the wind blowing through the broken glass.

Queen's continued its classes, well removed from the mainstream of the war that still could flow over New Brunswick at any moment, but "Elizabeth-Town Academy," hardly more than a good stone's throw across the river from the enemy, reopened in its old location, inviting the young of both sexes to become proficient in "reading with propriety and gracefulness, oratory, writing, arithmetic, navigation and mathematical branches in general; also geography and philosophy, besides the Greek and Latin languages." The Academy was inviting future raiders to put it to the torch and in this respect was not disappointed.

* * *

The Battle of Monmouth brought on a period of stalemate. For months at a time the war seemed to cease. One reason for

this lull was the strict orders Sir Henry Clinton received to
avoid offensive land actions and so contented himself with widely
separated seaport raids on Egg Harbor in New Jersey, New
Bedford and Fairhaven in Massachusetts, and Vineyard Haven
on Martha's Vineyard.

One land operation of significance occurred in the summer
of 1778 when Washington moved from New Brunswick in "easy
marches" that suggested either an extensive assault on the British in New York or a partial one against Newport, Rhode Island. Washington returned to his old encampment at White
Plains. The issue actually was settled for him by Vice-Admiral
Charles Hector, Count d'Estaing, who decided that New York
Harbor could not accommodate his deep-draught warships and
so sailed for Newport, Rhode Island.

Washington responded cheerfully, sending two of his best
brigades to Providence under Lafayette and designating Nathanael Greene and John Sullivan to command the expedition.
John Hancock in his first military role led 7,000 New England
militia to join the campaign. The British under General Robert
Pigot were on an island off the mainland. Seaconnet Passage
protected them on the east, Narragansett Bay on the west and
narrow straits on the north, while Newport stood on the south.
Ferries to Tiverton on the east and to Bristol on the west connected the mainland with the two roads on the northern end of
the British-occupied island.

The overoptimistic Sullivan was days late in meeting the
overcautious Estaing, the first ill omen. Plans were concerted,
however, and August 10 set for the joint attack. Sullivan occupied the north end of Rhode Island before discovering the
enemy had abandoned their works there, the second ill omen.
But the worst omen appeared after 4,000 French troops had
landed, when thirty sail of Lord Richard Howe's fleet were
sighted. Sullivan's Irish temper could not deter Estaing from
reloading his troops and setting sail to engage Howe. Sullivan
decided to fight Pigot anyhow. Meanwhile the two fleets ma-
neuvered into a near hurricane. Both were scattered and badly
damaged. With Greene wringing his hands on the admiral's

ship and moaning, "The devil has got into the fleet," Estaing declined to rejoin the mutual assault. Despite the fact that an all-Negro Rhode Island regiment beat off "furious onsets" of Hessians, Sullivan's offense was doomed.

The expedition almost grew into an international incident of damaging proportions. Sullivan spoke of the French with a scorn usually reserved by a Corkman to describe a Dubliner. Sullivan said that he "yet hopes the event will prove America is able to procure with her own arms that which her allies refused to assist her in obtaining"—a statement that so outraged Lafayette he forced Sullivan into issuing a sullen retraction. Then Estaing's Frenchmen opened a bakery in Boston (where flour was scarcer than sound Continental currency) and when the troops refused to share their bread with civilians, a riot erupted. Bostonians who understood no French jabbered indignantly at Frenchmen who understood no English. John Hancock's gifts of diplomacy solved this dilemma, blaming the entire uproar on a plot of British origin. Washington warned that warmth of friendship must govern American behavior toward the French. Meanwhile a French aide to Lafayette ridiculed Hancock's militia as a "laughable spectacle": "All the tailors and apothecaries in the country must have been called out. . . . They were mounted on bad nags and looked like a flock of ducks in cross-belts."

*   *   *

Once this diplomatic tempest had calmed and it became obvious that Sir Henry Clinton planned no further northern excursions, Washington was happy to return to New Jersey. His cavalry outposts fanned out from his headquarters at Middlebrook to Danbury, Connecticut, in the north and to Winchester, Virginia, in the south, so acute was his shortage of forage. Pressure was placed on the Commander-in-Chief to pass the winter in Philadelphia, and if he had, perhaps he would have sensed the forewarnings of a future heartbreak.

When Washington had followed Clinton to Monmouth, General Benedict Arnold had been given command of the American occupation forces in the Quaker City. Arnold, a widower and the father of three sons, was a druggist and bookseller in New Haven and a person of consequence in the Connecticut militia at the outbreak of the war. His black hair and dark complexion were the more marked for his light blue eyes. His chief characteristics, which made him one of the outstanding heroes at Saratoga, were unusual strength, agility, and physical endurance.

Secret fires of ambition raged rather than smoldered within Arnold. Philadelphia gave him the opportunity to expand. A housekeeper, a coachman, a groom, and seven other servants were quickly engaged. When he rode through the city's streets he was driven by a handsome team of four and liveried attendants. Arnold occupied the same mansion as had Lord Howe and was determined to demonstrate that he was as much of a social light as that discarded nobleman. Two traditions became part of his elaborate dinners—the finest wines and the presence of beautiful Peggy Shippen.

The fact that Peggy invariably had been the belle of the ball during the British occupation of Philadelphia did not deter Arnold. The blonde, gray-eyed Peggy won his heart almost at once.

My passion [he wrote his new love], is not founded on personal charms only; that sweetness of disposition and goodness of heart, that sentiment and sensibility which so strongly mark the character of the lovely Miss P. Shippen, renders her amiable beyond expression, and will ever retain the heart she has once captivated. . . .

Cupid must have blinded Arnold to Peggy's strong loyalist sympathies and wide acquaintance with British officers. Benjamin Franklin's daughter wrote her father in France: "You can think of how fond of kissing she is, and she gives such old-fashioned smacks Gen. Arnold says he would give a great deal to have her for a schoolmistress to teach the young ladies how to kiss."

Edward Shippen, a successful Philadelphia merchant, vigorously opposed his daughter's marriage to the general, but even in a cry-baby mood Arnold could be a persistent suitor: "Con-

sider before you doom me to misery, which I have not deserved
but by loving you too extravagantly." The couple were wed,
not too successfully, for Arnold's arrogance—plus the fact that
he was living far beyond his means—was reflected in his frequent outbursts of temper. He could not afford the magnificent
country seat on the Schuylkill, Mount Pleasant, where he took
Peggy to live. Here he met an old beau of Peggy's, Major John
André, whose excellent pencil sketch of her is now in the Yale
University Art Gallery.

What would have alerted Washington at the time was the
gossip of the Council of Philadelphia. Arnold was accused of
employing his military aides for personal gains. It was said that
he used the Pennsylvania militia "for menial service and for
his own personal work." He allowed an enemy vessel to leave
an American port, and the debt-ridden Arnold, a New England
Protestant, hated America's alliance with Catholic France, or
so the hostile Philadelphia Council intimated.

Thus did the form of the arch-traitor of the Revolution
emerge.

*   *   *

In December Washington marched through Bedminster on
his way to his winter headquarters in the Wallace home in Middlebrook where Martha Washington joined him. Israel Putnam
wintered his division at Middlebrook Heights near Chimney
Rock. Greene was located on the banks of the Raritan between
Bound Brook and Somerville and Wayne encamped south of the
river. Knox filled Pluckemin with the guns and men of the artillery
but the general, his wife, and their three children required com-
modious accommodations on a farm below Bedminster Church.
Steuben wintered in a house on a shady lane a mile south of the
Raritan, but his daily drills, lasting six or seven hours and well
spiced with profanity, were held in Pluckemin.

Washington's good humor became infectious. Not only were
the men in fine spirits and health, as he wrote Lafayette, who
had returned to France to attend his pregnant wife, but never
had the army generally been in better condition. The severe
cold ended by the tenth of January and the mild weather seemed

nature's effort to compensate for last year's miserable winter at Valley Forge. Farmers in the region predicted an early spring.

In an effort to become more intimately acquainted with his brigadiers, Washington held a series of nightly dinners. The service of queen's ware that could not be found in Philadelphia was easily purchased in New Brunswick through the knowledge of Lady Stirling. Washington would not wait longer than five minutes for a tardy guest, saying jocularly: "Gentlemen, I have a cook who never asks whether the company has come, but whether the hour has come." Washington treated all with the same cordiality, but after a few glasses of wine usually retired to the chores of the writing desk, leaving his company to the hospitality of his two most trusted aides, Colonels Alexander Hamilton and Tench Tilghman. A frequent guest was Governor Livingston with his two unmarried daughters, Kitty and Betsy, and his daughter Sarah who had wed John Jay, Lauren's successor as president of Congress.

Knox used the old academy in Pluckemin to deliver lectures on tactics, gunnery, and related military subjects. Mrs. Knox was pregnant—or "fatter than ever," as Greene phrased it—but the baby became the seventh of her ten children to die in infancy.

Frequent formal balls were held at Pluckemin, giving the loiterers at Eoff's Tavern weeks of gossip. Washington was a glamorous sight on such occasions: clothed in black velvet, silver buckles on his knees and shoes, a steel rapier at his side, his hair powdered and gathered in back in a black silk bag on which there was a rosette.

Spring stretched into the summer months of June and July. But as Washington opened a ball with Mrs. Knox holding his arm, he little realized how closely he approached the gloomiest year of the war.

*   *   *

Actually the outward gaiety at the various Continental quarters in New Jersey was a delusion. Just before Christmas Washington had been summoned to Philadelphia to plan the campaign for 1779. He had arrived in a fretful mood over the financial circumstances of the country—"a rat, in the shape of a horse," he told Congressman Gouverneur Morris, "is not to be bought at this time for less than £200"—and he was shocked by the attitudes of the leaders in Philadelphia.

Where were the great men—a Mason, a Wythe, a Jefferson—who had inspired the Revolution? Why had they been supplanted by men noted only for "speculation, peculation, and a thirst for riches?" Party disputes and personal quarrels ruled the day—why? "Your money," Washington told Congress, "is now sinking five percent a day in this city, and I shall not be surprised if in the course of a few months a total stop is put to the currency of it." Yet Congress would spend four hundred pounds on an assembly, a concert, a dinner, or supper as the officers of its army were "sinking by sure degrees into beggary and want."

Washington's admonitions were shared by John White, a merchant of Salem, Massachusetts, who believed "Our country is too poor to be a separate nation," adding:

"I am now above sixty-six years old and am glad and rejoice my trial is almost over."

With Washington's withdrawal, a new trial beset New Jersey.

*   *   *

John Graves Simcoe was unusual among British leaders in America. His father, a navy captain, was killed at Quebec during the French and Indian War. At the beginning of the Revolution, John bought a British captaincy with the 40th Regiment. He was wounded at Brandywine and again at Monmouth.

Simcoe decided to make his own military future. He raised and drilled a Tory cavalry battalion called the Queen's Rangers. Never was any group better trained in military behavior. His actions in the South won such distinction that in late June, 1779, Sir Henry Clinton raised him to lieutenant colonel.

Simcoe's Rangers operated out of Staten Island in late October, 1779. One night—on the 25th of October, most witnesses said—the hoofbeats of his horses were heard running hard down the road toward Metuchen and New Market. Sounds approaching in the night alarmed a householder; sounds receding brought a comfortable relief.

The British raiders' first objective was the home of Derrick van Veghten on the Raritan, where General Greene had passed the winter. Several flatboats, collected for the future use of the Continentals, had their bottoms ripped. Nearby a Dutch Church was burned. At Somerset the courthouse shot flames across a spark-speckled sky.

Simcoe rode through Eastern Precinct (Franklin Township), intending to recross the Raritan. Around him rose Rebel militiamen. Simcoe, thrown from his horse, landed unconscious upon the ground. After a spirited skirmish with Middlesex County militiamen, the Tory raiders continued on to New Brunswick.

The fighting now grew ferocious. First, Tories and militiamen contested the occupation of the town street by street. As the conflict heightened, musket shots were exchanged from house to house. Captain Peter Voorhees lost his balance when his horse tried to jump a fence. Behind him the Presbyterian Church illuminated the sky as a pillar of fire. Around Voorhees gathered Britishers who beat him to death with their swords.

Simcoe's raiders rode on to Perth Amboy and crossed to Staten Island. Tradition insists that the wounded Simcoe, whom militiamen wished to kill in retaliation for Voorhees' murder, was spared by a graduate of Queen's College, who once had been treated kindly as a British prisoner. Simcoe was returned to New Brunswick and hidden in a building at the corner of Neilson and Albany streets which generations called "Washington's Headquarters." Through the help of his captors he found his way back to the British lines and fought again at Yorktown.

PART THREE

Treason and Triumph

"The weather was cold enough
to cut a man in two."

Joseph Plumb Martin

Prelude

1778–1779

The enduring impact of war, both on individuals and a nation, is not always gauged by the number of its belligerents. The fighting on the western frontier was at its mightiest a remote echo to most Americans. Likely very few even had heard of the British commander at Fort Detroit, Colonel Henry Hamilton, who was called the "Hair Buyer" although there is grave doubt that he promised a reward to any Indian who brought him the scalp of an American frontiersman. The specter of even a legendary Hamilton, however, was real enough to those Virginians who lived beyond the barriers of the Appalachians.

Governor Patrick Henry looked into the "black, penetrating, sparkling eyes" of a twenty-four-year-old giant named George Rogers Clark, gave him the rank of lieutenant-colonel, a few flatboats, and 175 frontiersmen, and told him, if possible, to carry his campaign all the way to Detroit. Four days later Clark had traveled up the Tennessee River to a point where only by an 110-mile march overland could he hope to surprise Kaskaskia, a strategic Indian community at the mouth of the river whose name it bore.

An epic journey ensued—"through a drowned country in the depth of winter," to use the commander's phrase—but despite rivers that had overflowed their banks and muddy prairies, Clark pressed on. The last twenty miles, where two branches of the Little Wabash River flowed together that icy February of 1779, presented a harrowing prospect for exhausted men. A friendly fur trader informed Clark that Hamilton had come down to Vincennes with 500 troops and the young lieutenant-colonel changed his objective on the spot: he was by-passing Kaskaskia and going after Hamilton at Vincennes, the key to Detroit.

Men shivered wading through water three feet deep, but "a little drummer afforded them great diversion by floating on his drum." After four days they discovered the flooded land extended nine miles farther than they had thought. They plunged on as though their chattering teeth were the drum beats of a march. The water rose breast high and the smaller men floated on logs or straddled the backs of their taller friends.

On February 23, ten days after they reached the "drowned country," they came to a knoll and looked down on Vincennes. Clark sent a note warning the inhabitants to stay indoors for he intended to attack the outpost that evening. Then he waded through the overflow of the Embarrass River to the high ground of the community.

Flags flew and drums beat. There was, wrote one of Clark's captains, "smart firing on both sides." Cannon the Americans had floated on a raft "played smartly." There were no casualties. Clark demanded Hamilton's surrender and was huffily refused, but by noon the "Hair Buyer" changed his mind and asked for a meeting in the town church. Again Hamilton was outraged at Clark's demand for an unconditional capitulation. Indians returning from a scouting trip were captured, tied, placed in a circle within view of the fort and massacred with the single exception of a captain who begged Clark for his life. Hamilton had seen enough. He surrendered.

*   *   *

Before breaking camp at Middlebrook, Washington planned an active campaign against the northern Indians. A worse time to move against the redskins could not be imagined. Officers and men were far in arrears on their pay. A colonel could not supply his horse with oats or an enlisted man buy his family a bushel of wheat.

Still Washington had to face the truth that where the "Hair Buyer," and his Indians from Detroit, had menaced the frontiersmen of Virginia, 400 Tories and 500 Senecas from the ferocious Six Nations, led by John Butler and operating from Fort Niagara on Lake Ontario, were an equal threat to Pennsylvanians in that state's luxuriant Wyoming Valley. In 1778 a thousand homes were burned, and the scalpings of 227 residents attested to the barbaric treatment of these settlers. Under a notorious half-white, Joseph Brant, New York's Mohawk Valley was ravished in September and a pretty village, Cherry Valley, fifty miles from Albany, suffered the same calamity in November.

Gates, offered the command of an expedition against the Indians, found that age and his dwindling strength made him "entirely unequal" to the task, so that explosive Irishman, John Sullivan, who matched thirty-eight years against Gates' fifty, cheerfully accepted Washington's assignment—the country of the Six Nations was not to be "merely overrun but completely destroyed."

Sullivan totally ravaged the Indian villages as he directed two columns of men from the Wyoming Valley to the Susquehanna and from the Mohawk Valley to the Conajoharie. He slaughtered without conscience or compassion; and an American commented: "Not all the infernals of the prince of darkness, could they have been let loose from the bottomless pit, would have borne any comparison to these demons of the forest." A charge up a hill left twelve men dead and only two prisoners, one white, one Negro. The white man had painted his face, pretending to be black; he was washed and killed on the spot. Lieutenant William Barton of the 1st New Jersey Regiment told what happened when a party was sent to search for dead and wounded Indians: "Towards noon they found them and skinned two of them from their hips down for boot legs, one pair for the major, the other for myself."

Sullivan encountered little serious opposition. Forty Indian towns were destroyed. When a party of twenty-one Americans was ambushed and the head of their lieutenant cut off, the red-skinned raiders were discovered within three days and "toma-hawked, scalped, and butchered." Frontier warfare did not trouble with niceties. Washington had hoped for hostages to insure future good behavior among the Indians of the Six Nations. He received none.

*   *   *

The Articles of Confederation, passed in 1777 and still not approved by all the states, gave Congress the power to declare war but not to levy taxes to finance a war. Requisitions by Congress upon states for soldiers and money were of no more importance than the individual legislatures chose to make them. The willful actions of the states—all but one decided to maintain their own navies—caused Greene to moan: "God knows what the consequences will be." State politicians, at least as Greene observed them in Boston, carried their self-indulgence to the point of dissipation and "were no more to compare with those now prevailing in Philadelphia than an infant babe to a full-grown man."

*   *   *

Discipline, especially when the weather turned mild, was Washington's ever-present problem. Deserters who were apprehended received one hundred lashes. Major Henry Lee recommended cutting off their heads, but Washington was not that bloodthirsty. Except for minor raids into New Jersey and Connecticut during the long American encampment around Middlebrook, Sir Henry Clinton could have turned into a pillar of salt.

To Washington the logical move for Clinton would be to seize West Point, the fortress of the Hudson. By moving St. Clair's division to Springfield, Lord Stirling's and John De Kalb's forces to Pompton, and with several brigades under Alexander Mc-Dougall already in the Highlands, Washington began shifting his army toward thwarting this suspected plan. To everyone's confusion, Clinton, who had occupied a little fort at Verplanck's Point on the east side of the Hudson and was constructing works at Stony Point on the opposite shore—vital locations in dividing New England and the middle colonies—apparently was willing to leave these forces to their own devices while he pulled back to New York.

If the truth were known, the War Office in London verged at this moment on driving Sir Henry out of his mind with its complexity of suggestions concerning how Clinton might force Washington into an open fight. "For God's sakes, my lord," Sir Henry wrote snappishly to Germain, "if you should wish that I do anything, leave me to myself and let me adapt my efforts to the hourly change of circumstances."

Only "by indirect maneuvers," Clinton said sharply, could he hope "to force Washington to an action upon terms tolerably equal." The deed was more easily proposed than achieved without the reinforcements Clinton required to attack West Point, even after the British had assaulted the forts guarding King's Ferry, where Sir Henry expected the American Commander-in-Chief to appear. But Washington was a patient man where military tactics were involved. Clinton contemplated hitting Washington from behind by striking his supply depots at Easton and Trenton and knew, intuitively, he could not carry off that plan. As an abortive alternative Sir Henry pillaged and burned such Connecticut towns as New Haven, Fairfield, and Norwalk. Washington refused to be lured into a precipitate retaliation.

Just how much humiliation Washington could endure was problematical, however. On June 15 Henry Lee was sent to scout Stony Point and found a formidable bastion on a promontory extending a half mile into the Hudson. On one side a sheer, wooded slope rose fifty feet; the other three sides were covered by river marshes so that at high tide Stony Point was as effective as an island. Washington called Wayne from a furlough at home and the Pennsylvanian, still smarting from the humiliation at Paoli, was eager to redeem his reputation.

Wayne's leadership was spectacular. In bright moonlight,

covered by Lieutenant Colonel Hardy Murfree's North Carolinians whose riflemen diverted St. Clair's defenders on Stony Point, Wayne led a bayonet attack on the flanks. Well might Wayne write a friend from "Springsteel's, 11 o'clock P.M., 15 July, 1779, near the hour and scene of carnage." Anyone who wavered was to be killed instantly by the soldier closest to him, the American general ordered. Felled by a scalp wound as he crossed the second abatis, Wayne begged his comrades: "Carry me up to the fort, boys! Let's go forward!"

The thoroughness of the whipping Wayne gave the British at Stony Point not only provided a lesson Clinton would long ponder but also demonstrated, in the judgment of the *New Hampshire Gazette,* that "Americans have soldiers equal to any in the world." Although Washington could not afford to maintain Stony Point, at the time the American people and Congress were excessively cheered. The starch appeared entirely knocked out of Clinton for further campaigning in 1779 except for a small but successful raid on Powle's Hook, a sandspit in the Hudson.

In December Washington began withdrawing to another winter encampment at Morristown.

CHAPTER ONE

A War on Sleds

December, 1779–January, 1780

Rare was the day this fall and winter when at one hour or another it neither hailed nor snowed. In mid-October, 1779, after burning the lighthouse and blowing up their works, the British abandoned Newport. Surgeon James Thacher and his regiment were ordered from Providence to Morristown. On November 23 they joined General Stark's brigade in Connecticut at Danbury, a once flourishing town that revealed the ravages of British raiders. In such wretched traveling weather the struggling troops weakened and died in unusual ways. One man succumbed after treating an itch with a mercurial ointment; another ended his life by drinking six gills of rum.

Finally, on December 14 the soldiers reached their encampment site at Jockey Hollow, three miles from Morristown. Already two feet of snow covered the ground. Thacher marveled at the good spirit with which soldiers without tents and blankets, some "actually barefooted and almost naked," threw up brushwood as their only defense against their unpleasant environment.

Private Joseph Plumb Martin marched down from Peekskill. He tried to look upon his adversity with philosophical resignation: "As the old woman said [to] her husband, when she baked him instead of his clothes, to kill the vermin, 'You must grin and bear it.' " Hungry and tired, Martin trudged through the deepening snow. Luckily his regiment still possessed tents. In howling winds they scooped away the snow and pitched their tents in facing groups of three or four so that all would be warmed by a fire in the center. An armful of buckwheat straw, if one were so fortunate as to secure such "a luxury," provided bedding for men living like "wild animals."

Washington reached Morristown in driving sleet and established his headquarters in the home of the widow of Colonel Jacob Ford, who had commanded a regiment of the local militia. This luxurious dwelling, situated about three-quarters of a mile from the village green, was on the turnpike between Morristown and Newark. Washington occupied all of the house except two rooms in the upstairs eastern sector, which were reserved for Mrs. Ford and her family. Two log additions to the mansion provided a kitchen and an office for the Commander-in-Chief and his aides, Alexander Hamilton and Tench Tilghman. In a meadow to the southeast rose the huts used for lodgings by Washington's personal guards under General William Colfax.

Every precaution was taken that Washington would not be surprised and captured by raiders from New York as Charles Lee had been at nearby Basking Ridge. Upon occasion, when a soldier sparking a local maiden tried to sneak past a sentinel because taps had long ago sounded, embarrassments occurred. The crunch of the soldier's step in the ice-coated snow alerted the sentinel, who fired a warning shot.

Up from the meadow rushed Washington's guards. Doors were barricaded and windows thrown open. In each room stood five sentinels with their muskets cocked and charged. The freezing drafts of the coldest winter in the memory of Jerseymen since 1755 gusted across the bedrooms where Mrs. Ford and Martha Washington shivered under their coverings. Likely their heads were buried under quilted comforters. Water froze in the pitchers that filled the washing basins.

Meanwhile a highly distraught soldier tried with all possible

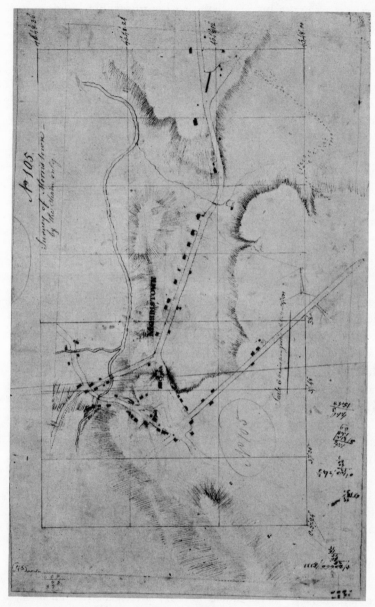

Robert Erskine's Map of the Morristown Area. *Courtesy of the New-York Historical Society, New York City*

noiselessness to make his way back to his miserable lodgings on the southern slope of Kemble Mountain.

*   *   *

Washington's plan for his army in Jockey Hollow was to build a "log-house city" as their winter encampment. Surgeon Thacher's heart was rent by the sight of hungry horses peeling bark from the trees to which they were tied, and when the matter under review was the pitiful condition of the men, General Anthony Wayne could describe the situation tartly:

I must confess that [the Light Infantry] would make a better appearance had they a sufficiency of *hats,* but as Congress don't seem to think *that* an essential . . . part of uniform, they mean to leave us uniformly bareheaded—as well as bare-footed—and if they find that we can *bare* it tolerably well in the two extremes, perhaps they may try it in the *center.*

The snowing seemed endless, and in time was to lie upon the ground to a depth of six feet. Still, as best they could, the men cut down the hard oaks and walnuts. For eight days the whole army went without "the staff of life"—"our only food," Surgeon Thacher wrote, "is miserable fresh beef, without bread, salt, or vegetables"—a circumstance that certainly did not increase the effectiveness of the axe-swingers. Sheer wonderment filled Thacher at the "heroic fortitude" of the troops. Since they were paid in Continental currency, which by the surgeon's estimate had become practically worthless at an exchange of thirty for one, "the people in the country are unwilling to sell the produce of their farms for this depreciated currency, and both the resources and the credit of Congress, appear to be almost exhausted."

Washington, it was said, fared no better than his troops, but Thacher overheard an anecdote at headquarters which somewhat contradicted this rumor:

"We have nothing but the rations to cook, Sir," said Mrs. Thomson, a very worthy Irish woman and house keeper to General Washington.

"Well, Mrs. Thomson, you must then cook the rations, for I have not a farthing to give you."

"If you please, Sir, let one of the gentlemen give me an order for six bushels of salt."

"Six bushels of salt, for what?"

"To preserve the fresh beef, Sir."

One of the aids [sic] gave the order, and the next day his Excellency's table was amply provided. Mrs. Thomson was sent for and told that she had done very wrong to expend her own money, for it was not known when she could be repaid.

"I owe you," said his Excellency, "too much already to permit the debt being increased, and our situation is not at this moment such as to induce very sanguine hope."

"Dear Sir," said the good old lady, "it is always darkest just before day light, and I hope your Excellency will forgive me for bartering the salt for other necessaries which are now on the table."

Salt was eight dollars a bushel, and it might always be exchanged with the country people for articles of provision.

*   *   *

Mrs. Thomson's shrewdness was one of the few bright spots in the beginning of a new year for Washington. Many of his generals showed the hard effects of war either by illness or loss of physical stamina. Sullivan retired from service along with Putnam, and Gates, refusing an assignment in the Highlands, returned to Virginia for the winter. McDougall suffered "alarming symptoms of the stone" and Jeremiah Wadsworth, a trustworthy commissary general, considered resigning. Countless three-year enlistments had less than half a year to run, another source of anguished contemplation for the Commander-in-Chief.

Impossible though it seemed, the weather worsened and a storm beginning on January 3 surpassed in its frigid fury any snowfall in the recollections of local residents. Surgeon Thacher recalled:

Several marquees were torn asunder and blown down over the officers' heads in the night, and some of the soldiers were actually covered while in their tents, and buried like sheep under the snow. My comrades and myself were roused from sleep by the calls from some officers for assistance; their marquee had blown down, and they were almost smothered in the storm, before they could reach our marquee, only a few yards, and their blankets and baggage were nearly buried in the snow. . . .

The suffering of the sentries on night duty could "scarcely be described." Soldiers who only had received two pounds of meat in the past ten days, and frequently had gone six or eight days without receiving any, Thacher wrote, were "so enfeebled from hunger and cold, as to be almost unable to perform their military duty, or labor in constructing huts." Private Martin, digging below the frost line, discovered "where toads take up their winter quarters." Appeals to New Jersey magistrates for provisions brought as ready a response as could be expected over snow-clogged roads.

A cheerful communication reached Washington from Lord Stirling. Although that general suffered severe pain while riding, Stirling had assumed Lincoln's old command. Now on January 7 he wrote a rousing report of how he had captured several spies and a number of men guilty of passing counterfeit Continental money. Indignantly he described local authorities who refused to incarcerate officially proven spies and urged Washington to write Governor Livingston on this subject.

Stirling next turned enthusiastic, urging a raid on Staten Island. The ice, he wrote, was so thickly frozen as to support men and sleds in a crossing from New Jersey to Staten Island. Washington, who had doubts of the success of the venture, replied simply that he was inclined "to Intrust the command and execution of it to your Lordship." Stirling answered on January 14 that the attack would be made at sunup next day.

*   *   *

The spectacle was unlike any scene ever observed on the North American continent: 800 soldiers in 500 sleds skimming over the snow! Lord Stirling had changed his mind and started at five o'clock when the winter darkness descended. The temperature dipped rapidly to zero, making every breath feel like a knife cut. Unless a musket were clutched in a gloved hand, the cold steel could peel away the skin. The sleds traversed knee-deep snow that would have exhausted a walking man in half an hour. Toes and fingers grew numb despite how snugly they were wrapped. Swiftly the sleds flashed over the ice between Elizabethtown and Staten Island. Coldness kept Stirling's men from cursing the twinkling stars at midnight that revealed their presence, but it was as well they saved their breath for a Tory spy already had informed the British of the expedition. A raid in the bitterest cold of winter was a kind of damn foolishness that the British found difficult to believe, even of Americans.

Stirling could not have asked for better luck, for the British only half prepared for the threatened assault. Once across the ice the snow grew deeper, but still when the Americans appeared the British outposts were surprised and their sentries driven in. Moving inland toward the central British camp, Stirling encountered stiffened resistance and knew his scheme had been revealed by spies. Still, part of the camp was occupied.

We then fell back a little distance [Private Martin reported], and took up our abode for the night upon a bare bleak hill, in full rake of the northwest wind, with no other covering or shelter than the canopy of the heavens, and no fuel but some old rotten rails which we dug up through the snow, which was two or three feet deep.

In weather "cold enough to cut a man in two," Lord Stirling also burned thirty-five tons of hay to keep the Americans from freezing. Originally, if the expedition had been a surprise, Stirling had planned to take captives, secure supplies and to destroy provisions and military stores in a hit-and-run raid. Pluck was needed to stay through the night, but no one ever had questioned Stirling's bravery.

Daylight revealed his Lordship's full danger since New York Bay was so firmly frozen that reinforcements easily could reach Staten Island from Clinton's encampment. Martin spoke of an armed brig lying in the ice with which a few shots were exchanged in a "morning's salutation." Even so, some prisoners (including a colonel) and some stores and blankets were taken.

Martin, retreating from the island at daylight, remembered:

The British were quickly in pursuit; they attacked our rear guard and made several of them prisoners, among whom was one of my particular associates. Poor young fellow! I have never seen or heard anything from

him since. We arrived at camp after a tedious and cold march of many
hours, some with frozen toes, some with frozen fingers and ears, and half-
starved into the bargain. Thus ended our Staten Island expedition.

But not for Lord Stirling, for whom the consequences approached tragedy. The British, as usual, exaggerated the number
of killed, wounded and captured among Stirling's men, but the
whole unhappy adventure loosened the tart tongue of John
Adams.

CHAPTER TWO

Huts in a Hollow

January–February, 1780

Lord Stirling and Washington shared a common detestation of
any soldier who stole private property. Now a cry arose that
many who had ridden to Staten Island on the sleds had pillaged
civilian homes. Where such looting could be proved, the property
was returned and the offenders severely punished.

But in Congress the lid was off the gossip kettle, so to speak.
One heard rumors of camp followers from Perth Amboy, who
had been the true culprits, and with frequent retelling one could
almost see Lord Stirling manipulating the ladle as he stirred up
a witches' brew. John Adams was among the worst spreaders of
falsehood, declaring that "some New Jersey people went over
[to Staten Island] at the same time and plundered without
mercy" while Stirling's little force "burned a few vessels and a
guardhouse, took a few prisoners, and brought off a few
deserters."

The pity was that Lord Stirling's military career had to end
on such a sour note. After the campaign on the sleds he confessed
to Washington: "I have not, for these two months, been able to
be on horseback with so firm a seat as was necessary in extreme
bad roads." He could no longer endure exposure to cold and
dampness—his fighting days were finished except in extreme
emergency.

Punishment of soldiers in camp who stole poultry, sheep, pigs, and even cattle from nearby farms Surgeon Thacher, somewhat unconvincingly, tried to justify by Washington's "inflexibility of purpose":

Death has been inflicted in a few instances of an atrocious nature, but in general, the punishment consists in a public whipping, and the number of stripes is proportioned to the degree of offence. The Law of Moses prescribes forty stripes save one, but this number has often been exceeded in our camp. In aggravated cases, and with old offenders, the culprit is sentenced to receive one hundred lashes, or more. It is always the duty of the drummers and fifers to inflict the chastisement, and the drum major must attend and see that the duty is faithfully performed. . . .

Tied to a tree, his back stripped to the skin, the accused awaited his punishment. Usually the whip consisted of several small knotted cords. At every stroke these knots could cut through the skin. The surgeon could not disguise his admiration for "a soldier [who] will often receive the severest stripes without uttering a groan, or once shrinking from the lash, even while the blood flows freely from his lacerated wounds. This must be ascribed to stubbornness or pride." Often the victims mitigated their pain "by putting between the teeth a leaden bullet, on which they chew while under the lash, till it is made quite flat and jagged."

So-called "incorrigible villains" were whipped at intervals of two or three days—"in which case the wounds are in a state of inflammation, and the skin rendered more sensibly [sensitively] tender; and the terror of the punishment is greatly aggravated." Another penalty in these cases was what Thacher called "running the *gantlet*." Soldiers faced one another in two lines. Each held a switch. Back naked, the "criminal" was made to run the path between. When soldiers favored the accused, and administered trivial punishment, the culprit was "ordered to hold a bayonet at his breast to impede his steps." A noncommissioned officer sentenced to corporal punishment always was demoted to private.

As a surgeon, whose life was dedicated to healing, Thacher tried to ameliorate American practice:

. . . in the British army, it has long been established in their military code, and it is not uncommon to sentence a criminal to receive a thousand lashes, and that they aggravate its horrors in the most cruel manner, by repeating the stripes from day to day, before the wounds are healed; and instances are not wanting of its having been attended with fatal consequences. . . .

Thacher could not be disloyal to the troops who shared with him the southern slopes of Kemble Mountain:

But amidst all the toils and hardships, there are charms in a military life: it is here that we witness heroic actions and deeds of military glory. The power of habit and the spirit of ambition, pervade the soldiers' ranks, and those who have been accustomed to active scenes, and found their social attachments, cannot without reluctance quit the tumult and the bustle of a camp, for the calm and quiet of domestic pursuits. There is to be found however, in the bosoms of our soldiers the purest principles of patriotism,— they glory in the noble cause of their country, and pride themselves in contributing to its successful termination. It is hoped they will not again be subjected to a starving condition.

*   *   *

After Stirling's raid on Staten Island, it was inevitable that the British should pay a return call on Morristown. They surprised the night pickets on January 27. Forty prisoners, including a major, were carried away.

*   *   *

Despite every adversity Washington's "log-house city" rose south of "Mr. Kemble's Mountain." Whether the troops had brought their own tools or "borrowed" them from farms in the neighborhood, Private Martin was not saying, but rare was the country-lad-turned-soldier who could not handle a crosscut saw, handsaw, froe, or auger. Usually the huts were built in groups of two in front and two in back, then a space of six or eight feet, then another group of four huts, and so on until provision had been made for a regiment. A street, twelve or fifteen feet wide, ran the length of the huts to the parade ground in front. Officers were housed in special huts in the rear.

The average soldier's hut was about fifteen or sixteen feet square and the notched sides rose to a height of seven feet.

Shingles, or more likely staves, four feet in length covered the
roofs; a chimney in back provided such warmth as was possible
in driving wind and snow; and berths for sleeping were hewn, as
Martin said, "for the reception of *gentlemen soldiers,* with all
their *rich* and *gay* furniture."

Starvation continued to haunt Jockey Hollow even though its
"log-house town" neared completion toward mid-February. For
four days and nights Martin lived on the black bark he could
pull from a stick of wood. He heard that some officers had killed
and eaten a pet dog.

John Kalb, who had sailed to America with Lafayette, believed that the suffering in this gloomy winter at Morristown far
exceeded the misery of Valley Forge. Kalb drilled divisions according to Steuben's directions whenever the weather permitted.
"It is so cold," Kalb wrote on February 12, "that the ink freezes
in my pen, while I am sitting close to the fire." Some drifts in the
road had reached a depth of twelve feet and the ice in the rivers
was six feet thick. Inflation added to Kalb's growing depression
which increased "from hour to hour":

A hat costs four hundred dollars, a pair of boots the same, and everything
else in proportion. The other day I was disposed to buy a pretty good horse.
A price was asked which my pay for ten years would not have covered. Of
course I did not take it, and shall try to get along with my other horses.
Money scatters like chaff before the wind, and expenses almost double from
one day to the next, while income, of course, remains stationary. I have
reduced my servants to the smallest number possible, which involves no
great self-denial, as almost all servants are lazy, addicted to drink, and
unreliable. The barber's compensation would at present consume all my pay;
I have, therefore, made up my mind to shave myself. Being entirely in rags,
I shall go to Philadelphia as soon as I can, to purchase new clothes, especially linen. The American officers have this advantage of us foreigners,
that they can go home on furlough, and there recruit and reëquip themselves. . . .

Washington, on constant alert against a surprise attack by
Clinton, persuaded Kalb to delay his journey to Philadelphia
until the ground thawed. Kalb was flattered by Washington's
attention—at the moment Kalb was one of the two major gen-

erals remaining at Morristown—but the foreigner was no less disdainful of the frequent "revolting churlishness" of native officers. A classic example was Brigadier General William Smallwood, who received a box from home which he guarded day and night so that Kalb could not touch it. The contents, in Smallwood's mind, "was intended for Marylanders only!" .

* * *

The winter distresses of Morristown were more or less spared Martin as a member of one of the two Connecticut brigades sent to Westfield and Springfield to share "the hardships and troubles" of guarding these communities. A detachment went to Elizabethtown, only six miles away from Martin and his First Brigade; another guard patrol was dispatched to Woodbridge. Somewhat grumpily Martin described the nature of his duties:

Suppose I went upon the Woodbridge guard. I must march from the parade at eight o'clock in the morning, go a distance of ten miles and relieve the guard already there, which would commonly bring it to about twelve o'clock; stay there two days and two nights, then be relieved and take up the afternoon of that day to reach our quarters at Westfield, where, as soon as I could get into my quarters, and, generally, before I could lay by my arms, warned for Elizabethtown the next day. Thus it was the whole time we lay there, which was from the middle of February to the latter part of May following. It was Woodbridge and Elizabethtown, Elizabethtown and Woodbridge, alternately, till I was absolutely sick of hearing the names mentioned.

Rations were sparse—nothing for bread except Indian corn meal and Indian corn flour—and Martin commented wryly: "Our Connecticut Yankees were as ignorant of making this meal or flour into bread as a wild Indian would be of making pound cake." A kind of "hasty pudding" resulted, washed down with milk or cider, for the whole mess "was as clammy as glue, and as insipid as starch." The inhabitants, as poor as the soldiers, had forgotten the meaning of "flesh meat."

At Woodbridge Martin lived in three houses—one empty, one the home of a parson, one the home of a farmer. Everyone was suspected of being a British spy, which was not true. One night Martin and his friends came upon British soldiers lying in a garden and dooryard. When, ultimately, the affair was culminated, the British escaped and the only peril anyone encountered was from a bullet lodged in the post of the bed in which the parson and his wife were sequestered. Again at Holstead's Point, about two miles from the main guard at Elizabethtown, Refugees (Tories) were expected to attack a farm at the setting of the moon, which would be about ten o'clock. They appeared on the dot of the announced time, killed a sentinel with twelve bayonet jabs, guaranteeing that he had been finished off with a flourish, and thus proceeded to the farm of Mr. Holstead, whose daughter revealed by candlelight that no Americans were loitering in the dwelling, and the young lady was not abused—to Martin "indeed a wonder." But Indian meal was strewn upon the floor, a circumstance that annoyed the Connecticut Yankees.

Martin recollected that during his time on patrol duty only one comrade was killed. Still Martin could scarcely contain his tears: "He lost his own life by endeavoring to save the lives of others; massacred by his own countrymen [Refugees or Tories], who ought to have been fighting in the common cause of the country instead of murdering him."

*   *   *

Lafayette wrote Washington from France. "I have a wife who is in love with you," the Marquis declared. Coyness tinged Washington's reply:

Tell her (if you have not made a mistake and offered your *own love,* instead of *hers,* to me) that I have a heart susceptible of the tenderest passion, and that it is already so strongly impressed with the most favorable ideas of her that she must be cautious of putting love's torch to it, as you must be in fanning the flame. But here again, methinks, I hear you say, I am not apprehensive of danger. My wife is young, you are growing old, and the Atlantic is between you. All this is true, but know, my good friend, that no distance can keep *anxious* lovers long asunder and that the Wonders of former ages may be revived in this. But alas! will you not remark that amidst all the wonders recorded in holy writ no instance can be produced where a young woman from *real* inclination has preferred an old man.

This is so much against me that I shall not be able, *I fear,* to contest the prize with you, yet under the encouragement you have given me I shall enter the list for so inestimable a jewel.

To Lafayette's hope that Washington one day would visit France the Commander-in-Chief answered sadly:

. . . remember, my good friend, that I am unacquainted with your language [and] am too far advanced in years to acquire a knowledge of it, and that to converse through the medium of an interpreter upon common occasions, especially with the *ladies,* must appear so extremely awkward, insipid, and uncouth, that I can scarce bear it in idea.

Another who was smitten with "the tenderest passion" that winter was Colonel Alexander Hamilton, who had fallen in love with Elizabeth, the twenty-two-year-old daughter of General Philip Schuyler. Everyone conceded that Elizabeth was a charmer and Hamilton was a devoted suitor who let no evening pass without pressing his courtship. Upon at least one occasion he returned to camp with his head so filled with thoughts of Elizabeth that he forgot the night's countersign for reentering the grounds at Morristown; he stood, embarrassed and irritated, a sentry's bayonet pressed against his breast, until someone came down from headquarters and whispered the proper "cabalistic" words in his ear. But all ended well: Hamilton married Elizabeth. She long outlived him and did not pass away until the age of ninety-two.

CHAPTER THREE

Death and Mutiny

March–May, 1780

March in Jockey Hollow continued the misery. Snow that apparently never would melt caused troops to slip and slide whenever they moved outdoors. Food was scanty and one old fellow boiled the sole of his shoe, declaring that he found it rather tasty. Surgeon Thacher realized that if conditions like the want of clothing and food did not end, everyone's patience would be exhausted.

In the belief that the devil finds work for idle hands, Washington determined that the troops must be kept busy. A high hill southwest of Morristown suited the Commander-in-Chief's purpose. Here his engineers planned an elaborate fortification. Every day details of soldiers appeared with their picks and shovels. Earthen mounds fringed the bastion. Embrasures for cannon gave the place an ominous look. How Washington expected to protect Morristown by building a defense that looked down directly on the town and could only be used effectively to blow Washington's headquarters to Kingdom Come baffled all speculation. The troops named the place Fort Nonsense.

Early April brought a different diversion—a nighttime surprise attack by the enemy. The assault fell upon a guard group under the command of Major Boyles of the Pennsylvania Line.

The air vibrated with the usual mixture of screamed curses, the sparks of clashing swords and bayonets, the little puffs of flame from charged muskets. Boyles fought furiously until he was mortally wounded, when his guard surrendered.

Enemy cheers were only a prelude to further deviltry. Flames pierced the night sky as houses were ignited by shadowy figures who rushed about with glowing torches. Among the fifty captives the British carried off were five or six officers.

The militia gave vigorous pursuit. Again there were exchanges of curses, sparking bayonets, and searing musket shots. A number of horses were retaken along with a considerable amount of valuable goods stolen from local residents.

*   *   *

The affray had scarcely ended when Morristown received distinguished visitors from afar. Washington journeyed to Philadelphia to meet his guests, and two hundred horsemen under Major Trescott formed a guard of honor as the General's party approached Morristown on April 19. The Chevalier de la Luzerne, minister of France, and another French gentleman acknowledged this salute. Also in the group was Don Juan de Miralles, a Spaniard considered to be of great distinction. The boom of thirteen cannon signaled their arrival. Riding in elegant carriages, the foreign dignitaries were greeted by virtually everyone living in the surrounding countryside. The object of the visit, Surgeon Thacher said, was "to take a distant view of the enemy's works, on York and Staten Islands, and of the different posts of our army."

Five days later a grand review was arranged under Baron von Steuben with four battalions of the Continental army. Governor Livingston "and his lady" were among those who sat on the stage erected for the occasion. Again there was a thirteen-gun salute. "Our troops," Thacher wrote, "exhibited a truly military performance, and performed the manœuvres and evolutions in a manner, which afforded much satisfaction to our Commander in Chief." As the troops passed the stage, the applause became thunderous.

A ball was held that night at the Morris Hotel. The artillery supplied an exhibition of fireworks. Unhappily Miralles came down with an illness which was called pulmonic fever. Five days later Luzerne again reviewed the troops before departing for Philadelphia and leaving his Spanish friend behind.

Miralles expired on April 28 and since he was a gentleman of rank in the Spanish court who had represented his country in America for almost a year, an extravagant funeral was arranged in Morristown. "The corpse was dressed in rich state, and exposed to public view, as is customary in Europe," Thacher reported. Thousands of people came from miles around to view the open coffin, which was lined with black velvet. The wealthy Spanish gentleman, who bequeathed to each of his three daughters one hundred pounds sterling, was laid out in a scarlet coat, embroidered with a heavy lace collar. A three-cornered hat sat upon his neatly cued wig and a costly watch, covered with diamonds, rested in his breast pocket. His legs were sheathed in white silk stockings and diamond buckles adorned his knees and shoes. His fingers were ornamented with numerous jeweled rings.

The cortege, led by Washington and members of Congress and followed by soldiers and civilians on foot, extended for more than a mile as it slowly progressed to the Presbyterian burying-ground. Here at the graveside a Spanish priest conducted the Roman Catholic service. A guard was posted at the grave "lest our soldiers should be tempted to dig for hidden treasure." Soldiers, bereft of so many necessities of life, naturally grumbled over so much wealth being buried underground.

Under an impoverished Congress, inflation continued to run rampant. In May, ordered to march to the South, Kalb again addressed himself to this bedevilment:

Provisions and other articles are growing dearer and dearer, being now double what they were a year ago, even if paid in gold, one dollar of which is now equal to sixty dollars in paper. My march costs me enormous sums. I cannot travel with my equipage, and am therefore compelled to resort to inns. My six months' earning will scarce defray the most indispensable outlay of a single day. Not long since I was compelled to take a night's lodging at a private house. For a bad supper and grog for myself, my three companions, and three servants, I was charged, on going off without a breakfast next day, the sum of eight hundred and fifty dollars. The lady of the house politely added that she had charged nothing for the rooms, and would leave the compensation for them to my discretion, although three or four hundred dollars would not be too much for the inconvenience to which she had been put by myself and my followers. And these are the people who talk about sacrificing their all in the cause of liberty! Everything else is in proportion to these figures; an ordinary horse is worth $20,000, I say twenty thousand dollars!

Early in May of a long-delayed spring, Lafayette returned to Morristown. The Marquis announced that he was now a proud father and had named his son George Washington Lafayette. The Commander-in-Chief joyously embraced the young nobleman.

* * *

Lafayette had other exciting news for Washington—six French ships of the line and 6,000 troops were sailing for Rhode Island under orders to join the Continentals in a joint attack upon the British in New York. D'Estaing would not lead the expedition, and both Washington and Lafayette could appreciate one estimate of that admiral: "Had only his seamanship equalled his courage!" The Marquis was most emphatic in his statement that Louis XVI expected these forces to act directly in accordance with Washington's wishes.

Washington needed to rest his military woes and hopes on Lafayette's young shoulders. As long ago as the late fall of 1778 what was vaingloriously called the American Southern Army—700 Continentals and 150 militia under General Robert Howe—had been routed by the British from Savannah in a battle Surgeon Thacher heard had required only fifty-five minutes. Thereafter Tory sentiment had spread across Georgia like weevils in a cotton patch. Cornwallis and Clinton then had put aside their mutual animosity to plan a combined land-and-naval campaign against Charleston, the Carolinas, and ultimately Virginia and Chesapeake Bay.

Howe was replaced in command by Benjamin Lincoln and reenforcements under Kalb sent to ease the tension in the Carolinas. In early April Clinton and Cornwallis had approached Charleston in a malicious mood, and Lincoln with only 1,200 troops of the South Carolina and Virginia Lines, plus 2,000 militia, had reason to toss in his sleep (if sleep, indeed, he ever had, once the full facts were ascertained). Clinton and Cornwallis had sailed on Charleston with about 8,500 troops, one third of whom were Loyalists. Ninety transports, escorted by fourteen men-of-war, had carried these invaders; what ships the infant American navy could spare—three frigates and a sloop-of-war—were sent to dispute the landing, which was like trying to put out a fire in a powder magazine with a handful of sand. The British completely befuddled Lincoln by disembarking the bulk of their forces on his unprotected land side. Still, the American general might have cut his way out had he acted quickly; but Lincoln loitered and by British estimate the fall of Charleston cost him 5,500 captives, including many armed or infirm civilians, and three Continental ships.

Where would Clinton and his ships next appear? Washington would not be able to answer that question until June 18, and before then considerable action nearer Morristown would keep the headquarters staff thoroughly occupied.

* * *

After hard months of snow that had killed fruit trees and winter wheat, the spring had continued cold and unpleasant, especially to hungry men who learned that cattle in the area were perishing for want of fodder. "One year rolls over another—and without some change—we are hastening to our ruin," Washington lamented.

Rumors of how many Jerseymen were reaping handsome profits from the war hardly lifted the spirits of soldiers near starvation in Jockey Hollow. It was well known that those who operated along the coast from Raritan Bay to Cape May were flourishing from privateering, a nice description of legalized piracy. Ports of minor account before the war like Toms River and Tuckerton were now thriving commercial centers. As many as thirty raiders crowded into Little Egg Harbor at one time and no vessel sailing the Jersey coast, unless armed or accompanied by a man-of-war, was safe from these marauders. Those who could endure a sun that broiled them like lobsters while the mosquitoes almost ate them alive became rich attending the salt vats in the numerous marshes. And for those with hard money all kinds of trade were profitable. Thus John Neilson, who had read the Declaration of Independence with such passion in the town square in New Brunswick, saw nothing wrong in buying salt in Toms River at fifteen dollars a bushel and selling it in Morristown at thirty-five dollars.

Discontent mounted in Jockey Hollow when, under pressure from Washington, Congress promised half pay for life and land grants to officers of the line who remained throughout the war. Why not give the same bounty to officers of the staff, among others? Perhaps Surgeon Thacher, who was not among the favored, voiced the most restrained complaint: "Equal justice should be the motto of every government."

May 25 was a pleasant day but still the men around Private Martin kept "growling like sore-headed dogs." Washington faced the first of three mutinies on New Jersey soil.

* * *

The Connecticut troops had returned to their old encampment, expecting to find life a little brighter, but, as Martin recollected, "the monster Hunger still attended us" and the best the Yankees received was "a little nasty bread and a little beef, about every other day." Men who "loved their country"—and Martin used the phrase without shallow sentimentality—were up against a bitter dilemma: "to starve to death, or break up the army, give all up and go home." The situation seemed unendurable. "Here was the army starved and naked," Martin wrote, "and there their country sitting still and expecting the army to do notable things while fainting from sheer starvation." Somewhere there had to come a breaking point.

It arrived unexpectedly at evening roll call on May 25. Men snapped back at their officers, disobeyed orders, and one soldier disputed an orderly sergeant who was giving details for next day. Before stomping from the parade ground the sergeant called the soldier "a mutinous rascal"; the accused man, in a passionate heat, banged the butt of his musket on the ground and called: "Who will parade with me?" To the soldier's astonishment the entire regiment fell in.

No one really knew what to do until the Fourth Regiment arrived to join in the parade. Now it was decided to ask the other regiments of the brigade, the Third and Sixth, to strengthen the demonstration. So that nobody could be singled out for court-martial while this recruiting proceeded, the drummer was given special instructions to enable all regiments to set off "with music playing." Officers came on the run, confused and cussing, for the night had turned quite dark. A guard was stationed so that the men could not return to the huts for their weapons; some scuffling resulted; and an extremely popular officer, Colonel Return Johnathan Meigs, was unintentionally wounded by a bayonet.

Anger increased when the rebellious troops discovered how the officers' guard kept them from returning to their huts. The brigade's grumbling was renewed on all sides. From the rear a soldier shouted:

"Halt in front!"

To this senseless bit of rebellion the officers reacted with equal senselessness; they jumped upon the culprit "like wolves on a sheep," intending to make of this "mutinous rascal" an example not to be forgotten, "but [as Martin reported] the bayonets of the men pointing at [the] breasts [of the officers] as thick as hatchel teeth, compelled them quickly to relinquish their hold of them." Even angry, hungry men valued dignity.

The officers turned from threats to trickery. One, feigning to have come down from headquarters, announced:

"There is good news for you, boys. There has just arrived a large drove of cattle."

"Go and butcher them," replied a skeptical voice in the ranks.

Lieutenant Colonel John Sumner of the Fourth Regiment de-

clared that he could "persuade" his boys to return peaceably to
quarters; he pleaded with his men, all of whom seemed to have
lost any sense of hearing, which threw their commander into a
violent rage; then calming down, Sumner again expended "a
whole quiver of the arrows of his rhetoric," which once more
brought the lieutenant colonel to the border of apoplexy, whereupon he left the field "chewing the cud of resentment all the
way." The other officers followed him. Meanwhile, Pennsylvania
troops, tricked by the darkness and actually believing they were
participating in the mutiny, were led by their officers to surround
the rebels from Connecticut. The ruse threatened not to work
once the Pennsylvanians understood the nature of the duplicity.

"Let us join them," they said. "Let us join the Yankees.
They are good fellows and have no notion of lying here like
fools and starving."

Rather than run the risk of having the mutiny spread to the
Pennsylvanians, the officers led their men back to the huts. The
Connecticut mutineers also decided to return to quarters, laying
by their arms and

venting our spleen at our country and government, then at our officers,
and then at ourselves for our imbecility in staying there and starving in
detail for an ungrateful people who did not care what became of us, so
they could enjoy themselves while we were keeping a cruel enemy from
them.

Colonel Walter Stewart—ladies in Philadelphia called him *"the
Irish Beauty"*—and other officers of the Pennsylvania Line arrived at the Connecticut camp to ascertain the source of the
trouble.

A galling dialogue ensued. The Yankees declared that they
were beyond bearing further "pusillanimity" when times were
growing worse instead of "mending." But Stewart also was told
the Connecticut regiments were "unwilling to desert the cause
of our country when in distress." Stewart asked why they had
not discussed the matter with their officers, which drew a stinging laugh. The Connecticut officers, Stewart insisted, were

"gentlemen" who could understand justified grievances; but the officers also suffered, he said, adding: "We all suffer." The other day he was offered a partridge for six pence, but had not the price. He praised the Connecticut troops for the "immortal honor" they had won and promised to consult personally with their officers. Some profit must have come from that interview for Martin reported: "Our stir did us some good in the end, for we had provisions directly after, so we had no great cause for complaint for some time."

The Connecticut disturbance shocked Washington who told Congress that the uprising "has given me more concern than any thing that has happened."

Next morning Martin and his comrades marched to the parade grounds in Morristown where they "performed a variety of military evolutions" under Steuben's direction. In an almost hilarious mood eight or ten fieldpieces were fired to make "a great noise." Each man was awarded a gill of rum, which, drunk on an empty stomach, produced some silly acts.

* * *

May 26 was a busy day at Jockey Hollow and Morristown. Eleven soldiers were condemned to die for various crimes. The three who were to be shot were pardoned by Washington, and the others marched to the gallows. Surgeon Thacher found the scene "most solemn and affecting." Carts bounced "the wretched criminals" to their place of execution where the chaplain, "in a very pathetic manner," impressed on them the "heinousness" of their crimes and the "justice" of their sentences. The tale was the type that Thacher loved to relate:

The criminals were placed side by side, on the scaffold, with halters around their necks, their coffins before their eyes, their graves open to their view, and thousands of spectators bemoaning their awful doom. The moment approaches when every eye is fixed in expectation of beholding the agonies of death,—the eyes of the victims are already closed from the light of this world. At this awful moment, while their fervent prayers are ascending to Heaven, an officer comes forward and reads a reprieve for seven of them, by the Commander in Chief. The trembling criminals are now divested of the implements of death, and their bleeding hearts leap for joy. . . .

One poor devil remained on the scaffold, a man guilty of forging discharges "by which he and more than a hundred soldiers had left the army." He was a cool rascal, counseling soldiers to remain faithful to their country and advising officers not to supply troops with excuses for mutiny.

He was very critical of his halter. The knot, he told the hangman, was not correctly made. He was too heavy a man, he added, for the strength of the rope. An adamant creature, the hangman gave no indication of hearing. The victim fixed the knot around his own neck and "he was swung off instantly." The rope broke and the forger was badly bruised. Calmly reascending the ladder, the condemned man called:

"I told you the rope was not strong enough. Do get a stronger one."

This time the victim was obliged and the nasty work finished.

So swung the pendulum of camp life at Morristown—from the death of a Spanish nobleman to that of a forger.

CHAPTER FOUR

Surprise at Springfield

June, 1780

Baron Wilhelm von Knyphausen, who had been left in charge
of New York when Clinton joined Cornwallis in the conquest
of Charleston, was still a vigorous, imaginative man in his sixty-
third year. His military training had been gained under Frederick the Great, and it is doubtful if in that age a better tutor
existed. Steuben's first claim to notoriety came when he sailed
to America with 12,000 German troops. Having no idea of
where the colonies were, he could not believe so many days
should pass before reaching his destination and asked the master
of his vessel, "Captain, ain't we hah past America?"

Once Knyphausen reached the colonies no one had to question
his whereabouts, for he fought with distinction in the battles at
Long Island, White Plains, Brandywine, and Monmouth. Among
his chief characteristics was a thorough mistrust of the fighting
qualities of mercenaries and native Tories. As the chilly spring
of 1780 arrived, New York Loyalists hounded the Baron to
cross the Hudson and rally New Jersey Tories to the cause.
Knyphausen indulged in little hit-and-run raids, so scattered and
often so pointless that Washington was as much confused by the
reports of his spies as by Knyphausen's actions.

A strong system of lookout stations supported Morristown.

Every high peak along the Watchung range possessed its signal station manned by local militia. Tar barrels nailed to shorn trees could signal alarm with smoke by day and flames at night. At Turkey Hill (Summit) stood "Old Sow," the big cannon carted from Princeton, whose boom at any hour could call farmers in the surrounding countryside to come running with their guns. The 3rd New Jersey Line under Colonel Elias Dayton, supported by militia, held the outpost at Elizabethtown; General Dickinson's 1,500 troops covered positions from Amboy to Hackensack. Washington's own forces protected the mountain passes to Morristown at Springfield, Scotch Plains, Middlebrook and Plainfield.

The pressure on Knyphausen to make a full-scale attack into New Jersey increased with mounting Loyalist confidence after the fall of Charleston. A confidential memorandum from Clinton, arriving on the same ship that brought news of the Charleston victory, outlined a two-pronged movement by which Washington's army could be trapped in Jockey Hollow and cut off from its base of supplies. While one wing forced the passes at Springfield, Clinton proposed, the other should slam shut Washington's "back door" by way of the gaps at Middlebrook and Plainfield, thus bringing Washington into the comparatively flat plain beyond the Watchungs. At the same time Clinton urged a feint in force up the Hudson.

Knyphausen was so intrigued by the plan that he missed an important point: Clinton intended to cooperate in this campaign. In this respect the Baron "jumped the gun." While troops on transports sailed up the Hudson, Knyphausen set out on the morning of June 6 to end the war.

*   *   *

Washington, who remained uninformed of Clinton's whereabouts, feared for both Morristown and West Point. His immediate concern, of course, was Knyphausen who had made a nighttime crossing from Staten Island.

As the sunrise burned through the morning mists of June 6 the force of Hessians and British appeared formidable. The

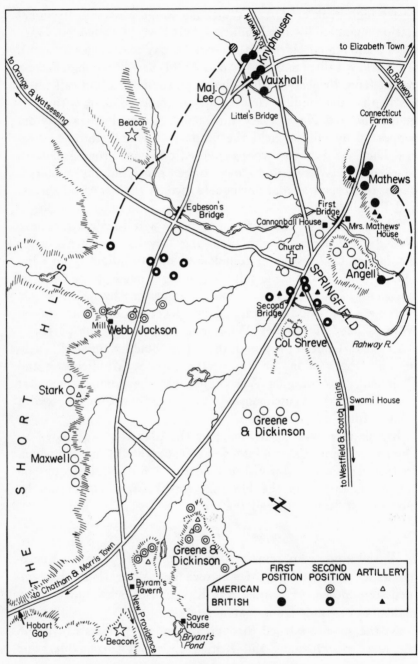

Battle of Springfield, June 23, 1780

competent General William Sterling led the advance on Elizabethtown, to which Simcoe's Tory Rangers already had crossed,
while General Edward Mathews commanded the center of the
line and General William Tryon the rear. In all 6,000 troops
were involved. A sparse equipage allowed only one fieldpiece to
a regiment and the invaders carried seven days' rations.

For young Sterling the battle quickly ended when he was
fatally wounded in the thigh by a sniper's musketball. Knyphausen strode forward to take command of the charge on Elizabethtown. The Baron's brigades were too numerous to justify a
serious stand by Dayton's 3rd New Jersey. Slowly, grudgingly,
reloading as they fell back along the road, Dayton's troops kept
their heads though the enemy fired briskly. As the mists evaporated, the Royal Artillery was rolled out.

But the big guns produced a result that Knyphausen had not
anticipated. Certainly the shots did little harm among Dayton's
retreating soldiers but the noise of the cannon warned the country around Springfield of the approaching danger. Soon "Old
Sow" shook the ground around Turkey Hill and tar barrels atop
their shorn trees on South Mountain sent columns of smoke
spiralling upward.

Farmers with their guns responded to the alarm. Simcoe's
Rangers, galloping ahead to disperse these rustics, encountered
a situation not unlike that which had overwhelmed the British
at Lexington in 1775. Every rock, tree, barn, stone wall, and
house shielded a defending rifleman. Men used to picking a
squirrel from the limb of a tree found Simcoe's masses a challenge a boy could handle. Quickly the farmers thinned the ranks
of the advancing rangers.

Knyphausen meanwhile found the opposition unexpectedly
stubborn as he pushed forward from Elizabethtown to Connecticut Farms (Union). Behind him the road was littered with
Hessian and British dead. Near the Farms was a knoll not more
than a mile and a half from where a bridge crossed the Rahway
River at Springfield. The knoll, providing a natural rallying
point, soon was aswarm with the troops of Dayton's 3rd New

Jersey. Meanwhile Ogden's militia and Maxwell's brigade supplied support on the Springfield side of the river.

Alarms still sounded, seemingly for miles away. Knyphausen halted and, in a sober mood, contemplated his next move. "After the European custom," his soldiers pillaged and burned the abandoned dwellings of Connecticut Farms. But the flames nowhere equaled the atrocity that befell the wife of Parson Caldwell. The British bore a particular grudge against Caldwell, who served as chaplain to Dayton's Jerseymen and once had been Washington's quartermaster. A burly Redcoat knocked in the door to the parsonage and found Mrs. Caldwell crouching in a corner with her infant. Two bullets, fired at "point blank" range, killed mother and child.

This barbarity, however, may have been induced by the stubbornness of American opposition, for as the Hessian Major Adjutant General Baurmeister noted, "At Connecticut Farms the Jägers met with unaccustomed resistence, the rebels holding off our vanguard with fixed bayonets."

Washington responded to the emergency with skill and speed. He accompanied a good part of his army into the Short Hills, prepared to cope with any situation. Riders were sped to Philadelphia, not only to summon the horsemen of Major "Light Horse Harry" Lee, but also to demand of Congress two hundred carts and wagons to carry the army's supplies to safety at Easton, Pennsylvania. The headquarters of the Commander-in-Chief at Bryant's (Byrams?) Tavern, in the rear of Springfield near Bryant's Pond, bustled with activity. Washington knew that he was being saved by half-starved and weary troops. The corps of Lafayette, Greene, Stirling, and Stark came forward to relieve the bone-tired soldiers of Maxwell and Dickinson.

Luckily—for Knyphausen as well as Washington—a thunderstorm ended the fighting at twilight. Baurmeister did not underrate the gameness of the American pursuit as Knyphausen fell back toward Elizabethtown: "The enemy followed, and, supposing that the greater part of our troops had already crossed over to Staten Island, fell upon our advanced post, the 22nd Regiment." What Baurmeister did not understand was that men who had seen their homes in flames intended to pepper their enemy as long as hope remained of gaining revenge. "Their attack," Baurmeister wrote, missing this point entirely, "was disorderly, and when our post was supported, the rebels withdrew on their own to the extreme end of Elizabethtown."

*   *   *

For more than a fortnight, Knyphausen remained virtually immobile with part of his force camped on Staten Island and part at Elizabethtown Point. New Jersey militia, numbering well over a thousand, tried to stir up a fight but gained little except the occasional shifting of outposts. A stone bridge over a creek at Elizabethtown divided the hostile pickets. Between lay "a no-man's land."

One evidence of Washington's perturbation was the placement of lookouts at intervals of fifty miles along the Jersey shore to watch for the return of Clinton's victorious armada. Washington, responding to military instinct, moved to West Point in preparation for a sudden assault up the Hudson. Did this judgment by Washington justify exposing Morristown with the provisions, baggage, and stores of his army to probable capture?

On June 17 Clinton and his fleet were sighted standing in for Sandy Hook. This news was relayed to Washington next morning. The Commander-in-Chief ordered the use of any means of transport available to remove all but immediately essential stores from northern New Jersey to Pennsylvania. Greene became a busy quartermaster general. Under instructions "to get this army in moving condition," Greene must hurry 1,700 barrels of flour from Trenton to the North River forts. Pleas to rally their militia sent galloping aides to the governors of New York and Connecticut and reinforcements were requested from the Council of Massachusetts.

"Ride night and day!" Washington urged his messengers.

All officers remaining in Morristown were ordered to join the Commander-in-Chief at Springfield.

To Washington's apprehensiveness was added a further report that Clinton had landed six of his vessels at Verplanck's

Point. "Light Horse Harry" Lee paced Washington's headquarters like a disciple of gloom, absolutely certain that Clinton
would be at West Point in less than forty-eight hours. On
June 21 Washington moved a large part of his army northward
to meet this contingency while the troops remaining at Springfield were placed under Greene's command.

Two days later, at Clinton's prodding, Knyphausen arose
from his seeming slumber, renewing the battle for Springfield
and Morristown.

                              *   *   *

"Old Sow" really was responsible for this invasion since her
three shots, telling Washington it was safe to move, also informed Clinton of his advantage in New Jersey. A rapid advance began on Elizabethtown and it was not until Connecticut
Farms that the Continentals offered any substantial resistance.
Clinton called out veterans who had fought from Bunker Hill
to Charleston—dragoons, regiments of the Foot, guards, Hessians of Landgrave, Bose, Anspach, Stern, Jaegers, and *chasseurs
du corps,* artillery, rangers—about 5,000 troops.

Spies told Greene what he must expect. The Rhode Islander's
defense did credit to the books on military science Henry Knox
had sold him years ago. In advance, Dayton's 3rd New Jersey
held off the enemy at Connecticut Farms while all the Americans retreated behind the barrier of the Rahway River at Springfield. Here on a hillock west of the river they posted a single
cannon, belonging to Colonel Angell's Rhode Island regiment.

The enemy now broke into two columns. Colonel Mathews
commanded the right, aided by Simcoe's Rangers and some of
Cortlandt Skinner's Tory volunteers. At Vauxhall, some distance
above Springfield, these forces crossed the river. Lee was waiting
for them and for a time the fighting was touch and go.

Meanwhile, since the flooring of the two bridges crossing the
river at Springfield had been torn up, Knyphausen with the left
and principal column wished he had never left Staten Island.
Angell's Rhode Islanders with their one cannon experienced
forty minutes of sheer joy. Jaegers trying to rush across the

cross pieces of the bridges danced a pretty ballet trying to dodge Angell's fire.

Angell cursed his luck when the Hessians discovered that the water in the river was only waist deep and could be forded. To add to this discouragement Mathews' column swung down the road from Vauxhall. Greene was not the sort of fool who would stand and see his forces squeezed to death: he withdrew all his troops to the heights controlling the passes. Angell had lost about a quarter of his men; he, least of all, could argue the wisdom in Greene's withdrawal.

Knyphausen by now had acquired a thorough respect for the quality of the American defense. Reserves under Maxwell and Stark, poised on the Short Hills, could disrupt any British attack by falling on the flanks. The ingenious Greene called Colonels Israel Shreve, Israel Angell and Elias Dayton to join him where the higher ground fronted crossing roads, inviting Mathews' forces, if they cared to advance, to march into the jaws of a trap with Greene on one side and Maxwell and Stark on the other.

For Knyphausen decisions became increasingly difficult and disheartening. The fact that his enemy had advanced without baggage told the Hessian the Americans did not fear for Morristown falling by a sudden *coup*.

Knyphausen rested his men in Springfield an hour and a half, thankful that the effectiveness of the American cannonade did not equal its liveliness. At this point, however, any cause for gratitude ended; even then, in all probability, there formed in the mind of one of Knyphausen's subordinates a sentence he later committed to paper: "I regret from the depths of my heart the great loss the Jägers took to no greater purpose."

The inevitable sign of a British retreat appeared—the flames of burning houses within their lines. Fire outlined the shape of the old Presbyterian Church and fields of ripening wheat were destroyed. Greene detached troops in an effort to prevent the destruction and pillaging of Springfield but only five dwellings remained when the enemy departed. The whole foray puzzled Greene as to why it had been attempted at all.

New Jersey soil, then and forever, impressed Knyphausen as a bed of red coals. His retreat this time was rapid and single-minded. There was no turnabout at Elizabethtown Point for a last-minute stand. British and Hessians alike fled over pontoon bridges to Staten Island. Clinton never could compose an explanation of the rout that satisfied the War Office in London.

New Jersey troops, on the edge of rebellion, found their spirits further depressed by the needless destruction of Springfield and, to a lesser extent, the devastation of Connecticut Farms. One militiaman spoke for all:

The whole scene was one of gloomy horror—a dead horse, a broken carriage of a fieldpiece, a town laid in ashes, the former inhabitants standing over the ruins of their dwellings, and the unburied dead, covered with blood and with the flies that were devouring it, filled me with melancholy feelings, till I was ready to say—Is the contest worth all this?

CHAPTER FIVE

Mutineers

July, 1780–January, 1781

A pasquinade posted in New York City ridiculed the British military invasion of New Jersey:

> Old Knip [Knyphausen]
> And old Clip [Gen. Robertson]
> Went to the Jersey shore
> The rebel rogues to beat;
> But at Yankee Farms
> They took the alarms
> At little harms,
> And quickly did retreat.
>
> Then after two days' wonder
> Marched boldly to Springfield town,
> And sure they'd knock the rebels down;
> But as their foes
> Gave them some blows,
> They, like the wind,
> Soon changed their mind,
> And in a crack
> Returned back
> From not one third their number!

The *Political Magazine* of London published the lampoon in August.

Generally the Continentals enjoyed their march northward. Colonel Alexander Hamilton's head reeled at the industrial possibilities of New Jersey once he beheld the falls of the Passaic. No more than the energy of nature needed to be harnessed to perform manufacturing wonders! The then powerful Passaic had cut clefts in the rock as deep as seventy feet. There was one part of the falls, the Continentals heard, the depth of which never had been ascertained. In wonder they watched the torrents of water rushing to "the huge cavities below." The cavern beneath this precipice was one of the deepest, and, wrote Surgeon Thacher, "Such is the astonishing depth of this receptacle, that the water neither foams nor forms whirlpools by the rushing current, but is calm and undisturbed."

Thacher came upon a discovery which he told with relish:

In the afternoon we were invited to visit another curiosity in the neighborhood. This is a monster in the human form. He is twenty seven years of age, his face from the upper part of his forehead to the end of his chin, measures twenty inches, and round the upper part of his head is twenty one inches, his eyes and nose are remarkably large and prominent, chin long and pointed. His features are coarse, irregular and disgusting, and his voice is rough and sonorous. His body is only twenty seven inches in length, his limbs are small, and much deformed, and he has the use of one hand only. He has never been able to stand, or sit up, as he cannot support the enormous weight of his head; but lies constantly in a large cradle, with his head supported on pillows. He is visited by great numbers of people, and is peculiarly fond of the company of clergymen, always inquiring for them among his visitors, and taking great pleasure in receiving religious instruction. General Washington made him a visit, and asked, "whether he was a whig or tory?" He replied, that, "he had never taken an *active* part on either side."

July brought the good news that a French fleet commanded by Admiral the Chevalier de Ternay had anchored at Rhode Island accompanied by 6,000 troops under the distinguished general, Jean Baptiste Donatien de Vimeur, Comte de Rochambeau. With his instinct for niceties, Washington "recommended to the officers of our army, to wear cockades of black and white, intermixed, as a symbol of friendship for our French allies, who wear white cockades." General Heath, sent to greet the Admiral and Count at Newport, missed his appointment and so for a night the Frenchmen walked empty streets stared at by "only a few sad and frightened faces in the windows." Rochambeau passed the night in a local inn. His gifts of Gallic chivalry must have been magnetic, for he convinced the town's authorities of the affection that had brought him to America. That night bells rang in Newport and fireworks illuminated the sky. Thereafter French sailors and soldiers were lavish in their praise of Rhode Island girls.

The arrival three days later off Sandy Hook of a six-ship British naval reenforcement under Admiral Thomas Graves weakened hopes of a combined French and American assault on New York. Washington, watching Clinton from New Jersey, asked Benedict Arnold to command his left wing, but Arnold, using a lame leg as an excuse, requested the easier command on the right at West Point. Washington consented. Greene took charge of the left wing. For the Americans there was no choice but to await further developments. Because of the scarcity of food Washington moved toward Fort Lee, a region that promised more bountiful supplies.

*   *   *

July, already celebrated by the arrival of the French, also marked the brief appearance of Tempe Wick in history. The Wick farm was located in Jockey Hollow, where some Continental troops remained. Tempe (Temperance?) was unafraid of these countrymen and rode her fine horse over the roads around Morristown. The girl had no notion of how these men, after a winter of hunger and deprivation, believed they were entitled to impress anything in the neighborhood that would serve them.

One day a group of Continentals blocked the road as Tempe was riding. One grabbed the bridle while the others, as though bickering at a sale, discussed the animal's fine points. Tempe listened in astonishment. Why these men, as bad as Hessian or British raiders, intended to steal her horse!

For a moment the hand that clutched the bridle relaxed its grasp. Tempe spurred her horse, smashing through the soldiers at a gallop. Accounts that say guns were fired in the air to frighten her are probably fictional, but, in any event, Tempe soon outdistanced her pursuers. The girl was perplexed. If she placed the horse in its stall, the soldiers would quickly steal it; if she hid it in the woods, they would follow its tracks. Tempe acted on impulse, leading her horse through kitchen and parlor into the downstairs guest bedroom where the window was kept shuttered when the room was unoccupied. She stroked the horse soothingly while the men, searching barn and woods, could not understand how they had been outwitted. For three weeks—or until the soldiers were ordered elsewhere—she kept her horse here, and since there was risk in going to the barn for oats, the animal was often indulged in such delicacies as biscuit and soft bread.

Had Washington remained in Morristown, Tempe probably would have given him a piece of her mind concerning the low character of his troops. But it was as well that the General was spared this lecture; not only was he stymied in the North, but sadness also tainted most of the dispatches he received from the South.

*   *   *

Cornwallis, at last gaining his own command at Charleston, hungered for fame, and he found a willing compatriot in Banastre Tarleton, whose only claim to military glory thus far was as one of the raiders who had captured General Charles Lee near Basking Ridge. Thickset and muscular, yet gross of manner and ungenerous of eye, this British cavalry leader added a new phrase to the English language—"Tarleton's quarter," meaning the wholesale butchery of opponents. Within three months Cornwallis and Tarleton practically smashed the patriot cause in South Carolina. They strung a line of fortified posts westward from Camden to within ninety-six miles of the frontier and added garrisons at Savannah and Port Royal to that at Charleston.

The Continental Congress made a political choice in selecting Horatio Gates for command of its Southern Department. The "Old Grandmother," advancing to battle at Camden with no more than 1,000 Continentals and 2,000 militia, seemed to be approaching military senility. Instead of marching through a well-stocked farmland that was only a few miles longer, Gates led famishing troops already ill from stuffing themselves on peaches, green corn, and raw meat after several foodless days, through hostile pine forests. Soldiers who added fatigue to hunger and dysentery were no match for Cornwallis. Camden, fought August 16, 1780, was a disaster from the moment the American militia broke before the first British bayonet charge. Although mortally wounded, Kalb tried to stem the collapse with the Maryland and Delaware Line. About sixty escaped, but nowhere as speedily as Gates, who leaped astride Dreadnought, one of the greatest racing horses in the South. Perhaps for practice, Tarleton shot a Quaker boy playing in his front yard.

Flushed with the laurels of Camden, Cornwallis, clearly eager to gain the supreme command, planned a new strategy. In late September he divided his army into three columns—one to protect his right and secure a base of supplies at Wilmington, North Carolina, and the Cape Fear River, another that he would lead to further glorious triumphs over Gates, and, on the left, a third under Major Patrick Ferguson whose Loyalist forces were to clear the western mountains of North Carolina of Rebels.

Atop King's Mountain with 1,400 troops, Ferguson "defied God Almighty and all the rebels out of hell to overcome him." Old Dan Morgan, awaking on the morning of October 7 and damning his arthritis, grew cheerful at Ferguson's challenge. Among boys as young as fourteen and men in their sixties, Dan limped about, telling each to stuff four or five musket balls in his mouth. Nothing was better for keeping the saliva flowing and slaking thirst, Dan declared. Morgan placed his riflemen behind trees and told them to show that plagued Scot, Ferguson, how frontiersmen fought. Afterward, Dan chuckled, the bullets had buzzed "like yellow jackets." Ferguson fell, wounded, and his anguish was eased by a "pocket pistol" in the hand of a friend. The British charged with demoniacal screams, but in less than an hour were waving the white flag and throwing down their arms. To the historian, Morison, King's Mountain was "the Trenton of the Southern campaign."

*   *   *

While neighborhood wolves and hogs gnawing on the loosely covered British carcasses on the slopes of King's Mountain became a shocking sight, the people were more thunderstruck by the news in October from the North. Three New York militiamen, trying to increase their incomes by robbing travelers in the so-called "neutral ground" of Tarrytown Road, fell upon a horseman who identified himself as John Anderson, a merchant. From the outset Clinton had warned Major John André, with his British rank, never to disguise himself as a civilian for then he could be executed as a spy. But with Washington approaching West Point for an inspection, Benedict Arnold had summoned André to an emergency meeting and had signed the pass by which he could enter American lines as John Anderson.

In one of André's boots were the plans by which for over a year Arnold and his wife had conspired to betray West Point to the British for the sum of $20,000. Arnold could give no excuse for what Greene called *"treason* of the blackest dye" except the excessive indebtedness he had contracted courting the former Peggy Shippen and supporting the three children by his first marriage. Arnold had even revealed the places Washington would be in case Clinton wished to send an expedition to capture the American Commander-in-Chief.

Nathanael Greene was quite right: Arnold was a thorough scoundrel. After chastising his hysterical wife for appearing in a morning gown too scanty "to be seen by a gentleman of the family, much less by many strangers," Arnold deserted Peggy and fled to his own safety aboard a British warship appropriately named the *Vulture*. When Washington reached West Point with André's plans that did not implicate Peggy Arnold, as she deserved to be, the General encountered a distraught woman who sobbed all day. Peggy's screeching denial that she knew anything of the conspiracy till Arnold had confessed that morning and declared "he must banish himself from his country and from her forever" wrenched Washington's heart with sympathy. Alexander Hamilton also was convinced by Peggy's theatrics; so much so, in fact, that Hamilton wrote his fiancée: "She received us in bed with every circumstance that would interest our sympathy, and her sufferings were so eloquent that I wished myself her brother to have a right to become her defender. . . ."

Washington could send Peggy home to Philadelphia with an escort and in time repair Arnold's long neglect of the interior of West Point, but he could not refuse to hang André as a spy. Clinton offered any exchange of prisoners Washington would accept to save André, but since Washington would consider Benedict Arnold as the only proper substitute, a betrayal of a betrayor that Clinton's military honor could not condone, André was doomed.

Surgeon Thacher, who apparently never missed a performance at the gibbet, saw a neat and poised André climb into a cart and stand upon his coffin. He took off his hat and stood with hands on hips. Thacher heard him say: "It will be but a momentary pang." The hangman arrived, his face hideously disguised by blackened grease. André put the halter around his own neck, tied a silk handkerchief about his eyes and handed another to his executioner for binding the major's arms behind his back. Wrote Thacher: "The wagon was very suddenly drawn from under the gallows, which, together with the length of rope, gave him a most tremendous swing back and forth, but in a few moments he hung entirely still. . . ."

*   *   *

The winter of 1780–81 has been called, quite correctly, "the nadir of the American cause." North and South a scattered army was festering under wounds too long unhealed. The Pennsylvania Line under Wayne remained at Morristown and the

New Jersey Line billeted within its own borders about Pompton. New England troops occupied West Point, among other strategic posts in the Highlands. The New York Line wintered at Albany. With Washington headquartered at New Windsor, across the Hudson from West Point, the Commander-in-Chief scarcely had intimate contact with his army.

The affair over Tempe Wick and her horse simply was a symptom of a deeper illness. Among the Pennsylvanians in Morristown that sickness was aggravated by the poverty of the veterans and the prosperity of new recruits who had agreed to short enlistments for attractive bounties. The Pennsylvanians were in "drooping spirits"—for want of liquor as much as anything—leading one historian to comment: "It was inevitable that the men should contrast their privations with the luxury of Philadelphia, known to them by report, and with the prosperity of the countryside about Morristown, flowing with milk and honey, or, more pertinently, hard cider and applejack."

Grumbles turned to growls and then to mutterings of mutiny. The revolt came on New Year's Day, 1781. Obviously the action had been well planned for that evening and was carried out almost as though every man among the 2,000 mutineers knew exactly what was expected of him. Ammunition and artillery were seized and two fieldpieces spiked. Four other fieldpieces were dragged along as the troops marched off for Philadelphia, determined that Congress must redress their grievances. Officers who tried to stop them were badly treated: one killed, two mortally wounded, others injured by muskets, bayonets or stones.

Not even Wayne's popularity could turn back his men. Once the General cocked his pistol and a dozen bayonets were pointed at his breast.

"We respect you and love you," the Pennsylvanians said. "Often you have led us into the field of battle, but we are no longer under your command. We warned you to be on your guard. If you fire your pistols, or attempt to enforce your commands, we shall put you instantly to death."

Pleading, cursing, expostulating, threatening, Wayne followed his mutineers to Princeton. Here for a time they occupied the

College, causing one student to write his aunt of rumors that "Nassau Hall has become a Nursery of Vice and irreligion rather than an institution of Virtue and morality"; but another authority insisted that the Pennsylvanians conducted themselves "with the greatest decorum."

Sir Henry Clinton never understood the nature of this rebellion, "one of the strangest mutinies in history." Two British messengers were dispatched with lavish inducements to promise the insurgents anything they wished, and said that soldiers had been placed on Staten Island with instructions to cross to Amboy and protect Wayne's malcontents in any necessary way. Two thousand Pennsylvanians had never felt more insulted.

Of Clinton a Pennsylvanian said indignantly:

"See, he takes us for traitors. Let us show him that the American army can furnish but one Arnold."

And the point was demonstrated by hanging the messengers at a crossroads near Trenton.

The mutineers entered Philadelphia where almost no one—in Congress or official state position—could deny that justice was on their side. Three-year enlistments, it was agreed, should expire at the end of the third year. So anxious was Pennsylvania to please its veterans that some were excused from service before their terms had been finished. Even some who had enlisted for the duration of the war were discharged. Nearly half the Pennsylvanians were mustered out and the others received furloughs of approximately two months. Wayne refused to identify horses stolen from his own stables.

Numerous Pennsylvanians offered to reenlist if given new bounties. As a result, most authorities doubt that the loss to the Pennsylvania Line had been of substantial consequence.

* * *

The mutiny of the New Jersey troops, scattered from Pompton to Chatham, occurred late in January. Shaken by the revolt of the Pennsylvania Line, the New Jersey Legislature appointed a committee of three to settle differences among its enlisted men "occasioned by the depreciation of Cont[inental] dollars" and, further, to investigate "any Uneasiness . . . among the Soldiers respecting the Term for which they had been engaged."

Apparently the Legislature had employed three blind mice for their investigators. In a masterpiece of silly complacency, the committee reported "that they knew of no Uneasiness in the Brigade; that very few had ever complained of being unjustly detained; and that therefore they conceived it unnecessary then to go into any Examination of the Subject." Moreover, while the committee investigated the encampment, numerous soldiers were uninformed that the legislators would hear their grievances.

Some were given back pay and soon the encampment was plentifully supplied with liquor. Drunkenness no doubt played a part in the mutiny, but the Jerseymen were praised by one commissioner for the "great Decency" with which they left camp "& discovered a great Affection for their Officers." The rebellion continued two days before the soldiers returned to camp upon promises of a pardon and a full airing of their complaints.

Washington, however, was indignant at this insubordination and sent 500 New Englanders under Major General Robert Howe to deal with the Jersey rascals. Howe struggled through miles of snow before surrounding the huts of the mutineers and aiming fieldpieces toward them. The punishment of the Jerseymen was far harsher than their behavior warranted. But Howe would hear of nothing but an immediate trial. Three soldiers—Grant, Tuttle, and Gilmore—were ordered executed by "twelve of the most guilty mutineers," although for reasons not clear Grant received a last-minute reprieve.

The two condemned to die revealed their terror of death. The twelve executioners, knowing that they were equally guilty, likewise were overwhelmed with pity. Tears streamed down their faces. But, as an eyewitness reported, "the wretched victims . . . had neither time nor . . . power to implore the mercy and forgiveness of God, and such was their agonizing condition, that no heart could refrain from emotions of sympathy and compassion." Howe then lectured the men on the dreadfulness of their crime, ordered the soldiers to beg for pardon from their officers, and considered his day's labors rather neatly finished.

These two flare-ups within months of assured victory marked how perilous was the tightwire between disaster and triumph over which the American states walked.

CHAPTER SIX

A Ride to Wethersfield

January–May, 1781

Within two months the New Jersey rebellion revived under circumstances that not only distressed Washington but also posed a danger to the American cause. This third outbreak of mutiny upset Washington at a time when he had gained the commander he wanted in the South by replacing Gates with Greene. The devoted Rhode Island Quaker admitted in January that "the appearance of the troops was wretched beyond description," but Greene possessed the alert mind of a man still in his late thirties. Cornwallis far from awed him. Greene divided his forces into two columns, taking charge of one and placing the other under the command of Dan Morgan. In addition, he was supported by the well-drilled cavalry of "Light Horse Harry" Lee.

Greene's rewards were almost immediate. On an open plain called Cowpens, and near the scene of the previous American victory at King's Mountain, Morgan engaged Tarleton's Tories and an infantry regiment of Scotsmen. The circumstances, as Dan saw them, required "downright fighting." He encouraged his boys with a promise should they turn back "Benny" Tarleton: "How the old folks will bless you and the girls kiss you." Red oak, hickory, and white pine supplied the type of cover Morgan's riflemen preferred; suitably they shouted an "Indian hallo" at the enemy's appearance. The steady marksmanship so decimated the British lines that after less than "an hour's wild fighting" about one-tenth of the attacking force escaped in panic.

In February Washington sent Lafayette south and told him to pick up a good part of the Jersey Brigade along the way. Due largely to the fact that the New Jersey Legislature had not yet been able to untangle the riddle of who had enlisted for three years or for the duration of the war, Lafayette had been asked to pluck a hornet's nest and carry it under his arm. Penitence can last just so long among soldiers, as the Jerseymen were now willing to prove. They sneered openly at the New Englanders who had intervened in their mutiny and one of the Jersey officers, Adjutant General Francis Barber, recalled the ruckus that occurred in Princeton:

The Jersey troops have behaved scandalously thus far. Last night, when at Princeton, they created a small riot with the Eastern troops. The grudge occasioned by the late subduction was the leading motive. After a little tumult they were dispersed to their quarters and all quiet after. This night many of them were drunk & very turbulent. They are clamorous about their money, meaning the fourth part of their depreciation, which they say is due tomorrow, the first of March. Several threaten not to march unless they receive it. This is the effect of liquor, and I hope when that is evaporated, they will be quiet. Our men I think are exceedingly altered for worse; from being almost the most orderly & subordinate soldiers in the army, they are become a set of drunken, and unworthy fellows. The situation of an officer among them is rendered more disagreeable than any other calling in life, even the most menial, can possibly be. . . . Nothing but the highest severity will reclaim them, and whether or not that will be effectual while they receive such countenance from the public, is very uncertain.

*   *   *

As Lafayette led his Jersey rebels to Philadelphia, where they boarded ships bound for Virginia, Morgan and Greene approached another climactic phase of the war in the South. By every rule of military good sense, Cornwallis should have retreated to Charleston after the disaster at Cowpens. Perhaps the kind of pride that goeth before a fall explained why he did not do so. Or perhaps illness warped Cornwallis' judgment, for he coughed and wheezed and his eyes were reddened through his efforts to write at night by flickering candlelight.

Morgan and Greene played a game of military hop, skip, and jump with Cornwallis, crossing the Dan River from North Carolina into Virginia and then back into North Carolina. In March, despite morning ground frost and occasional wet, cold days, the songs of mockingbirds and larks were sure harbingers of spring. Still Cornwallis' grumpiness did not lessen as several couriers brought reports of how by the hundreds former Tory militiamen were joining the patriots. Grumbling over the "sneaks" who fouled the ranks of the Loyalists, Cornwallis moved into battle at Guilford Court House on March 15. The old warrior shivered in the early morning mists and must have wondered what impulse had forced him to fight over this tiny village.

The battle opened with a British bayonet charge against the two front lines of Americans, one placed behind a zigzag fence and the other in a nearby woods. The Rebels broke, rushing "like a torrent through the woods" and scattering the ground with guns, knapsacks, and canteens. Greene, with the pick of his Continentals and two fieldpieces, waited patiently on a hillside for Cornwallis to come to the third line of American defenders. Stubbornly, after two horses were shot from under him, Cornwallis determined to "die or conquer" as Greene proceeded to "cut to pieces" his adversaries. Rifle fire ripped the British to a point of despair where British fieldpieces "opened upon friend as well as foe." By Cornwallis' estimate Guilford Court House was a stalemate, but Greene, smiling quietly as he faded from the engagement, knew how "severely" he had punished the British.

Greene and Morgan's mid-March showing at Guilford Court House heartened most Americans, but not that portion of the Jersey Brigade who had remained within the State. The stay-at-homers acted obnoxiously throughout the remainder of the spring and summer. The complaints against them included every-

thing from disobeying regimental orders to sleeping on sentry
duty. Some ignored officers, some deserted, some stole away from
camp after dark. Some ravished the property of civilian neighbors, some failed to bring their weapons to parade. Some out-
shouted their commanders so that drills could not be executed,
some fired their guns at inappropriate times. Fist fights became
commonplace.

Yet could the Jerseymen alone be blamed? The war had lasted
too long and had begun to drain the spirits of those who supported it with the greatest loyalty.

No other state [wrote Richard P. McCormick, perhaps New Jersey's
outstanding contemporary historian], so generally and continuously felt
the impact of the struggle for independence. The civil population, subjected
to the exactions of both friends and foes, was constantly reminded that
the State was a military frontier. State officials, harassed by internal strife
and by sudden military emergencies, were placed under severe trials. For
seven frightening years there was no peace for New Jersey.

* * *

At New Windsor on May 1, 1781, Washington began a military journal, recording: "I lament not having attempted it from
the commencement of the War, in aid of my memory." A pref-
atory statement deplored that without seizure by military force
—actions that "daily and hourly" led to "oppressing the people"
and "souring their tempers"—after five years of conflict his
army was virtually without food, clothing, military stores or
financial credit. Enlistments in "scarce any State in the Union"
had not, "at this hour, an eighth part of its quota in the field
and little prospect, that I can see, of ever getting more than
half." Where the Continentals should be contemplating "a
glorious offensive campaign" they faced instead "a bewildered
and gloomy defensive one" unless allies were generous in their
contributions of ships, land troops, and money—prospects, in
Washington's opinion, "too contingent to build upon." New
Jersey, which possessed the power of taxation, revealed dramati-
cally how far behind the needs of war a state could fall: by

1781 Essex, Monmouth, and Gloucester counties were just ful-
filling their 1775 quotas and Somerset and Gloucester were still
paying on their sinking fund commitments for 1776.

One week—any week—in the life of Washington disclosed
the astonishing range of problems confronting the American
Commander-in-Chief.

On May 1st, for example, Washington borrowed $9,000 from
Massachusetts with which to pay its own troops; he urged
Ezekiel Cornell, who represented Rhode Island in the Continental Congress, to scrounge around for arms and clothing that
could be sent to the army in the South; he authorized Major
Benjamin Tallmadge of the Second Continental Dragoons to
make payments to secret intelligence agents who operated
through headquarters; and he asked New Jersey's Colonel Dayton to open a line of correspondence with New York by way of
Elizabethtown so a closer check could be kept on Clinton's
movements.

May 2nd brought a happy entry: "No occurrence of note" and
the gale that day must have continued into the next for the 3rd
was also an uneventful day. Couriers from the South reached
New Windsor on the 4th. Steuben reported that enemy ships
had advanced up the James River as far as Jamestown and that
public stores had been moved from Richmond to the interior of
Virginia; a far cheerier Lafayette, about to march from Alexandria to Fredericksburg, reported that desertions had ceased
and "his detachment were in good spirits." (Originally Virginia
had been invaded by 1,700 Tories under Benedict Arnold, now
a British general, but Cornwallis, resupplied and newly reinforced, had entered Virginia as commander in late April.)

On May 5th Brigadier General James Clinton feared for the
safety of Fort Schuyler (formerly Stanwix) and warned Washington that he might have to abandon this post on the Mohawk
River unless Clinton received the flour and salted meat recently
requisitioned.

May 6th was a day Washington would have liked to skip.
First, the French stressed the point that they had not been
supplied as Benjamin Franklin had contracted before they left

France, and while they did not insist upon "immediate compliance," Washington found the circumstances "exceedingly embarassing." Second, Dayton had been asked to send a guard of Jerseymen to protect from a surprise Indian attack provisions at Sussex Court House (Orange County, New York). Third, John Flood of Lower Salem (Westchester County, New York) informed Washington of the location of recent ship arrivals. Fourth, the hunger of troops at Albany and posts above required dispatching a number of requisitions. Fifth, Washington resolved to send Major General William Heath to impress upon certain state legislatures how vital it was for them to measure up to their part in executing the war. On the 7th Washington fretted over a sou'easter that presumably damaged many ships along the coast.

These problems were a fair sampling of a week in Washington's life that spring. He dealt with the quandary at West Point where there was only enough meat to last two days; Dayton, "confirmed by two sensible deserters," reported ten ships of the line and as many as 4,000 troops sailing from New York to Rhode Island; an appointment was arranged to meet on the 21st with Rochambeau and Admiral de Barras at Wethersfield, Connecticut. There were reports of little raids in which Americans were "inhumanly murdered," secret messages with portions written in an invisible chemical ink, conflicting tallies on the ships passing Fort Lee and a prediction from Fort Schuyler that the British intended to invade northern New York, and an inquiry if it would not be wiser to move the garrison to German Flats, a productive valley on the west side of the Mohawk River. David Forman reported from New Jersey that seven British ships "of 60 Guns and upwards" with twelve large transports and ten topsail schooners had passed to the South.

Washington's relief well can be imagined when on May 18 he set off to confer with his French allies in Connecticut.

*   *   *

Situated on a bank of the Connecticut River, near Hartford, Wethersfield was one of the oldest and prettiest colonial settle-

ments in New England. Founded by independently thinking
people from Watertown, Massachusetts in 1634, the town's Indian name of Pyquag had been dropped three years later. Here
sturdy men and women had beaten back the forests to plant their
fields and build their homes and conquer the Pequot Indians,
who had been encouraged to take to the warpath by the jealous
Dutch, in one of the continent's earliest organized conflicts
with the redskins. Of the sons of the sons of the sons of such
stock had come Private Joseph Plumb Martin. Unlike Washington, who had been a member of the House of Burgesses and
for ten years had grown with the rebellion of mind and heart
that had turned the great men of Williamsburg, Virginia to
open war, young Martin knew nothing of how Thomas Jefferson
had matured under the leadership of a Washington or of an
outspoken country bumpkin in a greased pigtail named Patrick
Henry. So many like Martin, who year after year fought the
battles of the Revolution and suffered the terrible winters at
Valley Forge and Morristown, had no intimate association with
the philosophy of the war. They had absorbed a love of freedom
from the unshakable self-reliance of their forebears; in a way,
the force was as mysterious as the winds that pollinated the
crops they grew or the colorful wild flowers that spread their
patchwork quilts over the meadows.

As Washington rode to Wethersfield, the May air was sweet
and the countryside was beautiful with the bursting buds of
those wild flowers. He arrived on the 19th, two days before
his French allies were due, and found comfortable quarters in
the home of Joseph Webb. The next day was devoted to private
conversations with Jonathan Trumbull, the governor of Connecticut. Both agreed that a combined operation with the French
was of the utmost importance and, Washington noted, Trumbull
"had little doubt of our obtaining Men and Provisions adequate
to our wants." The Governor quoted Colonel Jeremiah Wadsworth, Commissary-General of Purchases of the Continental
Army, and other influential persons as concurring in this belief.

Admiral Barras did not appear next day because a British
fleet under Vice-Admiral Marriot Arbuthnot had arrived off

Block Island, at the eastern end of Long Island, and posed a threat to Rhode Island. As an adequate substitute Count Rochambeau brought François Jean, Chevalier de Chastellux, major-general of the French army in America. The meeting began at about noon and reached decisions that Washington clearly recalled:

—That the French Land force (except 200 Men) should March as soon as the Squadron could Sail for Boston [where it would be refitted] —to the North River—and there, in conjunction with the American, to commence an operation against New York (which in the present reduced State of the Garrison it was thought would fall, unless relieved; the doing which w[oul]d enfeeble their Southern operations, and in either case be productive of capital advantages) or to extend our views to the Southward as circumstances and a Naval superiority might render more necessary and eligable [sic].
—The aid which would be given to such an operation in this quarter.— the tardiness with which the Regiments would be filled for any other.—the insurmountable difficulty and expence of Land transportation—the waste of Men in long Marches (especially where there is a disinclination to the Service—objections to the climate &ca.) with other reasons too numerous to detail, induced to this opinion.
—The heavy Stores and Baggage of the French army were to be deposited at Providence under Guard of 200 Men (before mentioned)—and Newport Harbour and works were to be secured by 500 Militia—

Rochambeau departed the following morning. Washington wrote letters beseeching the four New England governors "to compleat [sic] their Continental Battalions for the Campaign." Massachusetts and Connecticut were asked for powder and means of transporting it to the army.

The Commander-in-Chief returned to New Windsor on May 25. As he might have expected, there was bad news— anxious letters telling of enemy landings at Crown Point, at the southern end of Lake Champlain, with the intention of penetrating the Hudson and Mohawk rivers. A regiment at West Point was alerted to be ready to move at an hour's warning. But next day brought cheerful news from Lieutenant-Colonel John Laurens, a special envoy to the Court of Versailles: France was lending the United States the sum of 6,000,000 livres for the purchase of arms and clothes and other necessities and a fleet of twenty French sail of the line had left for the West Indies. The Courts of St. Petersburg and Vienna had offered "their Mediation in settling the present troubles" which the king of France would not accept "without consulting his Allies."

To Washington the stars over New Windsor must have seemed brighter.

CHAPTER SEVEN

March to Glory

August–September, 1781

The secret of Washington's military genius rested in his gifts for improvisation. His alert, flexible mind relished new challenges. Thus after weeks of maneuvering for a joint assault with the French upon New York, he could almost within moments scrap the entire operation and become excitedly involved in other stratagems.

On August 14 a dispatch from Admiral Barras informed Washington that the Comte de Grasse intended to depart soon from Cape François, San Domingo, with at least twenty-five sail of the line and 3,000 land troops, arriving off the capes of Chesapeake Bay by October 3. The reason the Count could not cooperate in the New York attack, Barras explained, was because Grasse would "be under a necessity from particular engagements with the Spaniards to be in the West Indies by the Middle of October . . ." Washington had no choice now but to invade Virginia and finish off Cornwallis. A courier fled to Lafayette, "requesting him to be in perfect readiness to second my views and to prevent if possible the Retreat of Cornwallis towards Carolina." On the 15th letters from Lafayette and others confirmed the fact that for the past nine days Cornwallis had been throwing up works at Yorktown and Gloucester Point at the tip of the Virginia peninsula off Chesapeake Bay. If de

Grasse outran the British to Capes Charles and Henry, Washington would have his adversary neatly trapped!

When necessity warranted, Washington became an extremely close-mouthed man, and in order that there could be no chance of a spy learning what he now proposed to do—to march the French and American armies across New Jersey with Clinton still believing their only objective was to attack New York and Staten Island—the Commander-in-Chief's sole confidant for many days was the Comte de Rochambeau. On the day before the army moved, Washington wrote the chief geographer of the allied forces, Simeon DeWitt, who had escaped from Queen's College with his musket and knapsack when Cornwallis first invaded New Brunswick in 1776:

> Immediately on receipt of this you will begin to Survey the road (if it has not been done already) to Princeton—thence through Maidenhead [Lawrenceville] to Trenton—thence to Philadelphia—thence to the head of Elk through Darby, Chester, Wilmington, Christiana bridge.
>
> At the head of Elk [the head of Chesapeake Bay in Maryland] you will receive further orders. I need not observe to you the necessity of noting Towns, villages and remarkable Houses and places but I must desire that you will give me the rough traces of your Survey as you proceed on as I have reasons for desiring this as soon as possible.

*   *   *

Meanwhile, unless Washington could secure fresh forage for his weary and hungry horses, he faced "a slow and disagreeable" march to the Head of Elk. The Americans that he sent forward were the light infantry under Scammell—Lafayette called him "Light Horse" Scammell—and

> two light companies of York to be joined by the like Number from the Connecticut line, the Remainder of the Jersey line, two Regiments of York, Hazens Regiment and the Regiment of Rhode Island, together with [Colonel John] Lambs Regiment of Artillery with Cannon and other Ordinance for the field and Siege.

Hazen, crossing at Dobbs Ferry with his regiment and the Jersey troops, marched to the heights between Springfield and Chatham. Here began the movements to deceive Sir Henry

Clinton. Tents were pitched, a warehouse and a long shed were constructed, together with ovens large enough to sustain any prolonged invasion of Staten Island and New York. The report of French troops joining the Americans here "still further excited the British." Every evidence was given of a long encampment. The troops retired at night; and when the morning mists vanished, suddenly resumed their march southward.

The French army, in their rainbow-colored uniforms, delighted onlookers as their route carried them through Bedminster. What a marked contrast they made to the poorly clad and equipped Continentals! The Frenchmen, by Mellick's report, dazzled those who watched from the roadside:

The view of such perfect phalanxes, thronging helms, and thick array of waving banners was a new military experience for Bedminster people, and when the *tambour majors,* resplendent in *panache,* aiguillette, and tinsel, flourished their ponderous batons, making the hills and valleys vocal with the melody of the Gallic bands, the acme of warlike splendor seemed to have been reached. The private soldiers in their handsome and varied uniforms appeared as neat as their officers; easy, debonair and with natures proverbially gay, they were not stern-looking, grim-visaged warriors, as though wielding the offensive blade from love of carnage or eager to sack cities and devastate and raze villages. . . .

The citizens "especially marveled" at the legion of the Duke of Luzon—a corps of 600 hussars and infantry, "the very pick of the French army." These soldiers, "sparkling with life and activity," saw a march as "a holiday excursion." All were young, tall, handsome, and wore mustaches, "which were quite new on this side of the ocean." These "laughter-loving *beaux sabreurs*" excited feminine hearts: "It is said that, following the impulses of their gay dispositions, more than once after a day's march their assurance and captivating manners secured for them partners for an evening dance."

Unhappily for the lassies of Bedminster, the Frenchmen had to march on to Princeton which one of their officers described as "a pretty village of about sixty houses." The inns were "handsome and clean."

*   *   *

Joseph Martin, who marched to Chatham to build ovens "for the accommodation of the French troops," was one of the bedraggled Continentals for whom no girlish hearts fluttered. Martin believed that Washington was about to attack New York, but instead, by rapid marches, he arrived at Trenton and by vessel, traveling from sunset to sunset, reached Philadelphia. Along with other "Sappers and Miners" Martin "packed off" shells, shot and other military stores. He received not only shirts, overalls and silk-and-oakum stockings, but "a MONTH'S PAY, in specie" borrowed from the French, the first money that Martin could recall receiving since 1776.

Washington played well his game of deception, deciding, under the illusion of moving to Sandy Hook to assist the French fleet in entering New York Bay, "our intentions could be concealed one March more." The "whole army" moved in three columns. The upper line marched through Morristown to Somerset Court House (Millstone), the middle line through Bound Brook, and the third through New Brunswick. The three columns converged at Princeton on August 30 and reached Trenton next day. Washington hurried ahead to meet his troops in Philadelphia.

Clinton meanwhile braced for the expected assault on New York and a feint on Staten Island.

If [this depressed and outwitted commander wrote], I had as many reasons to believe that Mr. Washington would move his army into Virginia without a covering fleet as I had to think he would not, I could not have prevented his passing the Hudson under the cover of his forts at Verplanck's and Stoney [*sic*] Point.

Washington received a hero's welcome at a dinner in Philadelphia on August 31. The Continentals arrived the following day only twenty-four hours ahead of the French under Rochambeau. The birthplace of the Declaration of Independence reacted wildly. The natty French soldiers were no less inspiring in Philadelphia than they had been at Bedminster. To the music of drums and fife the French raised a cloud of dust "like a smothering snow-storm." Every window was crowded with women waving handkerchiefs.

* * *

Washington left Philadelphia on September 5 and at Chester learned that Grasse, with twenty-eight sail of the line, four frigates and 3,000 land troops had safely arrived off the Chesapeake capes. These forces were to join with Lafayette at Jamestown, while the French fleet anchored off Hampton Roads in Lynnhaven Bay.

On the next three days the Americans and the French from New Jersey mingled at the Head of Elk. All troops received a month's "hard money," supplied by the French, and, as one gay-hearted spirit said:

"General Washington and his army are gone to take Lord Cornwallis in his mousetrap."

Rochambeau remembered Washington "waving his hat at me with demonstrative gestures of the greatest joy."

Postlude

1781–1783

Tench Tilghman, Washington's devoted aide, rode into Philadelphia on October 24, cursing the stupidity of the ferry pilot who had delayed the journey a night by running aground in Chesapeake Bay. Now, two days after the event, Tilghman informed Congress of the surrender of Cornwallis and his army at Yorktown. That afternoon the delegates attended the Dutch Lutheran Church to "return thanks to Almighty God for crowning the allied arms of the United States and France with success." Then, according to Elias Boudinot, since the national treasury was short of hard money, each delegate drew a dollar from his pocket to pay Tilghman's expenses in bringing them this momentous news.

Celebrations were held throughout the colonies, but none quite equalled that in Newburgh, New York. Here it was proposed to burn an effigy of Benedict Arnold until someone remembered this general had lost a leg fighting as an American. The limb was removed and laid carefully on the ground; then the remainder of the effigy was ignited.

Wars end raggedly, and the American Revolution was no exception. Numerous raids upon New Jersey communities by Tories from New York inflamed local citizens until this non-

sense ended when Sir Henry Clinton was replaced in command
by Sir Guy Carleton. Hatreds between neighborhood Rebels and
Tories often had become so deeply rooted that they endured at
least a generation; residents of Monmouth County petitioned
the Legislature to prevent refugee Loyalists, who were labeled
as "Bloodthirsty Robbers" and "Atrocious monsters," from returning to their homes; and in Swedesboro Rebels were so an-
gered by the sight of their former enemies at church services
that these Patriots stayed away, "unable to worship."

The high hopes that after Yorktown the war had ended and
the army would soon disband gave way as the weeks dragged
on to a sense of apathetic depression. Washington, as adept at
diplomacy as he was at martial affairs, stood firm against breaking up his army, telling his critics that "an old and true maxim"
in making a good peace required a nation "to be well prepared
to carry on the war." After Yorktown, Rochambeau wintered
in Virginia and the Continentals occupied the Hudson and New
Jersey. Arthur St. Clair led the Pennsylvania, Maryland, and
Virginia forces southward to strengthen Nathanael Greene.
Washington rode northward to confer with members of Congress.

News of the British disaster did not reach London until November 25.

"Oh, God!" Germain cried to Lord North. "It is all over!"

*   *   *

George III was disinclined to accept this view. Not "the
smallest alteration," the King said, should be made in "those
principles" which had directed his past conduct. North was sick
of the war and would gladly have bestowed independence on
America, but he was a lonely figure in the King's council in this
respect. Washington, finishing his discussions with Congress, set
up headquarters at Newburgh where he faced problems similar
to those of 1775 : a lack of everything.

International events intervened to aid the American cause.
France smashed its way to victory in the West Indies. Minorca
was lost to the British and Gibraltar besieged. There was re-

volt in India. In the wake of these disasters citizens throughout the British Isles strongly petitioned George III to abandon all struggles in America. Lord North resigned and the Whig ministry of the Marquis of Rockingham was warm in its feelings toward its cousins across the seas.

On August 4, 1782, Clinton's successor, General Carleton, notified Washington that peace negotiations had opened in Paris. All "hostilities," Carleton wrote later, were suspended. Then the Marquis of Rockingham died, and the situation changed radically. Washington lamented: "That the King will push the war as long as the nation will find men or money admits not of a doubt in my mind."

Carleton's belief in an approaching peace led to the evacuation of Savannah, but with a change of ministries such withdrawals ended and there were isolated outbreaks of skirmishing. Charles Lee died, gasping in one of his last breaths that Washington remained a "puffed-up charlatan."

Wintry winds from Canada added to the dejections of 1783. In March, officers, whose salaries were long overdue, journeyed to Philadelphia to rebel against Congress and virtually threatened a mutiny at a meeting in the Temple, a building used for public occasions. Washington rushed to the national capital and at his appearance in the Temple the officers fell silent. Said one major: "Every eye was fixed upon this illustrious man."

Washington acknowledged the just grievances of the officers and pleaded with them to be patient a few months longer. The dignity of such conduct, he said, they owed to posterity. The revolt was averted, and next month, on the eighth birthday of the fighting at Lexington, came an announcement of "the cessation of hostilities between the United States of America and the King of Great Britain."

*   *   *

After half a century Joseph Plumb Martin attempted to recall how he felt at the close of the war. The moment, Martin thought, had contained "as much sorrow as joy" for men who "had lived together as a family of brothers." Surely there had

been little squabbles—all families had them—but they had
fought and suffered together, sharing hardships, sickness and
dangers; they had been for better or worse as "strict a band of
brotherhood as Masons."

"And now," Martin reflected, "we were to be, the greater part
of us, parted forever; as unconditionally separated as though
the grave lay between us." He doubted "if there was a corps
in the army that parted with more regret than ours did, the New
Englanders in particular. Ah! it was a serious time."

In this spirit Martin bade his "Dutch friends adieu" and set
his face "to the eastward," journeying to the country that would
later be the state of Maine, where he lived out the remainder of
his many years.

*   *   *

Life in the sleepy village of Princeton was not the same after
Congress, fleeing from the near-mutinous officers in Philadelphia,
occupied the Library Room in Nassau Hall. Thereafter came the
excitement of dignitaries alighting from every stagecoach stopover between Trenton and New Brunswick.

In September Washington and the Marquis de la Luzerne,
the French Minister, attended the commencement exercises in the
Presbyterian Church. Seven signers of the Declaration of Independence and nine signers of the Articles of Confederation
listened to serious student harangues on "Was Brutus justified
in killing Caesar?" or "Can any measure that is morally evil be
politically good?" Yet Washington was quite unprepared when
Ashbel Greene, the valedictorian, turned toward the Commander-in-Chief and predicted how history would judge him:

". . . Some future bard . . . shall tell in all the majesty of
epic song the man whose gallant sword taught the tyrants of
the earth to fear oppression and opened an asylum for the
virtuous and free."

Washington presented the college with a gift of fifty guineas.
The trustees voted that Charles Wilson Peale should be commissioned to paint the portrait of Washington so that it could

hang in place of that of George II, which had been decapitated in the Battle of Princeton.

Washington moved to Rocky Hill where he resided at Rockingham, then known as the "Higgens farm," about four miles from Princeton. Here from August 23 through November 10, 1783, Washington lived. Some days he gazed down the slope from house to river as he composed his farewell address to the army. William Dunlap, who won acclaim as a playwright, theatrical manager, painter and historian, described Washington at this time as "the man of whom all men spoke—whom all wished to see."

Appropriately, today, adjacent to Morven, stands a memorial, the inscription of which in thirteen magnificent lines recaptures the glory of that age when America reached toward military victory and human ennoblement:

> Here Memory Lingers
> To Recall
> The Guiding Mind
> Whose Daring Plan
> Outflanked the Foe
> And Turned Dismay to Hope
> When Washington
> With Swift Resolve
> Marched Through the Night
> To Fight at Dawn
> And Venture All
> In One Victorious Battle
> For Our Freedom

Notes and Comments

Preface

For David Ramsay's exceptional summation of the significance of the War for Independence see his enduring *The History of the American Revolution* (Philadelphia: R. Aitken & Son, 1789, 2 vols.); and the story of Charley Morgan is related in Louis Gottschalk's *Lafayette and the Close of the American Revolution* (Chicago: University of Chicago Press, 1942), 290.

Introduction

In writing a book an author acquires so many obligations that it is better to omit all than to forget one. Yet every good rule deserves an exception. In this case gratitude must be expressed to the staff of the Rutgers University Library—and especially Donald A. Sinclair and Oliver K. Westling, Clark Beck, Jr. and Irene K. Lionikis—for understanding that only an honest sympathy can ignite the heart of a lonely student in search of the approximate truth.

The source for the events of the adoption of the Declaration of Independence, as here related, is reconstructed from Catherine Drinker Bowen's splendid *John Adams and the American Revolution* (Boston: Little Brown and Company, 1950), 588, 594, 596. *George III and the Mad Business* by Ida Macalpine and Richard A. Hunter (New York: Pantheon Books, 1969), 176, is a work of psychiatrists who have invaded the realm of history. Truly to understand Britain's pitiful military structure at the outbreak of the Revolution, the opening chapter of Edward E. Curtis's *The Organiza-*

tion of the British Army in the American Revolution (New Haven: Yale University Press, 1926), is unsurpassed and New Jersey's basic reaction to the Stamp Act is drawn from Richard P. McCormick's *New Jersey From Colony to State, 1609–1789* (New Brunswick: Rutgers University Press, 1964), 111.

PART ONE: *Respite After Trenton and Princeton*

Prelude: 1774–1776

When first I met George F. Scheer in Chapel Hill, North Carolina, he was engrossed in writing a biography of Francis Marion and I insist that what little editorial acclaim I deserve arises from persuading George to collaborate with Hugh F. Rankin (now at Tulane) in recreating the entire Revolutionary War from contemporary sources. The result was a splendid volume, *Rebels and Redcoats* (Cleveland: The World Publishing Company, 1957) in which the Quaker gives his command on p. 66 [hereafter *Scheer-Rankin*]. The two quotations from Samuel Eliot Morison are in *The Oxford History of the American People* (New York: Oxford University Press, 1965), 224, 236. For attitudes in New Brunswick and Princeton as the war approached, see Earl Schenck Miers' *Where the Raritan Flows* (New Brunswick: Rutgers University Press, 1964), 23 [hereafter *Miers*], and Thomas J. Wertenbaker's *Princeton, 1746–1896* (Princeton: Princeton University Press, 1946), 57 [hereafter *Wertenbaker*]. Franklin characterizes his "common-law" son in *The Writings of Benjamin Franklin,* edited by Albert H. Smyth (New York: The Macmillan Company, 1907, 10 vols.), VI, 144. For the events leading to William Franklin's exile see Cornelius C. Vermeule's "Some Revolutionary Incidents in the Raritan Valley," *Proceedings of the New Jersey Historical Society,* New Series, VI (1921), 74 [hereafter Vermeule, *Incidents, NJHSP*]. For New Jersey's reaction to fighting at Lexington and Concord, consult Wertenbaker, *op cit,* 48 *et seq* and *The Lives of Eighteen at Princeton,* edited by Willard Thorp (Princeton: Princeton University Press, 1946), 57. Cornelius C. Vermeule, "Service of the New Jersey Militia in the Revolutionary War," *NJHSP,* New Series, 235 [hereafter Vermeule, *Militia, NJHSP*], describes the raising of a State Army; also Vermeule, *Incidents, NJHSP,* 75. For Witherspoon's activities in the Second Continental Congress see Wertenbaker, *op cit,* 56, 58.

Vermeule, *Incidents, NJHSP,* 79, Wertenbaker, *op cit,* 57 and Miers, *op cit,* 28–9 describe New Jersey's reaction to the Declaration of Independence. Washington's correspondence with Reed is in his *Writings,* edited by Worthington C. Ford (New York: G. P. Putnam's Sons, 1890, 14 vols.), V, 125 [hereafter *WW-f*] and *Scheer-Rankin,* 103. The climax of events in Boston and Canada is documented in Frank Moore's *Diary of the American Revolution* (New York: Charles Scribner, 1859–60, 2 vols.), I, 219, *Scheer-Rankin,* 110 and Vermeule, *Militia, NJHSP,* 236. For arrival of the Howes in New York, the sources are Morison, *op cit,* 239 and Ambrose Serle's *The American Journal . . . Secretary to Lord Howe,* edited by Edward H. Tatum, Jr. (San Marino: The Huntington Library, 1940), 28–9.

Unique among eyewitness accounts of the war is Joseph Plumb Martin's *Private Yankee Doodle . . . A Narrative . . . of a Revolutionary Soldier,* edited by George F. Scheer (Boston: Little Brown and Company, 1962), 21–5. Although originally published anonymously in Hallowell, Maine, when Martin was seventy, this book was virtually forgotten when Francis S. Ronalds, Superintendent of the Morristown National Historical Park, told Scheer of the work's existence. Historians can only be grateful for this literary resurrection; it is, as Scheer avers, "the best of all surviving first-person accounts of the life and times of a private soldier"; and Douglas Southall Freeman consulted it with delight while working on his definitive biography of George Washington.

John Valentine's *Lord Stirling* (New York: Oxford University Press, 1969), 95, 188–89, is distinguished and readable. *The Dictionary of American Biography* [hereafter *DAB*] states that Stirling's home in Basking Ridge burned in 1920. The action at Gowanus Creek is described in Martin, *op cit,* 26.

CHAPTER ONE: *The River Forts: November, 1776*

Fletcher Pratt, gentleman and literary historian known to fellow New Jersey craftsmen as the "Sage of Keyport," drew an excellent short military sketch of Nathanael Greene in *Eleven Generals* (New York: William Sloane Associates, 1949), 3, 4. All descriptions of weather are drawn from "[William] Bamford's Diary," *Maryland Historical Magazine,* XXVIII (1933), 9 *et seq.* For Washington's emotions as a correspondent during this period see *WW-f,* V, 1*n,* 4, 7*n,* 8–9, 11*n.* For Andreas Wiederhold's "The Capture of Fort Washington," see *Pennsylvania Magazine of History,* XXIII (1851), 95.

A model of local history in the grand tradition is Adrian C. Leiby's *The Revolutionary War in the Hackensack Valley* (New Brunswick: Rutgers University Press, 1962), vii, 7–8. Rall is the correct spelling; variations include Rohl, Ralle, Roll, Rhal, Rawle. The nature of the assault on Fort Washington also is described in Adjutant Major General Baurmeister's *Revolution in America: Confidential Letters and Journals,* edited by Bernard A. Uhlendorf (New Brunswick: Rutgers University Press, 1957), 69. The sad closing events of this struggle are told in Leiby, *op cit,* 59, 61–2; Baurmeister, *op cit,* 71; *WW-f,* V, 36–41, 44–50; *Scheer-Rankin,* 202–3; Moore, *op cit,* I, 350. An additional source is Hugh R. Rankin's

"Charles Lord Cornwallis," in *George Washington's Opponents,* edited by George A. Billias (New York: William Morris & Co., 1969), 193–94 [hereafter *Billias*].

CHAPTER TWO: *Flight: November–December, 1776*

A "Flying Camp" (first organized in New Jersey at Perth Amboy on June 3, 1776) was a mobile force expected to meet the British at any point of emergency.

For the flight as far as New Brunswick see *WW-f,* V, 51, 60n; Vermeule, *op cit,* 239 and Bamford, *op cit,* 18. The background of events at New Brunswick is drawn from William P. McMichaels, "Diary," *Pennsylvania Magazine of History,* XVI (1892), 139; William H. S. Demarest, *A History of Rutgers College, 1766–1924* (New Brunswick: Rutgers College, 1924), 103; Valentine, *op cit,* 193; *WW-f,* V, 54–7, 57n, 58–9, 61, 62n.

Originally Durham boats, built in Easton, Pennsylvania, were designed to carry ore over the shallow water where the Susquehanna River empties into Chesapeake Bay. They ranged from 40 to 60 feet in length and 8 feet in width, drawing only 20 inches of water when fully loaded. They could not pass into the Chesapeake, however, to the embarrassment of many colonial investors who dreamed of converting Baltimore into an international seaport.

In continuing the flight through Princeton, the sources used were Wertenbaker, *op cit,* 59; *WW-f,* V, 63; and C. H. Hunter, "Morven—The Princeton Home of the Stockton Family," *NJHSP,* IX (1924), 126, 131. The events leading to the capture of the enigmatic Lee were found in Frank R. Stockton, *Stories of New Jersey* (New Brunswick: Rutgers University Press, 1961), 119 (Stockton, living near Morristown, was thoroughly familiar with its local lore); Alfred Hoyt Bill, *The Campaign of Princeton, 1776–1777* (Princeton: Princeton University Press, 1948), 20–23; and the splendid reminiscences of Andrew D. Mellick, Jr. Mellick's work was originally titled *The Story of an Old Farm* and was published in 1889. The book—the unparalleled source in recounting the war in the Raritan Valley—became rare and its pages usually were deteriorated by the thumb marks of repeated use. The edition now cited, condensed and edited by Hubert G. Schmidt, was retitled *Lesser Crossroads* (New Brunswick: Rutgers University Press, 1948), 193–94 [hereafter *Schmidt*]. Washington crosses the Delaware from Trenton in *WW-f,* V, 64–5.

CHAPTER THREE: *Mount Holly: An Ace in the Hole: December, 1776*

Mifflin's activities are described in *Scheer-Rankin,* 206; for the harrowing tale of the refugees from Philadelphia see William Young, "Journal," *Pennsylvania Magazine of History,* VIII (1884), 255–56; and for the enlargement of Washington's authority, General W. W. H. Davis, "Washington on the West Bank of the Delaware, 1776," *Pennsylvania Magazine of History*, IV (1880), 136 and *WW-f*, V, 140*n*. Davis, *op cit*, 145 is again quoted and the inebriated horse is in Young, *op cit*, 255. *Scheer-Rankin*, 208, covers the fatal argument between Donop and Rall. Young, *op cit*, 142 tells the delightful glass of cider story and the subsequent experience with Rosebrough, Davis, *op cit*, 143–5.

Little known but of extreme value in understanding the later success at Trenton is William A. Slaughter's "Battle of Iron Works Hill at Mount Holly, New Jersey, December, 1776," *NJHSP*, IV (1909), 19–32. During the Revolution principal salt works were located at Toms River, Squan (Manasquan), Barnegat Bay, Burlington, and Sandy Hook. All repulsed Tory raids. Benson J. Lossing, *The Pictorial Field-Book of the American Revolution* (New York: Harper and Brothers, 1860, 2 vols.), II, 22, 23, is accurate concerning Cadwalader's dilemma. Few writers of American history excel the versatility of Lossing whom Laurence S. Mayo describes in *DAB* as "wood-engraver, author, editor." Lossing was Dutch and stolid, and often repeated an inaccurate story if it pleased his preconceived notion of events. Five years were consumed in writing and illustrating his *Field-Book*. More than forty titles flowed from his pen, not always correct but never failing in interest. His *Field-Book* was his masterpiece and as Mayo comments, "It was an original idea well executed, and the antiquarian of today turns to it for details which cannot be found elsewhere." See also *WW-f*, V, 134.

CHAPTER FOUR: *Surprise at Trenton: December, 1776*

For documentation supporting Washington's crossing of the Delaware, and his advance on Trenton, see Bill, *op cit*, 10–26; *WW-f*, V, 126–27, 129–30; Davis, *op cit*, 152, 154, 158; *WW-f*, V, 133.

Was John Honeyman among the spies who informed Washington of the problems he faced in attacking Trenton? The story, written by a grandson, was published almost a century later, and was attributed by him to "Aunt Jane" who was the eldest of John Honeyman's seven children [Elizabeth G. C. Menzies, *Millstone Valley* (New Brunswick: Rutgers University Press, 1969), 80–81]. The heart of a sentimental folklorist like Henry C. Beck could no more resist the story of Honeyman as the "most celebrated of Washington's spies" [Beck, *The Roads of Home* (New Brunswick: Rutgers University Press, 1956), 96 *et seq*] than the romantic poet in Carl Sandburg could ignore the equally suspect tale of Abraham Lincoln's undying love for Ann Rutledge.

For the background of the Battle of Trenton consult Lossing, *op cit*, II, 20; Bill, *op cit*, 43 *et seq*, 58; Davis, *op cit*, 157, 159; Valentine, *op cit*, 197; and General Joseph Reed's "Narrative," *Pennsylvania Magazine of History*, VIII (1884), 301.

CHAPTER FIVE: *Rumors and Realities: December, 1776–January, 1777*

The interlude separating the battles of Trenton and Princeton is documented in Bill, *op cit,* 69, 72, and also 34–5; Reed, *op cit,* 397; and *WW-f,* V, 145.

Phillis Wheatley's ode to Washington appears in *WW-f,* V, 143n. African-born Phillis worked as a personal maid to a minister's wife in Boston and was manumitted and sent to England in 1773 because of failing health. Arrangements for the publication of Miss Wheatley's first volume, *Poems on Various Subjects, Religious and Moral,* were probably made at this time. See John Hope Franklin's *From Slavery to Freedom* (New York: Alfred A. Knopf, 1947), 154–55. The many-sided activities by which Dr. Jacob Green patched out his livelihood, cited in Joseph H. Kler's *God's Happy Cluster* (Bound Brook: privately printed, 1963), 51, is substantiated by the opinion of the times that rated surgeons as the least important professional men of the age; lawyers were scarcely a notch higher, and John Adams fretted for long hours because his legal background might prevent his marriage to the daughter of a prominent clergyman.

For Washington's return to Trenton and subsequent scuffle with Cornwallis, consult *WW-f,* V, 139n, 142; Sergeant "R," "The Battle of Princeton," *Pennsylvania Magazine of History,* XX (1896), 515–16 [the Sergeant's memoirs originally appeared in *The Phenix,* May 24, 1832, Wellsborough, Pa.]; Lossing, *op cit,* II, 25–6; Bill, *op cit,* 81; and Wertenbaker, *op cit,* 59–60.

CHAPTER SIX: *Fox Chase in Princeton: January, 1777*

The sources of Washington's advance on Princeton are *WW-f,* V, 148; Bill, *op cit,* 34, 105; and Sergeant "R," *op cit,* 515–16. Mellick's superb summary of the battle is in Schmidt, *op cit,* 205–6; but see also *WW-f,* V, 149. The story of the American withdrawal from Kingston into Jersey's western hills is based on *WW-f,* V, 150; the third edition of James and Margaret Cawley's *Exploring the Little Rivers of New Jersey* (New Brunswick: Rutgers University Press, 1971), 21; and Schmidt, *op cit,* 206–8, 209. Pluckemin is the correct spelling; a frequently encountered variant is Pluckamin, which is phonetical.

CHAPTER SEVEN: *Village Festival: January, 1777*

For Washington's stay in Pluckemin, consult Schmidt, *op cit,* 6, 209–11, 211–12 and *WW-f,* V, 152–53.

The gravestone, still standing, bears this inscription: "In memory of the Hon. Capt. Will. Leslie of the 17 British Regiment, son of the Earl of Leven in Scotland. He fell Jan. 3, 1777 aged 26 years at the Battle of Princeton. His friend Benj. Rush M.D. of Philadelphia hath caused this stone to be erected as a mark of his esteem for his worth and of his respect

for his noble family." The cornerstone of the original Lutheran Church, dated 1756, was found in a cistern under a blacksmith's shop in 1901 (author's notes).

The army's movement to Morristown and its settlement there are documented in an unsigned article, "Washington in Morristown During the Winters of 1776–77, 1779–80," *Harper's New Monthly Magazine,* XVIII (1859), 292–93; Andrew M. Sherman's "Washington's Army in Lowantica Valley, Morris County, New Jersey, Winter of 1776–1777," *American Historical Magazine,* III (1908), 581, 584, 587, 590, 595–96; Schmidt, *op cit,* 218–19; and *Scheer-Rankin,* 222–23.

The authoritative source on how inflation crippled the Continental army is Kenneth Scott's *Counterfeiting in Colonial Times* (New York: Oxford University Press, 1957), 253, 259–60, 260–61, 262. See also Friedrich Kapp, *The Life of John Kalb* (New York: privately printed, 1870), 184. For the problems confronting the Commander-in-Chief refer to *WW-f,* V, 159, 168, 176n, 180–81, 185, 188–89, 203n.

The map of Morristown, which appears on page 193, is significant because it is the work of Robert Erskine, described as "surveyor-general" of Washington's Army. Erskine ran an iron works, which he organized his own militia to protect in 1775, *Bulletin, New Jersey Historical Commission,* I (March, 1971), 3. Guy H. Burnham, writing in *DAB,* described Erskine as commissioned in the Bergen County militia whose men were exempted "from compulsory militia service in any other company." Washington offered him his high commission in 1777. Erskine's maps were invaluable, especially as they delineated the country around the Hudson River, and his death on October 2, 1780, resulting from an illness caused by exposure, grieved Washington's entire staff.

CHAPTER EIGHT: *A Lull Before a Storm: Winter, 1777*

For Martha Washington's arrival at Pluckemin, see Schmidt, *op cit,* 220. For Washington's personality, consult Martha Bland to Frances Randolph, May 12, 1777, *NJHSP,* LI (1933), 151–52; for objections of British deserters, Sherman, *op cit,* 594–95; for Washington's reactions this first winter at Morristown, *WW-f,* V, 218n, 219, 221, 222, 233n, 237, 245, 250, 256, 260, 263n, 265, 269, 276–77, 278n, 293, 298–99.

See also Schmidt, *op cit,* 232 *et seq,* and John Hyde Preston's *Anthony Wayne, A Gentleman Rebel* (Garden City: Garden City Publishing Co., 1930), 15, 16, 62.

CHAPTER NINE: *Impasse: Spring, 1777*

Among British authorities on Howe none is more perceptive than Maldwyn A. Jones, "Sir William Howe: Conventional Strategist," *Billias,* 39, 44–5. The controversial Lee, as here discussed, is documented in Bill, *op cit,*

22, and *Scheer-Rankin,* 226. Washington's state by state analysis of his military situation is in *WW-f,* V, 321–23.

For British activity around New Brunswick, before and after the fighting at Bound Brook, see Titus E. Davis, *The Battle of Bound Brook* (Bound Brook: The Chronicle Steam Printery, 1895, pamphlet), 4–8, 9 *et seq,* 25; Miers, *op cit,* 37–8, 41; *WW-f,* V, 325; Kler, *op cit,* 44–5; and Demarest, *op cit,* 106.

CHAPTER TEN: *Valley in Arms: May–June, 1777*

Lord Stirling's "indiscretion" is explained in Valentine, *op cit,* 202–3; Washington's conflicting problems are drawn from *WW-f,* V, 327, 329, 331, 333, 338, 342, 343*n*–44*n*; for Howe's effort to lure Washington from the mountains to an open battle, see Valentine, *op cit,* 204; *General Washington Bicentennial Celebration* (Bound Brook: The Chronicle Printery, 1932, pamphlet), unpaged and unsigned but attributed to George M. LaMonte from an address before the Washington Camp Ground Association; *WW-f,* V, 455, 460*n*; for Howe's withdrawal from New Brunswick, *WW-f,* V, 459*n*–60*n*.

PART TWO: *The Guns of Monmouth*

Prelude: 1777–1778

Depiction of Lafayette, *Scheer-Rankin,* 229 and Frederick Butler, *Memoirs of the Marquis de La Fayette* (Wethersfield: Deming & Francis, 1825), 13–23. The volume was a potboiler obviously written to capitalize on Lafayette's triumphal tour of the United States in 1824–25. Comment on army's marching style, John Adams, *Familiar Letters of John Adams and His Wife Abigail Adams* (New York: Hurd & Houghton, 1876), 298. Burgoyne was well judged by George Athan Billias, "John Burgoyne: Ambitious General," *Billias,* 142, 163. For the battle at Brandywine, *Scheer-Rankin,* 234; at Germantown, Martin, *op cit,* 73; Burgoyne's home problems, *Billias,* 174 *et seq.*

The authoritative source on Clinton is *The American Rebellion: Sir Henry Clinton's Narrative of his Campaigns,* edited by William B. Willcox (New Haven: Yale University Press, 1954), 59–61. See also *Billias,* 40, 199.

CHAPTER ONE: *Forts Along the Delaware: October–November, 1777*

The plight of the soldier, Martin, *op cit,* 74–83; Howe's pursuit of the Americans along the Delaware, Thomas F. Gordon, *The History of New Jersey from its Discovery by Europeans to the Adoption of its Federal Constitution* (Philadelphia: John C. Clark, 1834), 226 and Martin, *op cit,* 84; at Fort Mercer, George R. Prowell, *The History of Camden*

County, New Jersey (Philadelphia: L. J. Richards & Co., 1886), 48–9, 50, 51; Thomas Cushing and Charles E. Sheppard, *History of the Counties of Gloucester, Salem, and Cumberland, New Jersey* (Philadelphia: Everts & Peck, 1883), 24–5, 168; and Martin, *op cit,* 85. The "histories" of Prowell and Cushing-Sheppard are surprisingly good despite the fact that prominent individuals paid for the flattering illustrations and biographies they received.

Hog Island was a major ship-building center during World War II. For the battle there and at Fort Mifflin, see [Surgeon] Albigence Waldo, "Diary, Valley Forge, 1777–1778," *Pennsylvania Magazine of History,* XXI (1897), 300, 301 [hereafter *Waldo*]; and Prowell, *op cit,* 54.

CHAPTER TWO: *Conspiracy: Winter, 1777–1778*

At Valley Forge and the Conway Cabal, Waldo, *op cit,* 300 *et seq,* 309, 310–12, 318; *Scheer-Rankin,* 303; Martin, *op cit,* 104, 114–15; *Scheer-Rankin,* 293–94.

Also William S. Stryker, *The Battle of Monmouth,* edited by William Starr Myers (Princeton: Princeton University Press, 1927), 10. This work, published posthumously, claims special importance for the wide use it makes of testimony at Lee's court-martial.

See also *Scheer-Rankin,* 299–300.

CHAPTER THREE: *The Chase Starts: Spring, 1778*

For Howe's recall from Philadelphia and the failure of the British peace commissioners, see Stryker, *op cit,* 18, 34–6, 44. Congress dated its refusal of peace terms August 11, 1778. Also *WW-f,* V, 323. For arrival of Lee, *Scheer-Rankin,* 313; Stryker, *op cit,* 22; and Carl Van Doren, *Secret History of the American Revolution* (New York: The Viking Press, 1941), 34.

Clinton departs from Philadelphia, Willcox, *op cit,* 89; Theodore T. Thayer, "The Battle of Monmouth," *Plan . . . [for] Monmouth Battlefield State Historic Park* (Trenton: N. J. Department of Conservation, 1968), 34 [hereafter *Thayer*]; Stryker, *op cit,* 31, 32, 41, 49. The American pursuit, Martin, *op cit,* 123; Willcox, *op cit,* 14; Stryker, *op cit,* 77, 87; Thayer, *op cit,* 34.

The legend of the curious fate that befell William Tennent has been known in our family for generations and is well told in Henry Charlton Beck's *The Jersey Midlands* (New Brunswick: Rutgers University Press, 1962), 373–77. For the military topography of the country between Tennent and Freehold, see Stryker, *op cit,* 90, 94, 113–14.

CHAPTER FOUR: *The Enigma of Charles Lee: June, 1778*

Stryker, *op cit,* 107–9, Thayer, *op cit,* 37, and Martin, *op cit,* 125 supply details of the gathering of the army under Lee.

The documentation of Mary Ludwig Hays will be found in Earl Schenck Miers, "Molly Pitcher and Peggy Shippen: A Study in Contrasts," *The Philadelphia Inquirer,* October 20, 1967, Pt. 5, 1 [hereafter *Inquirer*] and also the sketch of Mary Ludwig Hays McCauley by Virginia Ronsaville in *DAB*.

Lee's circumstances as he approached the battle are described in Martin, *op cit,* 126–27; Thayer, *op cit,* 37, 40; Lossing, *op cit,* II, 151; and *Scheer-Rankin,* 331.

CHAPTER FIVE: *Forever Molly: June, 1778*

For Monmouth after Washington's arrival, consult Stryker, *op cit,* 180, 181, 185–86, 199; Thayer, *op cit,* 42–3; *WW-f,* VII, 84; Martin, *op cit,* 129–30.

A "Molly Corbin" served in the same capacity when her husband fell at Fort Washington in 1776, *Pennsylvania Archives,* XII, 34, and Maban and Hanna may be heroines of other battlefields, Stryker, *op cit,* 190. The libeling of Mary's character is drawn from Martin, *op cit,* 132–33 and is of relatively recent vintage. Otherwise see *Inquirer* note in previous chapter and *Pennsylvania Archives,* Second Series, II, 181. Molly Pitcher was married to a George McCauley after the war; she was honored on a United States postage stamp in 1928.

The thirsty soldier who was killed giving up his turn at the well: Stryker, *op cit,* 195; on Comb's Hill: Thayer, *op cit,* 46.

CHAPTER SIX: *Shadows in the Night: June–July, 1778*

The unfolding battle: Stryker, *op cit,* 209, 210–11, 212–13, 214–17; Thayer, *op cit,* 47, 48–9. Washington does not wish to stop: *WW-f,* VII, 83. British withdrawal: Schmidt, *op cit,* 263; Stryker, *op cit,* 218, 230; *WW-f,* VII, 89, 90. Charges against Lee: *Scheer-Rankin,* 334–35.

CHAPTER SEVEN: *A* Feu de Joie *and Other Matters: Summer, 1778–Spring, 1779*

Celebration in New Brunswick: Demarest, *op cit,* 108; Lossing, *op cit,* II, 158. Lee's court-martial: Stryker, *op cit,* 244–45; Thayer, *op cit,* 51. Effect of war on education: Wertenbaker, *op cit,* 61–2, 63; Demarest, *op cit,* 120; Leonard Lundin, *Cockpit of the Revolution: The War for Independence* (Princeton: Princeton University Press, 1940), 409. Frustrations and tempers: *Scheer-Rankin,* 340, 341–42; Arnold smitten by Peggy Shippen: *Inquirer,* note in Chapter 4.

Washington at Middlebrook and subsequent social life: Schmidt, *op cit,* 264 *et seq*. Washington's camp site here is found by approaching the Watchungs along Mountainside Avenue in Bound Brook and taking a sharp left turn onto the Middlebrook Road. Here every day from sunup to sundown flies the "Betsy Ross flag" [author's note].

John White's pessimism: *Scheer-Rankin*, 356–57. Simcoe's Raiders: Miers, *op cit*, 48–50.

PART THREE: *Treason and Triumph*

Prelude: 1778–1779

Victory over the "Hair Buyer": *Scheer-Rankin*, 344–50. Impact of Indian warfare in New York: Schmidt, *op cit*, 286; *Scheer-Rankin*, 350–53. Clinton's plan against Washington: *ibid*, 360.

CHAPTER ONE: *A War on Sleds: December, 1779–January, 1780*

Snow in Jockey Hollow: James Thacher, *Military Journal During the American Revolutionary War* (Boston: Richardson & Lord, 1823), 214–16. As Washington's surgeon-general throughout the war, Thacher wrote a charming, intimate memoir that richly deserves to be reprinted with appropriate annotation. See also Martin, *op cit*, 165–66; Lossing, *op cit*, I, 310; Anthony Wayne to William Irvine, December 14, 1779, *American Historical Magazine*, VI (1862), 322; Thacher, *op cit*, 216–17, 220, 221; Martin, *op cit*, 167. George Scheer and I tramped Jockey Hollow on a blustery day; we covered all the countryside around Morristown, and even climbed (I carrying my younger son on my shoulder) to the eminence of Fort Nonsense, the remnants of which were clearly discernible.

Sled raid on Staten Island: Valentine, *op cit*, 246–47; 257–58; Lossing, *op cit*, I, 311; Martin, *op cit*, 171–72. Sources that say 3,000 New Jersey troops engaged in this operation seem wildly exaggerated.

CHAPTER TWO: *Huts in a Hollow: January–February, 1780*

Stirling's sacrifice: Valentine, *op cit*, 248–49. Punishments: Thacher, *op cit*, 222–25. Aftermath of Staten Island raid: Martin, *op cit*, 168–69.

Hunger and inflation: Martin, *op cit*, 172; Kapp, *op cit*, 182–85. On picket duty: Martin, *op cit*, 174 *et seq*. Lafayette rejoins Washington, *Scheer-Rankin*, 366; *WW-f*, XIV, 372, 375–76; Gottschalk, *op cit*, 156–57; *Scheer-Rankin*, 366. Hamilton: Lossing, *op cit*, I, 315.

CHAPTER THREE: *Death and Mutiny: March–May, 1780*

April raids, Thacher, *op cit*, 228. Funeral of Miralles, Thacher, *op cit*, 229, 230–31; Lossing, *op cit*, I, 311; Schmidt, *op cit*, 306–7. Inflation: Kapp, *op cit*, 184. Discontent in Jockey Hollow: Lundin, *op cit*, 403–7, 425–26; Thacher, *op cit*, 232. Pennsylvania mutiny: Martin, *op cit*, 182 *et seq*, 188. Hanging: Thacher, *op cit*, 233–35.

CHAPTER FOUR: *Surprise at Springfield: June, 1780*

Hessian approach and mistakes: Edmund B. Shotwell, *The Battles of Connecticut Farms and Springfield, 1780* (Springfield: Springfield Sun

Publishing Co., undated, unpaged pamphlet); M. C. Diedrich, *The Battle of Springfield* (Springfield: Springfield Historical Society, undated, unpaged pamphlet). Hessian approach and battle: Baurmeister, *op cit,* 353, 354. Knyphausen ends inertia: Lundin, *op cit,* 430–31.

CHAPTER FIVE: *Mutineers: July, 1780–January, 1781*

London poem: E. D. Halsey, *History of Morris County, New Jersey* (New York: W. W. Munsell & Co., 1882), 127. Again "vanity publishing," but extremely well done. Hamilton at falls in Passaic: Thacher, *op cit,* 242–43. A "monster," *ibid,* 245. By far the best telling of the Tempe Wick story was written by Stockton, *op cit,* 155–61. Significance of King's Mountain: Morison, *op cit,* 259. Treason of Arnold: *Scheer-Rankin,* 384, 387. The war at its "nadir": Morison, *op cit,* 261; George Doremus, *The American Revolution and Morris County* (Rockaway: The Record Print, 1926), 83, 84, 85; Lundin, *op cit,* 439, 441, 442–43; Thacher, *op cit,* 297; and Julian P. Boyd, "History as Seen by College Men," *NJHSP,* LXI (1943), 84–5; Halsey, *op cit,* 128.

CHAPTER SIX: *A Ride to Wethersfield: January–May, 1781*

Uprisings among New Jersey troops: Lundin, *op cit,* 444. Possible justification, McCormick, *op cit,* 139. Washington at New Windsor, *Washington's Diaries,* edited by John C. Fitzpatrick (Boston: Houghton Mifflin Company, 1925, 4 vols.), II, 207–8 [hereafter *WD*]. The Commander-in-Chief did not find the time to make diary entries from the outbreak of the war until May 1, 1781, a period of essentially six years. If a letter referred to in *Washington's Diaries* is not found in the collections of his writings edited by Worthington C. Ford or Jared Sparks, it usually is included in the Presidential Collection in the Manuscript Division of the Library of Congress. For other problems plaguing Washington in the spring of 1781 see Lundin, *op cit,* 445–46; *WD,* II, 208–11, 216–20; *WW-f,* IX, 256.

CHAPTER SEVEN: *March to Glory: August–September, 1781*

Plans altered by arrival of Cornwallis in Virginia, *WD,* II, 233–35, 255; Demarest, *op cit,* 111. Clinton outwitted in New Jersey, Doremus, *op cit,* 88–9; Schmidt, *op cit,* 322–25; Martin, *op cit,* 222; *WD,* II, 257–59.

Postlude: 1781–1783

Philadelphia learns of victory at Yorktown and raids in New Jersey, Lundin, *op cit,* 451. Carleton replaces Clinton, *Scheer-Rankin,* 498–99. Break-up of army, Martin, *op cit,* 280–81, 283. Washington at Princeton, Wertenbaker, *op cit,* 65–6. Writes farewell to army, Menzies, *op cit,* 124 (illustrations, 150). Rockingham has been twice moved since Washington stayed here; now restored and beautifully refurnished in keeping with colonial times, Rockingham is one of New Jersey's proudest historic sites.

Maps

The map of Revolutionary New Brunswick on page 33 is reproduced from William H. Benedict, "Early Taverns in New Brunswick," *Proceedings of the New Jersey Historical Society,* New Series (1918), III, No. 3, 132. "Trenton, 1777," reproduced on page 49, is from Benson J. Lossing, *The Pictorial Field Book of the Revolution,* 1860, II, 21. "Operations on the Delaware" and the plan of Fort Mercer on pages 116 and 117 are from George R. Prowell, *The History of Camden County,* Philadelphia, 1886, 49 and 50.

Index

Aberdeen, University of, 61
Adams, John, 6, 198; quoted, 3, 9, 58, 78, 103, 129, 199
Adams, Samuel, 6
Africa, 55
Albany, New York, 26, 32, 187, 232, 241; British threats to, 103, 104, 109
Alexander, Catherine, 81
Alexander, James, 14–15
Alexander, William, see Stirling, William Alexander, Lord
Alexandria, Virginia, 86, 137, 240
Allentown, New Jersey, 54, 139, 142
Amboy, New Jersey, 71, 80, 95, 97, 217, 233. See also Perth Amboy; South Amboy
American Crisis, The (Paine), 40, 45
American Light Horse, 139
Anderson, John, see André, John
Anderson, Richard Clough, 51

Anderson, Robert, 51
André, John, 178, 230–31
Angell, Israel, 222–23
Annapolis, Maryland, 86, 137
Appalachian Mountains, 185
Aquackamong Bridge, 28, 29
Arbuthnot, Marriot, 242–43
Armstrong, John, 97
Arnold, Benedict, 84, 95, 233, 240, 251; in Philadelphia, 139, 176–78; at Saratoga battle, 110–11, 177; at West Point, 227, 230–31
Arnold, Peggy Shippen (Mrs. Benedict Arnold), 177–78, 230–31
Arnold's Tavern, Morristown, 70, 98
Articles of Confederation (1777), 188, 254
Assunpink Creek, 48, 50, 51, 57, 59, 61
Auckland, William Eden, Lord, 136
Augusta (vessel), 123–24

Austria, 244
Auvergne, France, 101

Bahamas, 17
Baltimore, Maryland, 39, 73, 137
Bamford, William, quoted, 30–31
Barber, Francis, quoted, 237
Barnes, James, 166
Barras, Admiral de, 241, 242, 245
Barren Hill, Pennsylvania, 114
Barton, William, quoted, 187
Basking Ridge, New Jersey, 15, 36, 69, 92, 157, 192, 228
Battery House, Bound Brook, 89
Baurmeister, Carl Leopold, 169; quoted, 25, 220–21
Baylor, George, 73
Bear Swamp, 61
Bear Tavern, 47
Beaumarchais, Pierre Augustin Caron de, 132
Bedminster (Lesser Cross Roads), New Jersey, 66, 67, 82, 178; French in, 247, 248
Bemis Heights, battle of, 110, 111
Bennington, battle of, 105–106, 109
Bergen County, New Jersey, 5, 69
Berkeley County, Virginia, 36
Bernardsville (Veal Town), New Jersey, 36
Big Timber Creek, 118
Billingsport, New Jersey, 115, 118, 121
Bingley, Lord, 104
Birmingham Meeting House, 107
Black Horse (Columbus), New Jersey, 43
Black Watch, 139

Bland, Martha Dangerfield (Mrs. Theodorick Bland), quoted, 76–77
Bland, Theodorick, 76
Block Island, New York, 243
Blue Hills (Plainfield), New Jersey, 95, 217
Bonhamtown (Edison), New Jersey, 32, 96
Bordeaux, France, 102
Bordentown, New Jersey, 41, 42, 50, 52, 54, 57, 139
Boston, Massachusetts, 19, 32, 55, 57; French in, 176, 243; Morgan in, 83–84; port closing, 4; Washington in, 10, 12–13, 21, 29
Boston Gazette (newspaper), 90
Boston Tea Party, 4
Bottle Neck (Madison), New Jersey, 70
Boudinot, Elias, 251; quoted, 137
Bound Brook, New Jersey, 6–9, 30, 88–91, 92, 178, 248
Boyles, Major, 206–207
Brandywine, battle of, 106–108, 129, 141, 145, 172, 180, 216
Brandywine Creek, 106–107
Brant, Joseph, 187
Briar Hill, 150, 152–53
Bristol, Connecticut, 175
Bristol, Pennsylvania, 42, 46, 54, 108, 115
British Light Dragoons, 50
Brooklyn, New York, 13, 14, 16, 17, 96, 107
Brown, Daniel Isaac, 26
Brown, Mountford, 17
Brown, Stephen, 123
Bryant's Tavern, Springfield, 220
Buckingham, Pennsylvania, 42

Bucks County, Pennsylvania, 83
Bunch of Grapes, Philadelphia, 135
Bunker Hill, battle of, 5, 10, 68, 105, 118, 222
Bunner, Rudolph, 165
Bunting, Mrs., of Crosswicks, 141
Burgoyne, John, 95, 97–98, 103; quoted, 104, 105; Bennington and, 105–106, 109; Saratoga and, 110–11, 112, 124, 135
Burlington, New Jersey, 30, 41, 42, 56, 60, 115
Burlington County, New Jersey, 5
Burr, Aaron, 94, 165
Butler, John, 187
Butler, Richard, 150

Cadwalader, John, 42, 57, 61, 131; at Monmouth, 156, 162; Trenton and, 44, 47, 51, 54, 56
Cadwalader, Lambert, 56
Caldwell, Parson and Mrs., 220
Cambridge University, 27
Camden, New Jersey, 115
Camden, South Carolina, 228, 229
Campbell, Archibald, 23, 28
Canada, 12, 14, 27, 29, 95, 131; Burgoyne command, 103, 105, 109
Canajoharie, New York, 187
Cape Charles, 246, 249
Cape Fear River, 229
Cape François, San Domingo, 245
Cape Henry, 246, 249
Cape May, New Jersey, 210
Carleton, Guy, 252; quoted, 253
Carlisle, Frederick Howard, Earl of, 136
Carlisle, Pennsylvania, 146–47
Carrington, Edward, 162

Catherine the Great, empress of Russia, 111
Catholic Cemetery, Freehold, 153
"Cato," 174
Chad's Ford, 107
Charles Edward, Prince of Scotland, 61
Charleston, South Carolina: British in, 209, 210, 216, 217, 222, 228, 237
Charlestown Neck, Massachusetts, 83–84
Chastellux, François Jean, Marquis de, 118–19, 243
Chatham, New Jersey, 70, 233, 246, 248
Chavaniac, Chateau of, 101
Cheney, Squire, 107
Cherokee Indians, 79
Cherry Valley, New York, 187
Chesapeake Bay, *ix*, 103, 209, 245, 251; French fleet on, 246, 249
Chester, Pennsylvania, 108, 115, 246, 249
Chimney Rock, 178
Christiana Bridge, 246
Cilly, Joseph, 164, 165; quoted, 158
City Tavern, New York City, 53
City Tavern, Philadelphia, 135
Clark, Abraham, quoted, 75
Clark, George Rogers, 185–86
Clinton, George, 111; quoted, 136
Clinton, Henry, *ix*, 14, 26, 111–12, 135, 197, 224; American mutineers and, 233; Arnold and, 230, 231; command of, 135, 138–40, 252, 253; counterfeiting and, 73; Hudson defense, 188–89, 190, 217, 221–22, 227; on Lee court martial, 173; at Monmouth, 152,

153, 154, 157, 158, 163, 165, 166, 167, 169, 172; Peace Commission of, 136; Rhode Island and, 40, 176; seaport raids (1778), 175; Simcoe and, 180; Southern campaign of, 209–10, 216, 217, 240, 246; Washington pursuit (1778) of, 140–44; Yorktown and, 245–47, 248

Clinton, James, 240

Clothier, Mrs. James, 43

Clymer, George, 37

Coldstream Guards, 139, 152

Colfax, William, 192

Collège du Plessis, Paris, 101

Colonial Assembly of the Jerseys, 4

Columbia University, 15

Columbus (Black Horse), New Jersey, 43

Comb's Hill, 162–63

Committees of Correspondence, 4

Concord, battle of, 5, 10

Connecticut, 13, 136, 189, 241–44; militia, 46, 87, 108, 114, 122, 123, 158, 177, 203, 204, 211–14, 221, 243, 246. *See also specific placenames*

Connecticut Farms (Union), New Jersey, 219, 220, 222, 224, 225

Connecticut River, 241

Continental Army, *viii, ix,* 6, 16–37, 85–86; disbandment hopes of, 252, 253; flogging in, 188, 200–201; looting charges and, 199–200, 227–28; massacres by, 186–88; mutinies in, 211–15, 232–35, 236, 237, 238–39, 240, 253, 254; payment of, 93–94, 194, 202, 211, 214, 233–34, 237, 240, 248, 249, 253; Southern Army of, 209, 229,

231, 236–41, 252; supply of, 194–96, 201–202, 203, 206, 208–209, 210, 211–14, 229, 232, 240–41; Washington command, 39–40, 74–75, 78, 93, 103, 107–108, 129–30, 131–32, 133, 139, 145, 154. *See also specific battles*

Continental Congress, *viii,* 6, 9, 16, 21, 26, 41, 57, 179, 208; army uniforms and, 194, 240; Brandywine and, 108; British Peace Commissioners and, 136; Conway and, 129, 130, 131; Delaware Crossing and, 37, 38; Delaware forts and, 115, 121; flag adoption, 96; Fort Lee loss and, 28; Germantown and, 109; Indians and, 79, 81; Knyphausen and, 220; Lafayette and, 102; Lee and, 34, 36; Monmouth and, 157, 166–67, 173; Morristown mutinies and, 214, 232, 233; oaths of allegiance and, 75; pensions and, 211; Philadelphia (1777–1778) and, 80, 127, 138, 179–80; Princeton battle and, 64, 68; protests (1783) in, 253, 254; Southern Department, 229; Stark and, 105–106; Steuben and, 133; taxation powers and, 188; Trenton battle and, 46, 48, 54–55, 60; Washington powers and, 39–40, 78; Washington problem-list (1777) and, 87–88, 92–94; Yorktown and, 251, 252

Continental House, Morristown, 70

Conway, Thomas, 128–31, 133, 154, 170

Cooke, Nicholas, 74

Cooper's Ferry, 119

Cornell, Ezekiel, 240

Cornwallis, Charles, *ix,* 16, 26–28, 112, 139; at Brandywine, 107; at Monmouth, 150, 152, 163, 164; in New Brunswick (New Jersey), 71, 88, 89, 90, 91, 96–97, 246; New Jersey pursuit of Washington, 30–31, 34–35, 36, 37, 38; in Philadelphia, 108; Southern campaign of, 209–10, 216, 228–30, 236–38, 240, 245, 249; surrender, 251; Trenton battle and, 58–59, 60, 61

Cornwallis, Jemima (Mrs. Charles Cornwallis), 27, 31, 35, 112

Coryell's Ferry (Lambertville), New Jersey, 42, 140

Court of Saint James, London, 53

Covenhoven, William, 144

Coventry, Rhode Island, 19

Cowpens, battle of, 236–37

Cox, John, iron-works owner, 43

Cranbury, New Jersey, 54, 145

Crosswicks, New Jersey, 57, 61, 68, 141

Croton River, 121

Crown Point, 243

Cumberland County, Pennsylvania, 147

Custis, John Parke, 74–75

Danbury, Connecticut, 86, 176, 191

Dan River, 238

Dayton, Elias, 12, 240, 241; quoted, 74; Springfield and, 217, 219–20, 222, 223

Deane, Silas, 93, 101–102, 129, 132

Declaration of Independence, 6–9, 29, 39, 69, 211, 248; anniversaries, 98, 131, 171, 172; Lafa-yette and, 101; signers, 35, 37, 58, 75, 254

De Groot, Jacob, 90

De Heister, Philip von, 16, 96

De Kalb, John, *see* Kalb, John

Delaware, 39; militia, 17, 87, 95, 229

Delaware Bay, 103

Delaware River, 32, 34, 35, 45, 46, 70, 95, 103; Clinton crossing (1778), 139, 167; forts of, 113–24; Lowantica encampment on, 77; Washington crossings, 37, 38, 41, 42, 44, 47, 52, 55, 115

Derby, Pennsylvania, 129, 246

Detroit, Michigan, 185–86, 187

Dewitt, Simeon, 88, 246

Dickinson, John, 39

Dickinson, Philemon, 46, 148, 150, 217, 220

Dobbs Ferry, 21, 26, 68, 246

Donop, Carl von, 119, 120–21

Donop, Emil Kurt von, 41, 42, 44, 50, 52, 54, 57, 59

Dunk's Ferry, 42, 44

Dunlap, William, quoted, 255

Duponceau, Pierre, 132, 137

Duportail, Louis, 153, 173

Durham Iron Works, 83

Dutch Reformed Church, New Brunswick, 88

Eagle (vessel), 16

Eastern Precinct (Franklin Township), New Jersey, 181

East Jersey, 6

Easton, Pennsylvania, 36, 189, 220

East River, 13

Eden, William, 136

Edinburgh, University of, 136

Edison (Bonhamtown), New Jersey, 32, 96

Egg-Harbor, New Jersey, 175

Eight-Mile Ferry (McKonkey's Ferry, Taylorsville), 42, 46, 47

Elizabeth, New Jersey, 32

Elizabethtown, New Jersey, 22, 30, 196, 203, 204, 240; Knyphausen and, 217, 219, 220, 221, 222, 224

Elizabethtown Academy, 174

Elkton River, 106

Embarrass River, 186

England: colonial revolt and, 3–17, 85–86; counterfeiting and, 72, 73; Lafayette and, 101; New Jersey "invasion," 18–37, 38–39, 40–44, 45–52, 112; peace initiatives of, 135–37; smallpox inoculation in, 71; Yorktown and, 352–53. *See also specific battles*

England. Parliament, 4, 27, 85, 104

Englishtown, New Jersey, 145, 146, 160, 170

Eoff's Tavern, Pluckemin, 66, 67, 69, 76, 179

Erskine, William, 59

Essex County, New Jersey, 5, 240

Estaing, Charles Hector, Count d', 175–76, 209

Eton College, 27

Ewald, Johann, 43

Ewing, James, 42, 44

Fairfield, Connecticut, 189

Fairhaven, Massachusetts, 175

Farmer, Lewis, 158

Fauntleroy, Henry, 162

Ferguson, Adam, 136

Ferguson, Patrick, 229–30

Finderne, New Jersey, 95

Fisher, Hendrick, 6–8

Fitzgerald, John, 63–64, 77

Fleury, François Louis de, 121, 122

Flood, John, 241

Florida, 17

Ford, Jacob, 12, 192

Ford's Mill, 70

Forest, Captain, 50

Forman, David, 148, 155, 173, 241

Forman, Samuel, 12

Fort Constitution, *see* Fort Lee, New Jersey

Fort Detroit, *see* Detroit, Michigan

Fortieth British Regiment, 63

Fort Independence, 21, 71

Fort Lee, New Jersey, 16, 227, 241; American defeat at, 19–28, 29, 45

Fort Mercer, 115, 118–21, 122, 123

Fort Mifflin, 121–24

Fort Niagara, 187

Fort Nonsense, 206

Fort Oswego, 109

Fort Schuyler (Fort Stanwix), 74, 109, 110, 240, 241

Fort Stirling, 16

Fort Sumter, 51

Fort Washington, 16, 19, 21, 29, 31; Magaw command, 22, 23–24, 25–26

France, *ix,* 42, 81, 93, 104, 128, 132; Arnold and, 178; Lafayette in, 101, 178, 204–205; Luzerne embassy from, 207–208; naval aid from, 209, 226–27; Rhode Island engagements and, 175, 176, 209; troop supply and, 240–41; United States recognition by, 135, 136, 141; Wethersfield Con-

ference (1781), 241–44, 245;
Yorktown and, 247–49

Franklin, Benjamin, 39, 132, 177, 240; quoted, 4, 72, 136

Franklin, William, 4, 12; quoted, 5

Franklin Township (Eastern Precinct), New Jersey, 181

Frederick the Great, king of Prussia, 111, 132, 216

Fredericksburg, Virginia, 62, 240

Freehold (Monmouth Court House), New Jersey, *viii,* 140, 142–44, 145, 148, 150, 152, 153, 154; British evacuation of, 167, 169, 172

Freeman, Douglas Southall, quoted, 16

Frelinghuysen, Frederick, 12

Frelinghuysen House, Bound Brook, 6–8

French and Indian Wars, 15, 35, 62, 83, 85, 106, 180

Gage, Thomas, 10

Gallic Wars (Caesar), 19

Gansevoort, Peter, 110

Gates, Horatio, 36, 41, 46, 81, 138, 187, 195; Conway and, 130–31; Saratoga and, 110–11, 129; Southern command, 229, 236

George I, king of England, 86

George II, king of England, 64, 142, 255

George III, king of England, 4, 69, 104, 112, 138; Declaration of Independence on, 7–8; mercenaries and, 111–12; peace offers (1778), 135–37; Ticonderoga and, 105; Yorktown and, 252–53

Georgia, 209, 228, 253

Germain, George, Lord, 73, 104, 109, 135, 189; quoted, 2, 112, 252

German Battalion, 46

German Flats, New York, 241

Germantown, battle of, 108–109, 113, 129, 141, 145

Germany, 112, 128, 216

Gibbs, Caleb, 77

Gibraltar, 252

Gilmore (mutineer), 234

Gloucester, New Jersey, 115, 121

Gloucester County, New Jersey, 43, 240

Gloucester Point, Pennsylvania, 245

Glover, John, 44, 47

Gordon, Cosmo, 139, 163

Gowanus Creek, 17

Grant (mutineer), 234

Grant, James, 16, 53, 59; quoted, 54

Grasse, François Joseph Paul, Comte de, *ix,* 245–46, 249

Graves, Thomas, *ix,* 227

Grayson, William, 148, 150, 152

Great Mud Island, 121

Green, Jacob, 56

Greene, Ashbel, quoted, 254

Greene, Christopher, 118, 119, 120, 121

Greene, Nathanael, 29, 38, 67, 81, 94, 96, 118, 129, 188, 227; Arnold and, 230; at Brandywine, 106, 107; Clinton pursuit and, 141; at Fort Lee, 19–28, 45; at Monmouth, 160, 162–63, 164, 165; at Morristown, 70, 71; on New Jersey retreat, 34; Raritan encampment (1778), 178, 181; in Rhode Island, 175–76; South-

ern campaign and, 236–37, 238, 252; at Springfield, 220, 221, 222, 223; at Trenton, 47, 59
Greene, Mrs. Nathanael, 137
Green Mountains, 105, 106
Green Village, New Jersey, 69
Grenadiers, 139; at Monmouth, 152, 157, 163, 164, 165, 166
Griffin, Samuel, 43
Griggstown, New Jersey, 65
Guilford Court House, battle of, 238–39
Gulf Creek, 125
Gulph, The, 125

Hackensack, New Jersey, *ix,* 217; Washington in, 23, 24, 26, 28, 88
Hackensack River, 29
Haddonfield, New Jersey, 30, 115, 119, 121, 139
Halifax, Nova Scotia, 12
Hamilton, Alexander, 21, 31–32, 51, 77, 142; quoted, 96, 141, 156, 164, 231; at Middlebrook (1778), 179; in Morristown (1779), 192, 205; Passaic Falls and, 226
Hamilton, Elizabeth Schuyler (Mrs. Alexander Hamilton), 205
Hamilton, Henry, 185–86, 187
Hampton Roads, Virginia, 249
Hancock, John, 6, 115, 175, 176
Hand's Riflemen, 64
Hannibal, 82
Hanover, New Jersey, 69
Harcourt, William, 157
Harlem Heights, battle of, 17, 21, 43
Hartford, Connecticut, 241

Hartshorne and Bowne (firm), 93
Harvard University, 12
Haverstraw, New York, 31
Hays, John Caspar, 147
Hays, Mary Ludwig ("Molly Pitcher," Mrs. John Caspar Hays), 146–47, 159–60
Hazen, Moses, 95, 246
Head of Elk, Chesapeake Bay, 246, 249
Heard, Nathaniel, 4, 12
Heath, William, 22, 68, 78, 81, 87, 227, 241; quoted, 71
Henry VII, king of England, 111
Henry, Patrick, 87, 131, 185, 242
Herkimer, Nicholas, 110
Hesse-Cassel, Germany, 112
Hessians, *viii,* 16, 38, 79, 86, 112; Burgoyne use of, 105, 106, 111; Clinton and, 139, 140, 157, 169, 222; Delaware River forts and, 119–21; Hudson River forts and, 23, 24, 25; in New Jersey, 30, 32, 37, 41, 42, 43–44, 45–52, 54–55, 58, 59, 70, 71, 89, 96, 217, 220, 222–23; rebel Germans and, 82; in Rhode Island, 176
Highlands, The, New York, 22, 26, 68, 98, 195; West Point defense and, 188, 232
Hitchcock, Daniel, 55, 61, 64
Hog Island, 122
Holstead's Point, New Jersey, 204
Holy Roman Empire, 112
Hopewell, New Jersey, 54, 141
Horseshoe Cove, 167
Hortalez & Company, 132
Hospital Point, 122
Housler, David, 43
Howe, George, 85

Howe, Richard, 12, 13, 16, 136, 138, 175
Howe, Robert, 209, 234–35
Howe, William, 10, 12–13, 16, 17, 21, 26, 83, 85–86; at Brandywine, 107, 108; Clinton and, 111; Cornwallis and, 112; Delaware forts and, 118, 122, 124; Fort Washington and, 23–24, 25; New Jersey campaign and, 31, 32, 39, 40–41, 54, 57, 78–79, 89–90, 92, 95–97, 102, 107; oaths of allegiance and, 75; Philadelphia and, 46, 74, 80, 86, 95, 97, 98, 102, 103, 104, 106, 108, 113, 115, 127, 135, 177; recruitment bounties of, 93, 94; removal from command, 135, 138; Trenton and, 53
Howland's Ferry, 47
Hudson River (North River), 13, 17, 24, 25, 68, 97–98, 110, 138, 141, 252; Clinton threats and, 188–89, 190, 217, 221–22, 227; Cornwallis crossing of, 26, 27–28, 29, 36; French aid on, 243; Stony Point battle and, 189–90
Hudson Valley, 13. *See also specific placenames*
Hungary, 36
Hunt, Stephen, 12
Hunterdon County, New Jersey, 5, 83
Huntington, Jedediah, 162, 172
Hutchinson, Thomas, 4

India, 253
Indian Queen, Philadelphia, 135
Ireland, 27, 128
Iron Works Hill, battle of, 43–44

Iroquois (Six Nations) Indians: American massacre of, 187–88
Irvine, William, 146, 147
Irving, Washington, 35

Jacksonville (Slabtown), New Jersey, 43
Jaegers, 89, 90, 139, 157, 220, 222, 223
James I, king of England, 14
James River, 240
Jamestown, Virginia, 240, 249
Jay, John, 72, 179
Jay, Sarah Livingston (Mrs. John Jay), 179
Jefferson, Thomas, 6, 7, 165, 242
Jenner, Edward, 72
Jericho Mountain, 42
Jersey Blues, 140
Jockey Hollow, Morristown, 191, 194, 202, 206, 210, 211, 214, 217
Johnston, George John, 77
Johnstone, George, 136
Julius Caesar, 19, 82

Kalb, John, 93, 188, 210, 229; quoted, 202–203, 208–209
Kaskaskia, 185
Keith, William, 41–42
Kennett Square, Pennsylvania, 107
Kentish Guards, 21
King's Boys, 3
King's Bridge, 21, 22, 71
King's Ferry, New Jersey, 189
King's College (Columbia), 15
King's Mountain, 229–30, 236
Kingston, New Jersey, 54, 64
King's Volunteers, 26
Kirkland, Samuel, 81
Kitchel, Anna, 70

Knowles' Cove, Pennsylvania, 46

Knox, Henry, 19, 21, 26, 67, 129, 222; quoted, 51; Lee court martial and, 173; at Monmouth, 162; in Philadelphia, 139; Pluckemin camp (1778), 178, 179; at Princeton, 63

Knox, Mrs. Henry, 179

Knyphausen, Wilhelm von, 23, 24, 50, 216–24, 225

Lafayette, Marie Joseph Paul Yves Roch Gilbert du Motier, marquis de, *ix*, 93, 99, 101–102, 103, 118, 202; Brandywine and, 106, 107; Clinton pursuit and, 141–42, 144; Conway and, 131; in France, 101, 178, 204–205; Lee court martial and, 173; at Monmouth, 152, 153, 154, 156–57, 162, 169; Rhode Island expedition, 175–76; son of, 209; Southern campaign and, 237, 240, 245, 246, 249; at Springfield, 220

Lafayette, George Washington, 209

Lake Champlain, 29, 243

Lake George, 105, 109

Lake Ontario, 109, 187

Lamb, John, 246

Lambertville, New Jersey, 42, 140

Lamington, New Jersey, 66, 67

Lancaster, Pennsylvania, 108

Lane, Matthew, 67, 69

Laurens, Henry, 131, 150, 179; quoted, 133, 171

Laurens, John, 243

Lawrenceville, New Jersey, 54, 59, 246

Lee, Billy, 162

Lee, Charles, 22, 46, 81, 131, 139; Clinton and, 138, 141, 144; court

martial of, 170, 172–73; death of, 253; at Monmouth, 145–54, 155–56, 160, 162, 169–70; New Jersey campaign and, 28, 30, 34, 35–37, 40, 41, 192, 228; Prescott exchanged for, 87, 137; Washington efforts to retrieve, 74, 78, 86, 87, 137–38

Lee, Henry ("Light Horse Harry"), 188, 189, 220, 222, 236

Lee, Richard Henry, 130

Leslie, Alexander, 59, 139

Leslie, Charles, 68–69

Lesser Cross Roads, New Jersey, *see* Bedminster, New Jersey

Lexington, battle of, 5, 219

Leydecker's Farm, Hackensack, 23

Liberty Boys, 3

Liberty Corner, New Jersey, 66

Lincoln, Benjamin, 68, 88–89, 94, 96, 209–10

Little Egg Harbor, New Jersey, 211

Little Mud Island, 121

Little Wabash River, 186

Livingston, Betsy, 179

Livingston, Kitty, 179

Livingston, Sarah (Mrs. John Jay), 179

Livingston, William, 15, 29, 37, 137, 156, 207; daughters of, 179; Delaware fortification and, 115; recruitment and, 28, 30, 32, 80–81

Livingston, Mrs. William, 92, 207

Locke, John, 19

London, England, 112, 135, 225, 252

London Coffee House, Philadelphia, 135

Long Island, New York, 13–14, 243

Long Island, battle of, 14, 16–17, 21, 36, 38, 43, 52, 216
Long Island Ferry, 13–14
Loring, Mrs. Joshua, 53, 78, 86, 102
Louis XVI, king of France, 101, 102, 209, 244
Louisburg, battle of, 106
Lovell, James, quoted, 130
Lowantica Valley, 70, 71, 77–78
Lower Salem, New York, 241
Lutheran Church, Pluckemin, 67, 68–69
Luzerne, marquis de la, 207–208, 254
Luzon, Duke de, 247
Lynnhaven Bay, 249
Lyon, William, quoted, 65

McCormick, Richard P., quoted, 239
McDougall, Alexander, 188, 195
McHenry, James, quoted, 157
McKonkey's Ferry, Taylorsville, 42, 46, 47
McMichael, James, quoted, 31
Madison, New Jersey, 70
Magaw, Robert, 22, 23–24, 25–26
Maidenhead (Lawrenceville), New Jersey, 54, 59, 246
Maine, 254
Manalapan (Penelopen), New Jersey, 145
Marblehead, Massachusetts, 44, 47
Marie Antoinette, queen of France, 101
Marshall, John, 51
Marshall, Thomas, 51
Martha's Vineyard, Massachusetts, 175
Martin, Ephraim, 12

Martin, Joseph Plumb, 13–14, 242; quoted, 17, 108–109, 113, 114–15, 118, 121–22, 123, 127–28, 140, 183, 204; at Monmouth, 146, 147–48, 154, 158–59; in Morristown, 191–92, 196, 201, 202, 203, 211, 212, 214; on peace, 253–54; on Staten Island, 197–98; Yorktown and, 248
Maryland, 137, 246; Continental Congress in, 39; Howe in, 106; militia, 17, 30, 46, 87, 95, 156, 157, 229, 252. *See also specific placenames*
Massachusetts, 4, 12, 15, 32, 68, 79, 87, 152, 243; Clinton seaport raids in, 175; soldiers' pay and, 240. *See also specific placenames*
Massachusetts Assembly, 85
Massachusetts Council, 221
Mathews, Edward, 219, 222, 223
Mauduit, Duplessis, 163
Mawhood, Charles, 60, 63, 64
Maxwell, William, 12, 95, 96, 108, 173; Clinton's New Jersey march and, 140, 141; Knyphausen and, 220, 223; at Monmouth, 145, 152, 166
Meade, Richard K., 137
Meigs, Return Johnathan, 212
Mellick, Andrew, quoted, 63, 247
Mendham, New Jersey, 69
Mercer, Hugh, 42, 47, 50, 61–63
Mercersburg, Pennsylvania, 62
Merlin (vessel), 122, 123
Metuchen, New Jersey, 96–97, 180
Middlebrook, New Jersey, 94, 95, 176, 178–79, 186, 217
Middlebrook Heights, 178
Middlebush, New Jersey, 95

Middlesex County, New Jersey, 4, 5, 181
Middletown, New Jersey, 144, 148, 152, 167
Miers, John, *viii*
Mifflin, Thomas, 57, 81, 128, 129, 130; quoted, 38
Millege, Thomas, 69
Mill Hill, 57
Mill Pond, Trenton, 60
Millstone, New Jersey, 65, 95, 248
Millstone River, 64, 65
Minorca, 252
Miralles, Juan de, 207–208
Mohawk Indians, 35
Mohawk River, 109, 240, 241, 243
Mohawk Valley, 187
Molly Pitcher's Well, *vii*
Monckton, Henry, 165–66
Monmouth, battle of, *viii,* 142, 143, 171, 174–75, 216; Lee command at, 144, 145–54, 155–56, 160, 162, 169–70, 172–73; Washington action at, 155–63, 165, 166–69, 176
Monmouth County, New Jersey, 5, 93, 115, 142, 147, 240, 252
Monmouth Court House, *see* Freehold (Monmouth Court House), New Jersey
Monroe, James, 50; quoted, 48
Moore's Alley, Philadelphia, 135
Moorestown, 44
Morgan, Charles, *ix*
Morgan, Daniel, 83–84, 95, 96, 140; Clinton pursuit and, 141; at Saratoga, 110; Southern campaign and, 229–30, 236–37, 238
Morison, Samuel Eliot, quoted, 3, 230

Morris, Gouverneur, 180
Morris, Richard, quoted, 80
Morris, Robert, 58; quoted, 72, 136
Morris County, New Jersey, 93; militia, 5, 32, 34, 69–70, 77–78
Morris Hotel, Morristown, 208
Morristown, New Jersey, 13, 36, 68, 69, 231, 232; mutinies in, 211–15, 232–33; Washington in, 70–84, 89, 94, 98, 129, 190, 191, 192–96, 201–205, 206–15, 216–21, 227, 228, 242, 248
Morrisville, Pennsylvania, 37
Morven (Stockton house), Princeton, 35, 59, 255
Mount Holly, New Jersey, 43–44, 52, 124
Mount Independence, 74
Mount Joy, 126
Mount Pleasant (Arnold house), 178
Mount Pleasant, New Jersey, 95, 96
Mount Vernon, Virginia, 62, 76
Mount Whoredom, Boston, 10
Moylan, Stephen, 141, 157
Mud Islands, 121
Muhlenberg, John Peter Gabriel, 82, 83, 84, 96, 107, 162
Murfree, Hardy, 190

Narragansett Bay, 175
Narrows, The, 12
Nassau Hall, Princeton, 5, 9, 34, 35, 59; battle of Princeton and, 63, 64, 174; Continental Congress in, 254; mutineers in, 233
Navesink River, 140
Neilson, John, 9, 12, 211
Neshaminy River, 103

Newark, New Jersey, 28, 30, 32, 192
New Bedford, Massachusetts, 175
New Brunswick, New Jersey, 3, 4, 6, 9, 22, 40, 60, 64, 68, 211; British troops in, 53, 54, 59, 71, 88–91, 94, 95–97, 174, 246; Simcoe raid on, 181; Washington in, 30, 31–32, 34, 65, 170, 171–72, 175, 248
Newburgh, New York, 251, 252
New Castle, Delaware, 138
New Castle, New York, 22, 172
Newcomb, Silas, 12, 118, 120
New England, 13, 68, 138, 175, 231, 234, 237, 242, 254. *See also specific states*
New Germantown (Oldwick), New Jersey, 66, 82
New Hampshire, 41, 50, 87, 105; counterfeiters in, 73; militia, 158, 164
New Hampshire Gazette (newspaper), 190
New Haven, Connecticut, 177, 189
New Jersey, *ix,* 3–17; British invasion of, 17, 22, 23, 25–28, 29–37, 38, 39, 40–44, 54, 57, 74, 78–79, 80, 107; Clinton crossing (1778), 139–40; Delaware forts of, 113–24; Knyphausen raids on, 216–24, 225; New Brunswick British evacuation, 97, 102; postwar fate of Loyalists in, 252; Princeton victory and, 60–69; Trenton victory and, 45–52; Yorktown and, 246–49, 251. *See also specific placenames*
New Jersey, College of, *see* Princeton College
New Jersey Central Railroad, *vii*

New Jersey Gazette (newspaper), 139, 174
New Jersey Legislature (Provincial Congress), 5–6, 30, 80–81, 174, 252; mutinies and, 233–34, 237, 239–40
New Jersey Militia, 5–6, 9, 22, 80, 87, 192, 232; British evacuation of Philadelphia and, 139, 140; Delaware forts and, 118, 120; Indian slaughter by, 187; Knyphausen and, 217, 219–20, 221, 222; at Monmouth, 148, 157, 166; mutiny and, 233–35, 236, 237, 238–39, 240; New Jersey campaign and, 30, 32, 34, 74, 90
New Jersey Provincial Congress, *see* New Jersey Legislature (Provincial Congress)
New Market (Quibbletown), New Jersey, 95, 96, 180
Newport, Rhode Island, 40, 86–87, 175, 191, 227, 243
Newtown, Pennsylvania, 42, 52, 55
New Vernon, New Jersey, 69
New Windsor, New York, 232, 239, 240, 243–44
New York Bay, 13, 73; sled crossing of, 196–98, 199
New York City, 15; British occupation of, 12–14, 16, 17, 21, 23, 31, 53, 68, 86, 138, 139, 169, 175, 189, 207, 216, 227, 240; French plan against, 243, 245, 246, 247; Springfield battle and, 225
New York Mercury (newspaper), 90
New York State, 136, 241; militia, 87, 221, 230, 232, 246

Non-Importation Resolution (1765), 56

North, Frederick, 2nd earl of Guilford, Lord, 27, 136, 252, 253

Northampton County, Pennsylvania, 42

North Carolina, *ix,* 167, 190, 209, 229, 238

North River, *see* Hudson River

Norwalk, Connecticut, 189

Nottingham, England, 85

Nova Scotia, 12, 14, 83

Ogden, Aaron, 220

Old South Theatre, Philadelphia, 135

Old Tennent Church, Tennent, 142, 143, 145, 148, 159; Washington at, 155, 156, 162, 166

Oldwick (New Germantown), New Jersey, 66, 82

Olney, Jeremiah, 148

Oneida Indians, 81

Orange County, New York, 241

Orderly Book of Washington, 79

Oriskany, New York, 110

Oswald, Eleazer, 152

Paine, Thomas, 28, 45; quoted, 29, 30, 40, 50, 123

Paoli Tavern, 108, 189

Paramus, New Jersey, 172

Paris, France, 101, 253

Passaic Falls, 226

Passaic River, 28, 29, 70, 71, 226

Patten, Abraham, 91

Peale, Charles Wilson, 254–55

Peapack, New Jersey, 66, 67

Peekskill, New York, 22, 86, 87, 172, 191

Penelopen (Manalapan), New Jersey, 145

Pennington, New Jersey, 37, 41

Pennington Road, 47, 48

Penn's Neck, New Jersey, 54

Pennsylvania, 60, 160, 187, 221; militia, 30, 31, 34, 42, 46, 50, 56, 57, 61, 64, 80, 82, 83, 87, 107, 137, 141, 147, 150, 156, 157, 165, 166, 178, 213, 231, 232–33, 252; Washington in, 37, 38–44, 45–47, 106–109, 113–15. *See also specific placenames*

Pennsylvania, University of, 56

Pennsylvania Attorney General, quoted, 130

Pennsylvania Council on Safety, 74

Pennsylvania Evening Post (newspaper), 10, 12, 43–44

Pennypacker's Mill, Pennsylvania, 113

Pequea, Pennsylvania, 34

Pequot Indians, 242

Percy, Hugh, 24

Perth Amboy, New Jersey, 4, 22, 181, 199

Philadelphia, Pennsylvania, 3, 6, 9, 13, 58, 61, 202, 220, 237; Arnold in, 176–78; British approach to, 17, 32, 38–39, 40, 46, 74, 80, 86, 95, 97, 98, 102, 103, 104, 106, 108; British occupation of, 113, 114, 115, 118, 126–27, 135, 138–40, 177; British shipping in, 93, 115; counterfeiting in, 72, 127; Luzerne visit (1780), 207; mutineer missions to, 232, 233, 253; New Brunswick and, 88, 97, 172; Washington conference

(1778) in, 179–80; Wayne in, 82–83; Yorktown march and, 246, 248–49, 251

Philadelphia Committee of Safety, 56

Philadelphia Council, 178

Phoenix (vessel), 73

Pigot, Robert, 175

Piscataway, New Jersey, 96

"Pitcher, Molly" (Mary Ludwig Hays), 146–47, 159–60

Pittstown, New Jersey, 30, 32, 36

Plainfield (Blue Hills), New Jersey, 95, 217

Pluckemin, New Jersey, 65, 66–67, 76, 95; Knox encampment, 178, 179

Poland, 35

Political Magazine (London), 225

Pompton, New Jersey, 188, 232, 233

Poor, Enoch, 162, 167, 172

Port Royal, 228

Portugal, 35, 104

Potowomut (Warwick), Rhode Island, 19

Potts, Stacey, 50, 51

Powle's Hook, New York, 190

Prescott, Richard, 86–87, 137

Princeton, New Jersey, 6, 9, 30, 141, 217; British troops in, 34–35, 38, 41, 50, 52, 59, 60–65; Martin on, 140; Sullivan defense of, 95; Washington post-war rest in, 255; Yorktown march and, 246, 248

Princeton, battle of, 60–65, 70, 174; Pluckemin and, 66–69

Princeton College, 3–4, 5, 34, 35; commencement (1783), 254–55;

military exemptions and, 173–74; mutineer refuge in, 232–33, 237

Proctor's Pennsylvania Artillery, 147

Providence, Rhode Island, 175, 191, 243

Province Island, 122, 123

Prussia, 111, 132, 133, 216

Pulaski, Casimir, 93

Putnam, Israel, 13, 16, 24, 68, 78, 81, 91; in Middlebrook, 178; retirement of, 195

Pyle's Ford, 107

Quebec, Canada, 12, 84, 85, 180

Queens College (Rutgers), 9, 31, 65, 88, 174, 181, 246

Queen's Rangers (Simcoe's Rangers), 139, 219, 222; at Monmouth, 148, 150, 152, 166, 180; Staten Island headquarters of, 180–81

Quibbletown (New Market), New Jersey, 95, 96, 180

Rahway River, 219, 222

Rall, Johann, 24, 37, 41, 42; Trenton battle and, 44, 50, 51

Ramsay, David, quoted, *viii*

Ramsay, Nathaniel, 156, 157, 158

Randolph, Fanny, 76, 77

Raritan Bay, 210

Raritan River, 9, 31, 88, 89, 94, 96, 140, 144; Greene encampment (1778), 178, 181; Monmouth battle and, 171

Red Bank, New Jersey, 115, 118–21

Reed, Joseph, 10, 54, 61; quoted, 45–46, 52

Regulations for the Order and Discipline of Troops of the United States (Steuben), 133

Rhode Island, 19, 21, 32, 40, 241; French fleet off, 209, 226–27, 243; Lafayette and, 175–76, 209; militia, 74, 86–87, 122, 123, 148, 158, 176, 222, 240, 246

Rising Sun Tavern, 144

Robertson, British General, 225

Robin's Tavern, 142

Rochambeau, Jean Baptiste Donatien de Vimeur, Comte de, 226–27, 241, 243, 246, 248, 252

Roche de Fermoy, 42

Rockingham, Charles Watson-Wentworth, marquis of, 253

Rockingham, New Jersey, 255

Rocky Hill, New Jersey, 64, 255

Roebuck (vessel), 122

Rome, Ancient, 19, 82

Rosebrough, John, 42

Royal American Gazette (newspaper), 90

Rush, Benjamin, quoted, 130, 131

Russell, Lieut. Col., 122

Russia, 35, 111, 244

Rutgers University, *see* Queens College (Rutgers)

St. Clair, Arthur, 50, 61, 105, 188, 190, 252

St. Leger, Barry, 109, 110

St. Petersburg, Russia, 244

Salem, Massachusetts, 180

Salem County, New Jersey, 5, 43

San Domingo, 245

Sandy Hook, 12, 15, 102, 140, 221; British embarkation from, 167;

counterfeiters in, 73; French fleet off, 248; Graves fleet off, 227

Saratoga, battle of, 112, 124, 129, 135; Arnold at, 110–11, 177

Savannah, Georgia, 209, 228, 253

Savannah, battle of, 209

Scammell, "Light Horse," 246

Schuyler, Elizabeth (Mrs. Alexander Hamilton), 205

Schuyler, Philip, 78, 81, 97, 205

Schuylkill River, 113, 114, 125, 129, 137, 178

Scotch Plains, New Jersey, 96, 97, 217

Scotland, 5, 14, 61

Scots Foot Guards, 163, 164, 165

Scott, Charles, 141, 152, 153, 166, 169, 173; quoted, 154

Scott, Kenneth, quoted, 72

Scottish Rebellion of 1715, 14

Seaconnet Passage, 175

Second Continental Dragoons, 240

Seneca Indians, 187

"Sergeant R," 61

Serle, Ambrose, quoted, 12–13

Seven Years' War, 27, 101, 104

Shenandoah Valley, 82, 83

Shippen, Edward, 177

Shippen, Peggy (Mrs. Benedict Arnold), 177–78, 230–31

Shirley, William, 15

Short Hills, 77, 220, 223

Shreve, Israel, 223

Shrewsbury River, 167

Silk-Stocking Company, 56

Simcoe, John Graves, 180–81; Knyphausen and, 219, 222; at Monmouth, 148, 150, 152, 180

Simcoe's Rangers, *see* Queen's Rangers (Simcoe's Rangers)

Six Nations (Iroquois) Indians: American massacre of, 186–88

Skinner, Cortlandt, 222

Slabtown (Jacksonville), New Jersey, 43

Smallwood, William, 46, 95, 172, 203

Smith, Lieut. Col., 121, 122

Smith, Aaron, 43

Somerset, New Jersey, 181

Somerset County, New Jersey, 31, 66, 94; militia, 5, 82, 240

Somerset Courthouse (Millstone), 65, 95, 248

Somerville, New Jersey, 178

South Amboy, 30

South Carolina, *ix,* 102, 167; British in, 209, 210, 216, 228, 245

South Mountain, 219

South River, New Jersey, 170

Spain, 35, 102, 104, 245; Miralles visit and, 207, 208

Spencer, Joseph, General, 78

Spotswood Middle Brook, 148, 155, 162, 164, 165

Springfield, Massachusetts, 79

Springfield, New Jersey, 30, 32, 188, 203, 246; Knyphausen and, 217, 219–24

Springfield, battle of, 217–24, 225

Stamp Act, 15, 58

Stark, John, 50, 73, 191; in Bennington, 105–106; at Springfield, 220, 223

Staten Island, New York: British in, 12, 13, 31, 32, 41, 97, 140, 180–81, 207, 217, 220, 221, 222, 224, 233, 246, 247, 248; Stirling raid on, 196–98, 199, 201

Stephen, Adam, 42, 47

Sterling, Col., 115

Sterling, William, 219

Steuben, Friedrich Wilhelm, baron von, 93, 132–34, 137, 138, 202, 214; American voyage of, 216; Lee court martial and, 173; Luzerne entertainment, 207; at Monmouth, 162, 165; in Pluckemin, 178; in Virginia, 240

Stewart, Charles, 12

Stewart, Walter, 156, 157, 158, 213–14

Stiles, Ezra, 19

Stillwater, New York, 110

Stirling, William Alexander, Lord, 12, 14–17, 81, 94, 111, 188; at Amboy, 95; Clinton pursuit and, 141; on Conway, 128, 130, 131; Lee court martial and, 172; at Metuchen, 96–97; Mrs. Livingston and, 92; at Monmouth, 160, 162, 163, 164, 165, 166; in New Brunswick (New Jersey), 30, 31; in Pennsylvania, 42; in Princeton, 34–35; at Springfield, 220; Staten Island raid (1779), 196–98, 199, 201; Trenton battle and, 47, 50, 52, 55

Stirling, Lady, 137, 179

Stockton, Frank R., quoted, 35

Stockton, Richard, 35

Stony Brook, 61

Stony Point, New York, 22, 36, 248

Stony Point, battle of, 189–90

Strangers' Burying-ground, Woodbury, 121

Stuart dynasty, 14, 61

Sugar Hill, 105

Sullivan, John, 41, 48, 67, 81, 94, 95; Iroquois slaughter by, 187–

88; retirement of, 195; in Rhode Island, 175–76

Summit (Turkey Hill), New Jersey, 217, 219

Sumner, John, 212–13

Susquehanna River, 137, 187

Sussex County, New Jersey, 5, 34

Sussex Court House, Orange County, 241

Sutphin, General, 94

Sutton, Daniel, 71

Swedesboro, New Jersey, 252

Tallmadge, Benjamin, 240

Tarleton, Banastre, 228, 229, 236

Tarrytown Road, 230

Tennent, William, 142–43

Tennent, New Jersey, *viii. See also* Old Tennent Church

Tennessee River, 185

Ternay, Chevalier de, 226–27

Thacher, James, 191, 206; quoted, 194–95, 196, 200–201, 207, 208, 211, 214, 226, 231

Thayer, Maj., 122, 123–24

Thayer, Theodore, quoted, 148, 150

Thimble Mountain, 70

Thomas, Edward, 12

Thompson, David, quoted, 69–70

Thompson, Mark, 12

Thomson, Mrs., of Jockey Hollow, 194–95

Ticonderoga, New York, 41, 70, 85, 102, 105, 109

Tilghman, Tench, 77, 156, 179, 192, 251

Timber Creek, 119

Tiverton, New Jersey, 175

Tomson, Thomas, 144

Toms River, New Jersey, 210, 211

Trenton, New Jersey, *ix,* 5, 35, 37, 41, 42, 54, 61, 68, 95, 147, 233, 248; Mount Holly battle and, 43–44, 52; Washington supply office at, 189, 221

Trenton, battle of, 44, 45–52, 62, 105, 230; aftermath of, 53–59, 60, 64, 67

Trescott, Maj., 207

Trevelyan, George Otto, quoted, 51

Trinity Church, New York City, 53

Trout, Joab, quoted, 107

True American Inn, Trenton, 57

Trumbull, John, quoted, 172

Trumbull, Jonathan, quoted, 136, 242

Tryon, William, 219

Tuckerton, New Jersey, 43, 210

Turenne, Henri de La Tour d'Auvergne, vicomte de, 21

Turin, Italy, 27

Turkey, 35, 111

Turkey Hill (Summit), New Jersey, 217, 219

Tuttle (mutineer), 234

Union, New Jersey, *see* Connecticut Farms (Union), New Jersey

Valley Forge, 13, 126–34, 135, 147, 170, 179; Lee return to, 137–38; Morristown and, 202, 242

Van Buskirk, Abraham, 26

Van Cortland, Philip, 12

Van Doren, Mrs. John, 65

Van Harlingen House, New Brunswick, 65

Van Tilburgh's Inn, Kingston, 64

Varnum, James Mitchell, 87, 122

Vaughan, John, 71

Vauxhall, New Jersey, 222, 223

Veal Town (Bernardsville), New Jersey, 36

Veghten, Derrick van, 181

Verplank's Point, New York, 189, 221–22, 248

Versailles, France, 101, 243

Victoire, La (vessel), 102

Vienna, Austria, 244

Vincennes, Ohio, 186

Vineyard Haven, Massachusetts, 175

Virginia, *ix,* 6, 29, 195; British campaign in, 209, 210; Continental Army in, 237–39, 240, 245–46, 249, 251, 252; Indians and, 185, 187; militia of, 46, 51, 75, 82, 83, 87–88, 110, 137, 148, 162, 164, 166, 210, 252; Washington in, 62, 242, 245–46, 248, 249, 251. *See also specific placenames*

Virginia House of Burgesses, 242

Voorhees, Mynders, 172

Voorhees, Peter, 181

Vulture (vessel), 230

Wadsworth, Jeremiah, 195, 242

Waldo, Albigence, quoted, 122, 123, 124, 125–27, 128, 129, 160

Walker, Benjamin, 133

Wallace, William, 178

Ward, Andrew, 46

Warwick, Rhode Island, 19

Washington, *viii, ix,* 6, 10, 12, 13, 85–86, 91, 102, 103; Arnold betrayal of, 230–31; British occupation of Philadelphia and, 113, 118, 138; British peace offers and, 136; Clinton pursuit (1778) by, 140–44; Delaware forts and, 118, 124; disciplinary methods of, 188, 199–200, 214–15, 231, 234–35; French support, 209, 226–27, 241–44, 245–46, 247–49; Gulph encampment and, 125–26; Hudson River forts and, 21, 22, 23, 24, 25, 28; Indian massacre by, 186–88; Lee court martial and, 170, 172–73; Long Island battle and, 14, 16, 17, 43; Middlebrook winter quarters (1778), 178–79; military journal (1781) of, 239–41; Monmouth and, 145–70, 176; in Morristown, 70–84, 89, 94, 98, 129, 190, 191, 192–96, 201–205, 206–15, 216–21, 227, 228, 248; New Jersey retreat of, 29–37, 38, 39–40, 41; peace news (1783) and, 253; in Pluckemin, 66–69; Princeton and, 60–65, 254–55; problem list (1777), 87–88; Rhode Island expedition, 175–76; Stony Point battle and, 189–90; Trenton and, 44, 45–52, 53, 54–55, 56, 57–58, 59, 60; at Valley Forge, 126–34, 135, 137–38, 170, 179, 202; in Watchung Mountains, 94–97; Yorktown and, 251, 252

Washington, John Augustine, 25, 29, 169

Washington, Martha (Mrs. George Washington), 10, 76, 137, 178, 192

Washington, William, 50

Watchung Mountains, 94–95, 96, 97, 217

Watertown, Massachusetts, 242

Wayne, Anthony, 82–83, 84, 178, 231; quoted, 96, 194; at Brandywine, 107, 108; Clinton pursuit and, 141; Lee court martial and, 173; at Monmouth, 152, 153, 157, 162, 165, 166, 169; mutiny and, 232–33; at Stony Point, 189–90

Wayne, Gilbert, 82, 83

Wayne, Polly (Mrs. Anthony Wayne), 83

Waynesboro, Pennsylvania, 83

Webb, Joseph, 242

Weedon, George, 107, 162

Westchester County, New York, 121, 241

Westfield, New Jersey, 96, 97, 203

West Florida, 136

West Indies, 77, 244, 245, 252

West Jersey, 6

Westminster Abbey, London, 85

West Point, New York, 102, 188–89, 217, 221, 222, 232, 243; Arnold at, 227, 230–31; supply of, 241

West Virginia, 36

Wethersfield, Connecticut, 93, 241–44

Wheatley, Phillis, 57; quoted, 55

Wheatley, Susannah, 55

Whippany, New Jersey, 70

Whippany River, 70

White, John, quoted, 180

White Marsh, Pennsylvania, 113, 124

White Plains, New York, 23, 28, 175

White Plains, battle of, 17, 21–22, 86, 216

White's Tavern, Basking Ridge, 36

Wick, Tempe, 227–28, 232

Wiederhold, Andreas, quoted, 23, 24

Wilkinson, James, 51; quoted, 130

Williamsburg, Virginia, 242

Williamson, Isaac, 6

Williamson, Matthias, 6

Wilmington, Delaware, 106, 107, 246

Wilmington, North Carolina, 229

Winchester, Virginia, 176

Winds, William, 12

Wistar's Ford, 107

Witherspoon, John, 4–5, 6, 34, 173–74

Wolfe, James, 85

Woodbridge, New Jersey, 31, 32, 96, 203–204

Woodbury, New Jersey, 121

Woodbury Creek, 118

Woodford, William, 167, 172

Woodstock, Virginia, 82

Wrottsley, John, 163

Wyandot Panther, 105

Wyckoff, Peter, 153

Wyoming Valley, 187

Yale University, 19, 178

Yardley's Ferry, 42

Yeates, Bartholomew, 63

York, Pennsylvania, 108, 138

Yorktown, Virginia, 245

Yorktown, battle of, *ix,* 13, 181, 251, 252; march to, 245–49

Zabriskie, Peter, 23, 25, 26

ABOUT THE AUTHOR

Earl Schenck Miers has published 64 books since his first appeared in 1936. He is a graduate of Rutgers University and holds two honorary degrees from his alma mater and one from Lincoln University.

Mr. Miers has written numerous books for young people, principally on sports and American history. He was a pioneer in reviving interest in the American Civil War and Lincolniana, and while director of the Rutgers University Press from 1944 to 1949 laid the groundwork for the later publication of the monumental *Collected Works of Abraham Lincoln.* Among his important historical books are *Gettysburg* (1948), *The Living Lincoln* (1955), and *The Great Rebellion* (1958). His autobiography, *The Trouble Bush,* was published in 1966.

The text of this book was set in Caslon Lino-type and printed by offset on P & S Special XL manufactured by P. H. Glatfelter Co., Spring Grove, Pa. Composed, printed and bound by Quinn & Boden Company, Inc., Rahway, New Jersey. Jacket drawing and text drawings by Charles Waterhouse.